*C O V I*

MW00935643

**Submariner Sea Stories**

**By the men who served their country beneath the seas.**

Copyright © 2014 Jim Schenk

ISBN-13:978-1499265682

**COVER ART**

Original 12"x14" acrylic painting on canvas by the author March 2010.

**ACKNOWLEDGEMENTS**

Thanks to all of the voluntary submissions over the years from the Submariners that made this book possible, and to my ever-friend, Kay Blevins, author of, "SOUND OF ADVENTURE", who helped me bring this book to fruition.

Go to <u>iTunes</u> and catch Submariner Bill Nowicki's PodCast entitled, "Submarine Sea Stories".

### *DEDICATION*

**To:** all of the Sailors that have gone to sea in Submarines, whether or not they came back home.

Your country proudly honors you, and this fellow boatsailor respects you as a brother in arms.

**To:** all the lovers of their "ensured freedoms" due to your unselfish voluntary service.

*Thank you.*

## *The Submariner*

Only a submariner realizes to what great extent an entire ship depends on him as an individual. To a landsman this is not understandable, and sometimes it is even difficult for anyone to comprehend, but it is so!

A submarine at sea is a different world in herself, and in consideration of the protracted and distant operations of submarines, the Navy must place responsibility and trust in the hands of those who take such ships to sea.

In each submarine there are men who, in the hour of emergency or peril at sea, can turn to each other. These men are ultimately responsible to themselves and each to the other for all aspects of operation of their submarine. They are the crew. They are the ship.

This is perhaps the most difficult and demanding assignment in the Navy, and is on a volunteer basis only. There is not an instant during his tour as a submariner that he can escape the grasp of responsibility. His privileges in view of his obligations are almost ludicrously small, nevertheless, it is the spur which has given the Navy its greatest mariners; the men of the Submarine Service.

It is a duty, which most richly deserves the proud and time-honored title of…"SUBMARINER".

***THE TWENTY-THIRD PSALM*** *Adapted for Submariners*

*by John Cole, U.S.S. WHALE (SS-239)*

*further amended by James E. Schenk (SS-214)*

**"The Lord is my helmsman, I shall not drift.**

He maketh me lie down in deep green oceans.

He leadeth me through the dark waters.

He steereth me in the deep channels.

He keepeth my log.

He guideth me by the star of His holiness for His name's sake.

Yea, though I sail amid the thunders and tempests of life,

I shall fear no danger, for Thou are with me.

Thy love and Thy care, they shelter me.

**Thou preparest a harbor before me in the land of eternity.**

**Thou anointeth the waves with oil.**

**My boat rideth calmly.**

**Surely sunlight and starlight shall favor me on the Eternal Patrol I now take.**

**Then shall I rest my oar in the Port of God, forever.    AMEN."**

FROM: Anthony Liss nuke ETC(SS), USS FLORIDA SSBN-728 –

In the summer of 1999, I went on patrol on the USS FLORIDA as an ET2(SS) fully qualified and a bit of a smart ass. I was known on the boat as a practical joker. YN2(SS) Joe Hanson comes up to me on the mess decks and says, "Tony, I got a problem." He goes on to tell me that the XO had commented that he was tired of getting messed with for Half-Way Night, and was wondering what he could do to get the crew to leave him alone (he was tired of having his door stolen and being 'voted' into the scullery for Half-Way Night dinner). After much thought, I came up with a plan. We told the XO we would leave him alone for Half-Way Night if he would schedule an E-7 and above call, with the CO, in the Officers' Study on the evening before Half-Way Night, and he agreed. Myself, YN2 Hanson and four others were pre-staged in MCUL about a half hour before the CO's call. We had tool bags, web belts across our chests, with cordless drills, tools, and home-made ski masks. We had radios and a forward compartment spotter using call signs to let us know when all of the Chiefs had left the Goat Locker. We got the call that the Goats had flown the coop and we proceeded to the Goat Locker, humming the Mission

Impossible theme song. As we hit the Goat
Locker and verified it empty of all khakis,
we commenced our operation. We removed
the table tops to both tables, all cushions for
all seats, the power cords to all electronic
equipment, the mini-fridge, shower stall
doors, shower heads, toilet seats, and the
doors from the lounge into berthing (x2),
from berthing to the head (x2), and from the
lounge into the head (x1). We took all the
pictures and plaques from the wall, and
every other thing that was not actually
welded down. While on the way to the Goat
Locker we picked up about ten other guys
who wanted in on the action, so it was a
steady stream of stuff being removed from
the Goat Locker. It took us a total of 22
minutes to completely strip the Goat Locker.
After everything had been removed, and
sent to various hiding spots throughout the
boat, we Danger-tagged the front door to the
Goat Locker SHUT, and Caution-tagged the
escape scuttle "CO's permission required for
operation". The authorizing officer for the
tag-outs was the CO, who thought it was
pretty funny. After we finished I went to the
smoke pad to wait for the fireworks to start.

After the CO's call, the COB and EDMC came down for a smoke and about two minutes later the EMC came down, laughing so hard he could barely talk. He said, "Have you guys seen it?" "Seen what?", the COB asked. "The Locker, they stripped it, it's completely empty." Immediately the COB and EDMC turned toward me… "Liss, what the ____ did you do?" I, of course, disavowed all knowledge of what they were talking about. From here it kind of went down-hill. The Chiefs refused to relieve the watch, keeping the E-6's on watch, and they locked up all of the toilet paper on the boat (it was stored in the Goat Locker Head). The Deck LPO managed to scrounge up a case or so of TP and issued each blue-shirt a roll. E-Div decided to "adjust" the heat for the Goat Locker and raised it to about 120 degrees F. Unfortunately, the CO's stateroom was on the same circuit, so he got on the 1MC and told the Chiefs to relieve the watch, and the crew put the Goat Locker back together. It took us four hours to find everything and put it back together. All of the Chiefs congratulated us on our planning and performance of the practical joke, which they agreed was the best that they had ever seen. They also told us it would never be able to be done again, on any boat in the fleet, because the word would go out and the Chief's Quarters would never be left alone for that long ever again.

Fast forward to 2005; I was stationed at Nuke Field "A" School in Charleston, SC, and one of my students came up and said he had met a retired ICC(SS) who was working at a hotel, or something, in the area. They got to talking and he mentioned my name, to which the ICC stated laughing and told my student to ask me the story about raiding the Goat Locker for Half-Way Night. Amazing how Sea Stories make the rounds. This one beat me from Bangor, WA to Charleston, SC, and I, in turn, told it to several classes of Baby Nukes. While it may never be able to be done again, the story lives on. I have met several other people since who have heard of the story.

Now, being a Chief myself, all I can say is, "The Blue-Shirts will never be able to raid my Goat Locker. I know better than to go to a CO's call the night before Half-Way Night and leave it unattended.

FROM: Robin McAteer TM3(SS) –

In 1977 we were in the Caribbean area of the Atlantic Ocean. We were doing "sound trials" after an overhaul in Norfolk Shipyard. As any boatsailor knows, the post-shipyard tests are long and very tiring. Days filled with drills, critiques, more drills and more critiques.

Our CO, CDR Sibley L. Ward III (Slammin' Sam) decided that a respite was necessary after the Squadron dogs had departed. While off Andros Island, he authorized a swim call. Warm day, warm waters can equal sharks. And as all boatsailors know, any time there's a swim call, there has to be an armed shark watch on the sail. I volunteered for Shark Watch duty, so while my shipmates swam innocently in the warm blue waters, I was perched atop the sail with the OOD. After about half an hour of talking of just about everything under the sun, the OOD asked me, "McAteer, what would you do if you spotted a shark?" My quick response was, "I would blow this whistle and shout to everyone to clear the water. Then I would shoot the furthest swimmer, giving the rest of the crew a chance to get back on board." "McAteer, you're a sick puppy; I almost believe you would to that." With a friendly smile I replied, "Yes sir, and thank you...hopefully we'll never know whether I'm joking or not."

FROM: George Bass, WWII COB, 4 War Patrols aboard USS BOARFISH SS-327 –

When I was Chief of the Boat, I came through the watertight door into the After Torpedo Room and all of the Torpedomen suddenly became quiet. Too quiet, so I asked them, "OK, guys, what's going on in here?" Nobody volunteered any information. It was just then as I passed the Head that I heard a noise in there and knocked on the door and asked if anything was wrong, to which I received no response. Another noise prompted me to attempt opening the door to see what was wrong. It was unlocked and when I got an eyeful of what was in there I slammed the door shut. The guys had somehow acquired a live lion and placed it in the head. Now I knew what the hush-hush was all about and they had been caught red-handed. The next question was, "OK, what in the h*#l is a lion doing in that room?" The second class Torpedoman said, "Well, Chief, every ten minutes we open the door and whip that kitty with a pair of khaki pants, and we are waiting for the Weapons Officer to come back and use the Head!" My eyes narrowed and each man cowered as I said, in no uncertain terms, "I don't care what you do with that wild animal but you're going to have it off my boat post haste. I'm going to walk up to the Forward Torpedo Room and when I come back and it is still on board, you guys are gonna pay heavily." When I came back a little later, there was a nonchalant card game going on and no one even acknowledged me coming through the hatch. I looked in the Head and the animal was gone; I never found out how they got it aboard or how they got rid of it. Boys will be boys...

FROM: Jack Lemke –

In December of 1963, I was stationed aboard the USS CARBONERO SS-337, and was assigned as a mess cook. I was a 9901 fresh out of Sub School, and looking to get qualified in submarines so I could attend Nuclear Power School. The crew looked at a 9901 as a lot of work to get you qualified and then you were gone to bigger and better things, so they screwed with you any chance they got.

We were out in the Pacific off the coast of Japan operating with a Carrier Task Force providing a target for anti-submarine training. It was great duty as we would go to "silent running" and I could sit down and not make any noise. They would drop depth charges with a small charge in them (PDC's – Practice Depth Charges) and the Captain would evaluate how they did. The other great part of this duty was that the carrier delivered mail to us every day or so via helicopter. One crew member would don foul weather gear and go up to the sail and attach his "life belt" to the safety rail that ran the length of the boat and go aft and retrieve the mail. When he went down to the control room and removed the foul weather gear, he was given a ration of Brandy, because he was wet and cold, "Good Deal".

I was in the control room working on quals and the Chief of the Watch was getting things readied for the mail delivery. He needed someone to go up and get the mailbag from the chopper, and no one volunteered. He asked me if I wanted to do it and I jumped at the chance; it would be exciting and I would get some Brandy. So I donned the foul weather gear and the "life belt" and up through the sail I went. The seas were rough and the wind was blowing quite hard. Over the side of the sail I went and attached the safety line to the rail. There were a couple of important pieces of information I should have been given before I started this adventure. The first was when you grab the mail, grab the bag and not the cable hanging from the chopper as there is one hell of a static charge that you provide a ground path for.  I think the hook was isolated from the cable so when I grabbed for the mail the second time, I grabbed the bag and undid the hook with no shock.  As I turned around to head back to the sail, everyone that was topside had a big grin on their faces.  I took the mail down to the control room where the Yeoman was waiting, and removed the foul weather gear.  The Corpsman was there, I assumed, to give me the Brandy.  This is where the second piece of information was given, that I would have liked to have had before I went to retrieve the mail.  I asked for my Brandy and was told the last ration was used at the last mail delivery.  No wonder nobody volunteered when the Chief needed someone to go up and get the mail.

FROM: Tom Sheridan;

USS TANG SS-563 –

This prank was perpetrated on an NQP aboard the USS TANG circa 1971.  It involves a water slug and the "White Rat" sound powered phone monitoring system located in Maneuvering.

In order to acquaint this non-qual with 1250's, I had him fill out one for a water slug. We had a can which was duly marked "Water Slug", 1 each, with an FSN and location. I told him that it was a Pri-1 chit and that he had to get all of the appropriate signatures on it, including the CO's. After the usual several trips through the boat, the only sig left was the skipper's. We were under way returning from WestPac, and I always stood the 12 to 16's and the 00-04's in Maneuvering. The Skipper was sleeping, so I told him to just throw back the curtain on his stateroom and holler, "Captain, Captain", and that he would get up. Tommy McVey was Auxiliaryman of the watch, his eyes bugged open, and he said, "Oh, ____, I gotta listen!" He then waited in a secure place while the NQP woke up the Skipper. He said, "Captain, Captain, wake up. I have a Pri-1 chit for you to sign". The Captain asked, "What for?" He told him it was for a water slug. The Skipper picked up his sound-powered phone and hollered at us in Maneuvering, mainly me, "Sheridan, you SOB! What do you think you are doing?" We were laughing our asses off while the Skipper kept on squalling. Finally, I keyed our phone so he could listen to us. He paid me a visit, even though he was also laughing, and told me not to wake him up like that anymore.

While in transit from Pearl to San Diego for a change of homeports aboard TANG, it was, yup, 00-04, blow San tanks time. The wardroom Steward had just qualified on blowing sanitaries and it was his duty to blow the forward tank. The only thing he forgot was to vent. Fast forward to about 0500 – I was on my way to the Forward Room with a cup of coffee for Jim Freeman, the Forward Room watch, and was just passing the Sonar Shack when I heard a carroommph, followed by some of the most colorful sailor language I've ever heard. Being smart and not wanting to be the first one the Skipper saw after getting his morning dump packed back up his ass, I dived into Sonar, while, of course, laughing my ass off. The ping-jockeys asked what happened, and I told them. That poor bastard spent the next six weeks blowing all of the sanitaries under instruction! Oh, Jim's coffee got a bit cold, what was left of it. Submarine life is great.

FROM: Roger E. Carlton,

USS VON STEUBEN SSBN-632 –

My job on board the boat was that of Storekeeper which meant that I spent a lot of time driving the boat. The Control Room was a notorious place for pranks to originate (the COB helped). My favorite was when a rookie new recruit was asked to stand the mail buoy watch. We had a long pole made up with a hook on one end. We would send the recruit into the Control Room Trunk with instructions as to how he would use the pole once we got close enough to the surface. But he had to climb all the way to the top of the trunk so that when he opened the hatch, it would not give away our position. As soon as he started his ascent, we would close the lower hatch behind him. Do you know how dark and lonesome the Escape Trunk can be?

Then there is my favorite officer, LTjg (Splash) Shipway. Another place for the best pranks to brew was in the Engine Room. If you recall, the voice communication system between the upper and lower levels may have seemed a little antiquated, but due to the noise levels, that buzzer worked wonderfully. Well, the plan was to get "Splash", an engineering officer, to the lower level to look at a faulty valve. As he was evaluating the valve, he was called to the voice tube by the ringing of the buzzer. When he looked upward to speak, five gallons of fresh water came "splashing" down the tube. He was a terrific sport. It didn't dampen his spirits at all. He stood the remainder of the watch just a little damp around the edges.

But, the all-time favorite was breaking in a new Officer of the Deck (OOD). Without giving away too many details, patrol speed for the boats was not all that fast. Things like small temperature changes in the outside water or slight movement of the planes could affect the "trim" of the boat. Ideally, the trim should be kept just slightly above level. One of the best ways to mess with the trim was to muster as many guys as you could in the Torpedo Room. This made the bow tip downward, not good. When the Number One valve opened, which was very audible, to pump water from the bow to the stern, all the members of the "trim party" would follow the flow of the water aft. Now the problem has been compounded. There is at least twice as much water (with people) aft as there now should be. The trim angle of the boat is now much higher than desired. The rookie officer now pumps water forward to compensate. Again, the "trim party" follows the flow of water forward. After a couple of times doing this, the "trim party" marches through the Control Room so that the rookie OOD knows that he has been had. What a way to pass the time.

FROM: Dan White, USS STONEWALL JACKSON SSBN-734(B); USS OHIO SSBN-726(B) –

During ORSE, I think in 1993, we got "The Greenburgs" pretty good. We were getting tired of him talking to the pumps, so we donned EAB's and started yelling at him. He donned an EAB (in ERF, and then ran to Maneuvering) and ended up taking it off when an ORSE-Board member asked him why he was wearing it.

An ET (RO) was hanging "Diver's Tags" and actually attached a DANGER Tag to an energized bus (SPM fuses) with the fuses removed. The Diver received a jolt when his damp boots grounded out to bare metal on the deck.

I body-checked a "Butter-Bar" rider into the PTGLO sump when he played as a drill prop in ERLL. Not a good idea to stand between a man and an EAB port during a fire drill. I ran into him a couple of years later when he was an ORSE team member – he thanked me for the body check.

Squid in a sail boat running slalom in the channel entering Kings Bay. OOD decided to take out a buoy rather than the sail boat. Watch the sea buoy fly when caught by the screw. Can you say $2M screw?

Embarrassing moment: when the Captain sees something behind the piping tab on the 12K and grins when he pulls out a photo of the "Black Angus" in Puerto Rico. At least I didn't go to the donkey show.

An attempt at a burial at sea from a T-Hull. Who would have thought that ashes would stick that well to the damp fairwater planes? After three dives and surfaces the ashes still stuck. Upon returning, the Admiral made the mistake of taking the family of the departed on a tour of the refit pier while they were pressure-washing ashes off the planes.

An A-Ganger NUB approached the OOD requesting permission "to blow the DCA". The OOD was in fact the DCA.

Another A-Ganger on the fairwater planes was tapping on the digital depth gauge, when asked by a senior member what he was doing, he informed that, "sometimes the gauges stick".

An M-Divver providing his wife with PM cards for his personal vehicle for the time he was at sea. (start the car, change the oil, etc…).

After personally coming back after my first patrol on New Years, I got drunk with an A-Ganger whose wife had left him, then went out on the town. I was returned to base by Camden County's finest to the EHW by the Shore Patrol. I was carried across the brow by the OOD, and dropped down the MC LET after telling the OOD, whom I thought was another officer, "Mr. _____, you fat bag of ____, get your hands off me you ____. When I looked up from the MC deck at the bottom of the ladder, the misidentified officer had a halo around his head, (due to the light behind his head and my blurry eyes). I asked if he was GOD. Next day, the Captain called the boat and asked if there had been any other sightings of GOD on his boat.

The crew was meeting on the Mess Decks and I suggested to a shipmate to "write-in" D.B. Cooper on the attendees list. The COB apparently didn't like the idea. He yelled out, "Where in the Hell is D.B. Cooper?" A YN who was passing the Mess Decks on his way to the YN office heard him, stuck his head in and said, "I think I just passed him, he's probably in the laundry."

Welcome Aboard! (or how I met Captain Hicks).

In October 1981 I was freshly arrived on the "BILLY B.", a quiet kid trying to stay off the dink list and out of trouble. One of the first jobs I got to help out with involved tagging-out some valves in the Coolant Discharge system, one of those "back aft" things we nukes worried about. This particular valve line-up was pretty important, as some maintenance was in progress that would remove cooling water from a heat-exchanger that kept the ion-exchanger cooled. The resin in the ion-exchanger could be damaged if it was heated over a certain point, and the reactor coolant was much hotter than that, so without cooling water it was important not to put any water through the ion-exchanger. One of the qualified guys (I think I know who, but not really sure anymore), hung the red tags on the system. He needed someone to verify that the tags were hung on the correct valves, and this seemed like the perfect job for a new guy who wasn't qualified to do anything, so I was selected.

As luck would have it, one of the tags was hung on the wrong valve, and being new and nervous I did not pick up on this minor discrepancy. When a discharge was initiated, the ion-exchanger high-temperature alarm went off almost immediately. Of course, everything stopped at this point and there was an investigation, which quickly identified the source of the trouble.

Here I was, on board less than two weeks and already involved in a serious problem. This seemed like it was going to ruin my plans of "flying below the radar" for the next four years. There was nothing for me to do but stay at the Coolant Discharge station in Machinery 2 Lower Level, and answer questions that were asked, and just basically feel like a fool. But things were about to get much, much worse, because Captain Hicks was on his way aft to take charge of the situation.

Now anyone who remembers Captain Hicks can guess what came next, he proceeded to lay into that MM2 who had hung the tags. I remember thinking how he was using such colorful language, and his face was turning very red, and the veins on that bald head of his were bulging out on both sides. Most of all I remember thinking that I was not looking forward to my turn. But of course, eventually Captain Hicks was done yelling at my mentor, and turned his attention to me.

In a moment of inspiration, I decided that I could spare both myself and the Captain from an unpleasant situation, so I said to him, "Captain, I was standing right here listening to everything you said to him and you don't have to say anything. I get it. I ____ed up!" For a second or two I thought that I had said the magic words, but then I noticed that his face was getting much, much redder, and those veins on the side of his head now looked more like hoses, so much that I expected them to burst. And then Captain Hicks let loose with a roar, saying, "_____ up? You're ____-in A Tweety you ____ up!" And with that he turned on his heel and stormed off, still fuming.

After a few moments of stunned silence, my mentor and I burst out laughing. The assembled M-Divvers could not believe that I got away with such effrontery. I'm still not sure I'd call it "getting away" with anything, as even to this day I remember that event whenever I have to walk down a tag-out. And yeah, this story is a no-____er!

FROM:  Sean M. Gawne, MM1(SS),

USS WILLIAM H. BATES SSN-680 –

Submarine Damage Control Trainer.

Submarines are very complicated machines, so the crews get a lot of training on how to operate them.  Some of this training is unique to submarines, such as the submarine escape training at Sub School. One thing a lot of people don't realize is that nukes don't usually get to attend Sub School, so we missed out on a lot of the fun stuff.  It's also rather odd that most of the Engineering Department, with the exception of the officers and the auxiliary mechanics, never got the benefit of Submarine School training.  Perhaps this is why the submarine Damage Control Trainer was invented.

The Damage Control Trainer is a very special training simulator, designed to replicate the experience of flooding in a submarine.  Flooding is an awful thing on any ship, but at least for most sailors there has always been the option of jumping overboard or getting into a lifeboat. Submariners don't have those options. To make things worse, flooding on a submarine is a much more serious problem than on a surface ship. Most large ships have a great deal of extra buoyancy, so they can stay afloat even with a lot of extra water on board. Submarines are simply designed with very little extra buoyancy, which is a fancy way of saying we are already sunk, so sinking further is not a good idea. It only takes a very small amount of water to send you towards the bottom of the sea, where things only get worse.

As if that were not bad enough, modern submarines operate deep below the surface (last time I checked the exact values are still classified), where the pressure of the water outside can be hundreds of pounds per square inch (increasing 44 lbs./square inch per every 100 feet). This means that the smallest hole can cause a great inrush of water, and it takes both skill and speed to stop such a leak. It was important for submariners to know how to deal with this, and the only way to learn is by doing it, and practicing until you could do it right.

The simulator was built to look and feel like a typical compartment on a submarine. There is a collection of pipes, valves, and assorted equipment just like you would find on any submarine, along with the right colors of paint, lockers and cabinets, etc. Two things were very different from a real submarine, however. The first thing was the windows – the simulator had windows that allowed the trainers to observe what was going on inside, so that they could control the situation from outside. The other big difference was that the pipes, valves and other equipment were riddled with holes , cracks, loose flanges, and other things that would cause leakage of water into the compartment when the water pumps were turned on to simulate the pressure of the ocean.

Now I've never been to Sub School in Connecticut, but it only makes sense that the water up there is a lot colder than in San Diego, so I'm glad that my only experience in the Damage Control Trainer happened in San Diego. The Navy sent me to a lot of schools, but without a doubt the most memorable and fun school I ever attended was the Submarine Damage Control School. (It probably helped save my life and that of the whole crew, but that's a story for another day). The training was memorable because of the realism of the experience, but it was fun because I got to attend with a bunch of guys from the good old "Battlin' BILL BATES, some of the best guys I have ever worked with in my life. This is the story of our experience in the DC Trainer.

If you've never been to the Submarine DC trainer course, you really missed out on something special. Here's how it works: on the first day, you sit in a classroom for a few hours in the morning and some instructor tells you about how the machine works, how you are supposed to communicate with each other, how to signal to the simulator operators, and so forth. Then before you know it they are taking a group of you inside and LOCKING THE DOOR SHUT from the outside. And then they turn on the water pumps. You have a few minutes before the water starts to get really deep, while you are looking around to see what tools and equipment might be available to help you.

As the water level rises, you get colder and scramble about more madly. If your team is lucky enough to fix any of the leaks, it really doesn't matter much, because the pressure just keeps getting higher and higher (as it would if you were sinking in the ocean) and eventually everyone winds up the same, swimming just to keep your head above the water and hoping you don't drown. When the water level gets about a foot from the top they shut off the pumps, then the chamber is drained down and you get to come out, dry off and change clothes. It's called a pre-training assessment, but it's a darn good technique for getting your full attention. Looking back it's quite funny, but at the time it can be very frightening and the water is really cold.

So now that the instructors have your full attention, they spend the next several days teaching and demonstrating various techniques for stopping leaks and making emergency repairs to pipes and other things. Some of it may be things you already know about, some of it is new, but mostly all of it is things you don't practice very often. Knowing that on the last day of class you're going back into that chamber, and the pumps will be running at twice the pressure as on the first day, you study and practice very hard.

But the instructors tell you over and over that the most important thing you will learn is not the skills for patching and clamping, but the ability to work together as a team. No individual would have a chance to survive the kind of calamity that you are about to encounter, but as a team you can succeed. If you do not work well together, you may be highly trained individuals, but you will most assuredly find yourself up to your neck in cold water. This is one of the most important lessons about submarines and life in general that I ever learned. (If you've read some of my other sea stories, you can see that I was long overdue for such a lesson. I wish I had gone to this course much earlier in life).

The group that went to school with me that week was special in that we were all from the BATES, and we all worked in the Engineering Department. We knew each other, we were friends who respected each other and knew one another's strengths and weaknesses. Almost everyone in that group had been on the BATES for two years or more, so we had a pretty good idea about how to use most of the equipment. We were feeling pretty confident that this would give us an edge. By the end of the week, as our final exam was coming up, we were expressing our confidence to the trainers, telling them we were going to beat their machine. They told us they were going to run the pumps at full pressure, and we might be able to fix all the leaks if we applied everything we had learned, but we should plan on getting very wet.

When that final test came, we were totally prepared. We had discussed how we would work together, and everyone performed at the highest level. Despite the fact that they ran those water pumps at full speed, we were able to shut off all the leaks when the water level was just above my knees. It was one of the proudest accomplishments in my Navy career, made all the more special because it was a team effort, not just an individual accomplishment. Every one of us did a great job, and together we achieved something really special. The trainers told us that our performance may have been the best they had ever seen, nobody could recall a team of guys who beat the DC Trainer and got the water leaks shut off so quickly. The ravages of time have dimmed my memory, so that I can't name every guy in that trainer with me, but you all know who you are.

Those were the best of times, and we sure were lucky to have that time together.

"Fire in Machinery Two!"

"Fire in Machinery Two!!!" Those words came over the 1MC at about 0602 one Saturday morning in San Diego. I

remember it well, as I was just rolling out of
my bunk, as reveille had just been sounded a
few minutes earlier. I was looking forward
to breakfast, being on for the off-going duty
section, having been asleep since just after
midnight. With a groan I realized the
Engineer was Duty Officer and was up to his
usual game of making us all get up with a
drill to start the day. For the love of Pete,
this was Saturday! Could we ever get a
break?

Being the duty section leader for
engineering, as this was very near the end of
my tour on BATES, I was in charge of the
fire team. Being in no mood for a drill, I
wanted to just get this over with and get
some eggs and bacon in my belly, so I
pulled on my boon-dockers and headed aft
in my shorts and tee shirt. There were a
couple of guys trying to pull on firemen's
suits, but I walked right by them with a
snort. There were two or three guys in the
tunnel, and the after hatch was closed, but I
walked right up and swung it open. By now
I was really out of patience.

Imagine my horror when I was met with a thick cloud of acrid black smoke! There were angry orange flames shooting from somewhere up near the overhead at the aft end of the compartment, and little balls of burning plastic were falling to the floor of the upper level with a funny noise. As I stood there in my underwear, I suddenly felt extremely under-dressed, and more than a little foolish. Worse yet, the fire team was now arriving and asking me for directions, and although I made an attempt, those balls of falling fire scared the crap out of my near-naked self. Finally I had to tell someone else to take over for a few minutes while I put on some clothes.

This turned out to be a pretty bad fire in the shore power breaker, for those who remember that one. The cables in the overhead looked like a tar pot when it was finally out, and the breakers were a bunch of melted goo. We were on reduced electrical for months, as there were no spares to replace that old breaker. Our cooks got a lot of practice cooking barbeque on the pier, and we all got damned tired of the smell of diesel smoke. Must have run that diesel for months!

The fire took what seemed like hours to put out, and the fire team did just fine without my leadership, so the fact that it took me a few more minutes to respond might not have mattered that much, but I don't know if I've ever felt quite as dumb as I did that morning. That was the last time I ever assumed anything was a drill, believe me!


Toxic Gas in Machinery Two!

First, you lucky reader, you get a quick refresher course on Water Chemistry Control of Naval Nuclear Reactors. On the BATES, as in most Navy nuclear plants, we added Ammonium Hydroxide, more commonly known as ammonia, to the Reactor Coolant System to minimize corrosion. Inside the reactor, the neutron radiation would bombard the molecules of ammonia ($NH_3$), breaking it down into Nitrogen gas and Hydrogen gas. Since we already added Hydrogen gas to keep chemistry in a reduced condition, and Nitrogen is inert, this is okay. The only problem being that you had to keep adding more ammonia to maintain the system PH as high as you wanted.

Normally it was no challenge to keep the chemistry optimized, as the plant usually operated at a very low power. However, during those rare times when the boat ran at high speed for a long period, this chemistry control was more of a challenge, as the ammonia broke down faster at high power due to the higher flux of neutrons, which meant we had to add lots of ammonia at high power.

Okay, that's it for the Chemistry lesson. One WestPac cruise (I believe it was 1983 on the way to Australia), we were operating at high speeds like this for more than a few days and consuming lots of ammonia. This was no fun for the ELT folks as we had to add chemicals almost every day, which was more work than normal, and after each chemical-add we had to sample the reactor coolant water, which was more work. Adding chemicals to the reactor coolant could be simple, except that the chemical involved was ammonia, which is very volatile.

The brilliant engineers who designed the system created a "tank", which was really no more than a large-diameter pipe, to which you would add the chemicals that needed to go into the reactor coolant water. Then you used a high-pressure pump to force the chemicals into the reactor system. Pretty simple sounding stuff so far, but it got more complicated. You see, it was important to minimize the amount of oxygen that might get into the system (oops, more chemistry stuff), so the engineers added some heaters to the water supply for the pumps that charged water into the reactor. The water was kept at about 180 degrees F, which keeps air from dissolving. When you charged water into the system, the pipes all got very hot, because of the hot water. This included, of course, that wide pipe they called the Chemical Addition Pot, where we were supposed to add the ammonia.

Now, if you've ever used ammonia
or any other highly volatile chemicals, you
can figure out what happens when you try to
pour it into a container that is 180 degrees F.
The ammonia wants to expand very rapidly,
and much of it will turn into ammonia gas.
By the way, ammonia gas is toxic to humans
at fairly low levels. So you can see the
system was not designed to be user-friendly.

Anyone who remembers how much
the ELT's used to complain about adding
chemicals probably thought we were just
being lazy, and while I'll admit we could be
lazy there was more to it than that. It could
be a very sketchy evolution, and there was
one particular day that I will never forget,
and many of you may also remember. As
Paul Harvey would say, "this is the rest of
the story".

There we were, burning a hole in the
ocean as fast as we could go, and I had to
add chemicals to the reactor coolant almost
every day. After a few days of this routine
the ELT's learned that we were in for a
tough time, because while it was normally
not that hard to add one bottle of ammonia

to the system, it became quite complicated when you were doing it every day. You see, the pipes never got time to cool off, so the ammonia was always trying to flash to vapor. This was more than a minor problem, for we got the ammonia into the pot by siphoning it through a little plastic hose. If you did not siphon it really fast, it would heat up and come back out! It was a real problem.

Anyone who knows me will tell you that I love to solve problems, and sometimes I've been known to do things a little outside the rule book. One day, while adding a bottle of ammonia to the pot, I decided to try something different to speed things up. It occurred to me that if we pressurized the ammonia bottle it would go into that pot much faster, and then I could shut the valve quickly before the ammonia heated up. Sounds reasonable, right? But how does one pressurize a bottle of ammonia? The first thing that came to mind was to blow into the vent hose on the bottle, and it seemed to work great, the ammonia was flowing into that pot much faster than normal.

Then everything went wrong in a big way. The ammonia hit that pot and vaporized, raising the pressure and pushing hot ammonia back into the bottle. That in turn pushed hot ammonia through the vent hose into my mouth, before I could move away. You might think my first concern would be the fact that I was burning all the skin off the inside of my mouth, or the fact that I could not breathe, but actually I was scared to death that I would be in big trouble now. Terrified does not properly describe how I felt at that moment.

But I was not frozen in place; no, I was quick to act. My eyes were burning from the ammonia fumes, and it was hard to see, but I had placed a bottle of rinse water on the sink nearby, and I grabbed that to rinse out my mouth. Instantly I realized that what was supposed to be rinse water was in fact another bottle of ammonia, as I had grabbed the wrong bottle in my blind confusion. Now I really began to hurt. Quickly I turned on the water to the sample sink and stuck my head under the flowing water, letting it run into my mouth. It felt great, and I took big gulps of what felt like fresh air to me.

Now, around this time, the alarms started going off on the ship, and something came over the 1MC about "Toxic gas in Machinery Two." I was somewhat amused at the sight of people coming down the ladders in the EAB's, while there I was in the worst spot of all with no protection. Sheepishly I took an EAB out from the stowage locker and put it on, but I guess by this time I was pretty sure the air was not toxic enough to kill me. This incident did give me a renewed respect for ammonia, as my mouth was peeling for days. It was kind of like what happens when you bite a really hot pizza, but instead of just the top of your mouth this was the cheeks, gums, and everything. Good thing that stuff grows back really fast.

I don't think the little detail about my blowing into the vent tube ever came out during the investigation of that incident, and I'm sure I did not brag about it. Anyways, if you are one of those people who were riding along that day and had to put on an EAB,

and you have been wondering until now
how in the world an experienced ELT could
spill all that ammonia into Machinery Two
Lower Level, well now you know the truth.


Sasebo, Japan.  The Navy can take away
everything except our birthday…Oh No!

September 18, 1982.  I remember the
date so well, because it was supposed to be
my 21st birthday, a day that I had looked
forward to.  We were underway that
morning, soon to arrive in Sasebo, Japan.
Standing in line for breakfast, I took a look
at the POD, and to my shock and horror the
date said, "September 19".

The first paragraph had a note about
how the Quartermasters had set the clocks to
local time overnight, and so we were now on
Sasebo time, and had skipped September
18th.  The Old Salts had always told me that
the Navy could take away anything but my
birthday, and with a sinking feeling I
realized that not even this was sacred.  What
a way to start my first adventure in the

exotic eastern empire of Japan. For a few hours I was pretty mad. But soon we were making preparations for maneuvering watch and all was forgotten. Finally I was going to see the world!

Pulling into the harbor was an unexpected adventure, as we had loaded so many stores in Pearl Harbor that the boat was having a hard time staying on the surface. We had to keep up the speed and run the LP blower repeatedly. Then there was the issue of navigating through all those local boats to our mooring place in the harbor. The local officials were worried about our/their safety, so we were not allowed to pull up to a pier. The U.S Navy was kind enough to offer the services of the USS TUSCALOOSA to provide us with shore power so we could send the crew ashore for liberty.

Tying up to that thing was perhaps the most frightening experience of my life up to that point, (and this from someone who twice had someone try to shoot me at close range, once close enough to cause flash burns), we almost parted the lines several times due to the currents and the unfamiliarity of each crew with the other's type of vessel, the shore power cables fell in the drink and were badly grounded, it took hours and I was alternately laughing and fearing for my life.

One of the funniest things I've ever done happened just before we tied up. There is a rule that before anyone goes topside, the ELT has to survey for radioactive contamination on top of the boat. Coming into Japanese waters, this was a special concern. On that day, the waves were slapping pretty high, and the boat was drafting pretty deep due to the ballast problems, so I was nearly washed overboard several times. As if that was not bad enough, there were several helicopters from the local news channels trying to get a shot of the boat coming into port, and they were flying so close overhead that they kept blowing the "swipes" out of my hands. It was putting me into an especially foul mood. Then, because the reactor was going to be critical for a few hours we had to check for radiation. Of course there was an area around the reactor where the radiation levels were high enough that the law required me to post a sign. This was where the fun started.

The Captain was very concerned about avoiding an international incident, knowing the Japanese to be very sensitive about nuclear stuff. When he saw me doing the radiation survey, he asked me if maybe I could just skip the radiation sign. Now, I knew the regulations and I wasn't in the mood to break any rules at that time, especially not to please those wackos that had almost blown me into the water with their helicopters. So I told the Captain that, "the law was the law," and I really had to put up a sign, but I would go below and see if I could find something more suitable that would not upset the natives as much.

Always full of mischief, I went to the Nucleonics Laboratory and found the biggest, most brightly-colored Radiation Area Sign I had ever seen. It was brand new and bright yellow with the big purple trefoil symbol in the middle, and it must have been three feet high. I took it topside and hung it on the back of the sail. This was simply too much for the helicopter crews, who all tried to fly as close as they could to get a shot of this thing, all while a Japanese Defense Force helicopter tried to keep them away to protect us from any threat. I looked up at the CO, grinning, and the look on his face said it all: "International Incident".

After the fiasco of mooring to the TUSCALOOSA was complete, some of the crew started going ashore for liberty. I had duty that night so I was shutting down the reactor and taking down that big Radiation Area Sign. After dinner, someone switched on the TV and we saw the local news. I don't know what they were saying, but there I was with that big Radiation sign. Feeling a little embarrassed, I got up and switched the channel, but I was on that one too. In fact I think it was on five channels. By now I was beginning to realize my little joke had not worked out exactly as planned.

Fortunately for me, everyone's attention would soon be diverted to a much more serious incident. We had been warned that large crowds had gathered to protest the visit of a nuclear ship, and the presumed presence of nuclear weapons, which of course nobody can confirm nor deny. The crew was instructed not to say or do anything to upset these folks, and there was a large riot-police force present to keep the situation under control.

Our guys were going to shore on landing craft from the TUSCALOOSA. One of the guys, I believe a Torpedoman, but I don't recall his name, went to shore in one of those first liberty boats wearing a windbreaker. After landing at the pier, he got out and walked toward the gauntlet of riot-police and the huge crowd of protestors, he opened his jacket to reveal his tee-shirt with two mushroom clouds and the slogan, "USA 2 – JAPAN 0". Needless to say, a riot ensued, and my little stunt with the Radiation Area sign was quickly forgotten.

Adventures in Tijuana, Mexico.

Wow, I must be getting old because I can't remember all the details any more, but I'll do my best to recollect a very interesting experience that happened one night just south of the border in Tijuana, Mexico. Of course this could mean a lot of things, I personally had quite a few "interesting" experiences in Tijuana, mostly in sleazy night clubs or bars, but this is not that kind of story. I'll leave those donkey tales for someone else to tell. I've only heard of those things, never seen 'em myself.

No, on this night I was taking the rather unusual and slightly risky method of exploring Tijuana. I was driving my own vehicle. Most of the time when we would go shopping or sight-seeing we would either walk or catch a Mexican taxi, because the roads are not great and your American insurance probably won't cover anything that happens in Mexico. But for whatever reason we had decided that we would drive my old pickup down to Tijuana and do some shopping – probably wanted to save on cab fare, or something. One of my passengers was trying to teach me how to negotiate with those local vendors. He could drive a hard bargain, and I wanted to perfect that skill before the next WestPac cruise, as I knew it might come in handy in Thailand or elsewhere. I'm not sure who my other passenger was that night.

Well, the evening started out on a pretty sour note. Feeling a bit hungry, I stopped at a little café on the side of the road and ordered a taco and a beer. The taco meat did not taste right, and I should have stopped at the first bite but was really hungry and in those days felt super-human, so I ate the whole thing. What the heck, I was there to explore a foreign country; might as well sample the authentic cuisine, right? Quickly downing the beer, we walked up the street, but as I passed the alley something very disturbing caught my eye. Behind the little café where I'd just eaten were what appeared to be the skins of dead cats. Well, I guess I know why that taco tasted so odd! At that point I emptied the contents of my stomach in the alley, and we proceeded to explore some other parts of town.

Most of that night is but a dim memory now. I do recall practicing my negotiation skills with the owner of a leather shop, who was selling a jacket that I really wanted. My friend told me to never settle for a price more than half the original asking price. We started at $100.00 and I got this guy down to $55.00, but when I said no more than $50.00, he told me to get out. Later that night I tried to go back and get the jacket for $55.00, but he was so offended he refused to let me back into his shop. I guess I learned a valuable lesson about negotiating there, but I am not really sure what it was.

Here's where it really got interesting. After a full evening of sight-seeing, shopping, and more than a couple of beers, we decided we'd better head back home before it was too late. We jumped in my old pickup and headed northwards, generally. I was not very familiar with Tijuana, but basically just headed towards the brighter lights on the American side. After a few blocks, the red lights started flashing in my rear-view mirror. Uh-oh, it was the Tijuana Police. I was pretty sure I knew what was coming.

Doing my best to appear sober, I asked the officer what was wrong. He told me that he pulled me over for going through a stop sign. Looking back, I could not see any stop sign anywhere, and told him that, " I did not see any such sign. When did I drive through the sign?" This must have been the wrong thing to say, for he told us all to get out of the truck.

Now, it's not a good feeling to be standing on a lonely street in some third-world country with a corrupt policeman standing there with his hand on his gun, but I grew up in Arizona not far from the border so I was not surprised by this. I figured I would just pay him a small fine, perhaps ten dollars, and we would drive off. What I had not counted on was the help that my passengers would provide. They began to argue with the officer, insisting that there was no stop sign, and that this appeared to be no more than a shakedown of three American gringos because of my California license plates.

Now I was starting to get really nervous, partly because the cop was clearly getting angry, but more because I remembered that I had two rifles and a shotgun under the seat of my truck. Now the policeman was telling us that we had to follow him to the station house where we could talk to a judge. Knowing a thing or two about Mexican jails and the Napoleonic code of law, I knew that I was in a very dangerous situation. Unfortunately my passengers were oblivious to the danger, and kept on trying to bluff their way out of paying a fine. Of course, it did not help that my driver's license had been expired for more than a year.

Needless to say, by the time I was able to get everyone to settle down and talk the cop into a "field fine" the price had gone up to $100.00. My friend had to drive, as the cop would not let me get behind the wheel with an expired license. As we drove away, I explained to the other guys what was under the seat, and we all behaved until we got back across the border. After that, whenever we went to Tijuana, we parked on this side of the border and walked across the foot bridge, like normal folks.

But it wasn't a total loss, because I did go back later and get that leather jacket. And I also have a great way to teach our new students at the local nuke plant about the elements needed to cause two localized corrosion methods. We teach that Caustic Stress Corrosion requires Caustic, Austenitic Stainless Steel, high Temperature, and Stress (CATS) and Chloride Stress Corrosion requires high Temperature, Austenitic Stainless Steel, Chlorides, Oxygen and Stress (TACOS). Put them together and what have you got? CAT TACOS. I've been telling new students that story for almost 20 years and not one of them has ever forgotten it! Oh, and in case you are wondering, NO, they don't taste good. Not at all.

Hanging out with the locals in Hawaii.

Our first port call on the WestPac cruise of 1982 was not really a liberty port, but a stop for supplies. Still, we had a couple of days to spend in exotic, tropical Hawaii, and we were determined to make the best of it.  As this was technically my first port call ever, it promised to be very exciting.  Little did I suspect just how exciting.

I don't remember if it was the first or second day in port, but it was pretty early on that stop when I went out one evening with a friend, Mac, who was my mentor in M-Division, and some Nav-ET who shall remain nameless for the purpose of this story (as the reader will come to later understand).  Neither Mac nor I had any particular liking for his fellow, but he had a rental car, and we did not, so we swallowed our pride and hitched a ride.

We'd heard about these evening bay cruises that had open bars and dancing, which were supposed to be popular with tourist girls.  That sounded like a great chance to have some fun, and it turned out to be darn near as good as anything we could have imagined.  Well, that's how it seemed at first.  We got on this flat-bottomed boat with a bunch of tourists, and there were indeed some mighty good looking young girls.  Mac and I both hit it off pretty quickly with some lovely young things from somewhere in Canada, and it was starting to look like it was going to be a beautiful evening indeed. Somewhere around 8 p.m., however, we began to see the flaw in the logic of combining open seas, flat-bottomed boats and liquor. Our poor dance partners were turning a bit green, and here's a hint for you amateur sailors – seasickness is not an aphrodisiac! Needless to say, when the boat pulled into the dock, the girls headed straight for the nearest bathroom, and we had to be satisfied with having drunk as much free booze as possible in the previous 90 minutes.

Well, what do three well lubricated sailors do when left alone with a car? Why, drive around and look for some excitement, of course. Not knowing much at all about Oahu, we headed for some neighborhoods off the beaten path. This was our first serious mistake of the evening. (Apologies to those living in the 21st century, but in those days getting into a car with a Blood Alcohol Content of around 2.0 was not considered to be such a big deal, unless you were a traffic cop). Before long, we were beginning to think our driver was lost, and perhaps worse than that he was getting to be even more obnoxious than he was when sober (which was pretty obnoxious).

We stopped at a traffic light with one car in front of us. When the signal changed to green, the car did not move quickly enough for him, and he began to use the horn and flash the lights. This seemed to upset the people in front of us, and for a while we played some kind of silly game with them. Then at the next red light these two local guys, looking pretty Asian, got out of their car and came up to the windows of our car to "talk" about the horn thing. The language was not what one really expects a host to use when speaking to his guests and our obnoxious driver was throwing fuel on the flames. Pretty soon we were all engaged in a spirited discussion of the merits of our driver's abilities, and theirs. Around this time we were called "haolies" for the first, but certainly not the last time that night.

The two Japanese looking guys were really doing their best to lure us out of the car but we resisted the temptation, until for some reason they decided to escalate the situation to a physical confrontation. Not that blocking our way with their car wasn't physical, but I mean they started hitting Mac and our driver in the head through the window. Since I was in the back seat I was out of their range, but that did not matter. This had now become a matter of HONOR. There was no holding back now.

All three of us managed to bail out of the car and engaged with our opponents, except that it became clear very quickly that our driver's contribution was going to be limited to verbal jabs, whereas Mac and I were taking quite a lot of physical abuse. However, Mac was a very large dude and I was not exactly small either, so we had maybe 30 pounds advantage each over these punks. This was the first time I was in a real serious fight, one where you could say you might be fighting for your life, and I had no training as a pugilist, so I was pretty impressed to see Mac beating up on his opponent, but I was getting pretty annoyed that this dude kept punching me in the face.

My only skill was at wrestling, and finally this guy got close enough for me to get a good hold on him. I'll always remember that something inside me sort of snapped, and I just didn't want to stop choking this dude even when he was clearly passed out. Mac had to pull me off of him, or he would have been dead. Thanks for saving me from murder, Mac.

At this point we should have headed back to base, but we had just left these two local toughs lying on the pavement, and were feeling pretty tough ourselves. Plus, we were still not quite sure where the heck we were, so we drove around the town a bit, trying to figure out which way to go. That did not last long.

After driving around for a while it was clear we were going in circles, as we kept seeing the same landmarks. We were getting pretty mad at our hopelessly lost driver, but then we saw our Asian buddies again, and this time they were not just two guys in one car, but there were two other cars filled with much bigger looking Samoan dudes. This did not look like a good situation, and they were trying to get us to pull over, so we decided to get the heck out of there. Unfortunately we had no idea where to go in that neighborhood, and as lousy luck would have it we turned onto a dead-end street. As the driver was turning around we saw that the other three cars had blocked the road, cutting off our exit. We were trapped! There was nothing to do but get out and face them.

So, we got out of the car, and they got out of their cars. I think I counted about eight of the big Samoan guys, plus the original two. This already looked bad, but then we noticed that they were carrying a variety of sporting goods, such as baseball bats, tennis rackets, and such, and it was a little late at night for ball-playing. It looked like this was going to become a very interesting night, indeed. While Mac and I were taking all this in, we heard the slamming of the car door, as our driver locked himself in the rental car, leaving us outside to fend for ourselves.

The group of Samoan guys began to ask us why we had beaten up their buddies.

The two smaller guys, who were very clearly quite pissed at what had happened, were pushing their friends to even the score. Mac and I stood almost back to back in a defensive posture as the group circled us. We were both pretty drunk, so it was hard to dodge the occasional shot from a racket or bat. It was obvious how this was going to turn out, so I decided to try and reason with the biggest guy, who was clearly the leader of the group. In between whacks to the head, I pointed out that his two smaller friends were exceedingly rude and obnoxious, and seemed to be taking advantage of his friendship. I offered that perhaps Mac and I were the victims of the same sort of situation, as it was quite clear that our "friend" had thrown us to the wolves. The Samoan guy said it was unfortunate that he would have to beat the crap out of us, as we seemed to be generally stand-up guys, but he assured us that when they were done with us they would deliver an even worse beating to the guy in the car. Seizing on the only chance I could see to get out of this predicament, I offered to help them kill the SOB.

After a few more minutes of this, for some reason the Samoans saw some value in my arguments. As I recollect now, the thing that saved us was that this idiot in the car cracked open the window a little bit to shout further words of scorn upon our attackers. I was glad it did not go on much longer, for I was doing okay at dodging most of the blows but I could see Mac was bleeding pretty heavily now. And I was not kidding about wanting to kill that SOB.

A small group of the Samoans, led by the biggest guy, went over to the rental car. Some words were exchanged, and then that big guy stuck his fingers through the crack in the top of the window. The fool saw what was happening and tried to close the window, but it was too late. That big SOB started to bend the door frame with his bare hands, and other hands started reaching in to grab that driver. With a scream of terror he finally started the engine and started driving around wildly. He popped open the right door and Mac and I jumped inside, but he was panic-stricken. The street was blocked by three cars, there was no way out!  As a large gang of angry Samoans was chasing us we told him, "This is no time to be bothered with traffic laws, drive up on the darn lawns and get us the hell out of here!".  So we dented a few trash cans on the way out of there, but we were able to get away.

A few blocks later we saw a police car in the parking lot of a donut shop (of course), and pulled over to report what had happened.  The rental car looked like hell; it had many dents from baseball bats and the driver's door was bent way over.  There had also been some minor sideswipes during the earlier game of tag. We gave a good description of the perpetrators to these two police officers, expecting them to take prompt action.  They proceeded to laugh with contempt, asking us what the heck a bunch of "haolies" were doing in that neighborhood at night.  We could not believe it.  They were not going to do anything, we were lucky to get them to file a report for the insurance.

Disillusioned, we headed back to the base, followed by the police who had warned us they might arrest us if we headed in any other direction.  As all three of us were bleeding, we thought we should make a visit to the ER at the base hospital.  Once again we were in for a surprise.  The reception desk asked us a few questions and then called for the MP's.  After the shoddy treatment we had received from the local police, I was in no mood to be arrested, and as my head was only bleeding slightly and I've never really liked head stitches that much, I opted to run off and take my chances back on the BATES.

I guess there are some life-lessons in this story somewhere; like don't ever forget to have insurance on a rental car, in case some big Samoan dude gets a hankering to rip off the driver's door.  The night was one big rush, from the dance-cruise right up to the mad race from the MP's in the hospital.  Looking back on those days, I often wonder how the heck I ever lived through it all.  But like all these stories of mine, this one is a no- ____er.  You can take my word for it.

Getting a tan topside in San Diego.

Nobody could ever claim that I was a model sailor…far from it. Beginning from the time I was in boot camp, I seemed to be dead set to make trouble for myself whenever possible, often for no reason. So it was really no surprise that eventually it all caught up to me in 1983, right after I was promoted to first class petty officer. During the maneuvering watch coming out of Mare Island, I was caught sleeping and was busted for dereliction of duty. Probably because of my heretofore less than stellar record I had the book thrown at me and got busted down to third class, along with 60 days of restriction and extra duty. It offered me some time to think seriously about things, but of course I tried to make the best of it.

Being restricted to the boat between WestPac cruises really sucked. We did not get much liberty anyways, so I was not a happy camper. The CO was being really strict about the limits of restriction too. I remember that I was really mad when we did DSRV ops, and they told me I could not even go into the DSRV at 400 feet because that would be leaving the ship. Talk about playing tough! Monday through Friday I also had extra duties, but on the weekends I had a little bit of a break. At first I would watch movies in the crews' mess, but somebody decided that was not allowed during my restriction, so I had to find other means of entertaining myself. I wrote a lot of letters, exercised some, but was mostly bored. One sunny day I decided it would be a good idea to lie out on the aft deck and get a tan.

Of course I'm not generally known for my tan, as I tend to tan in shades of red, but I figured a few minutes of sun bathing would make me feel better. So I donned a bathing suit and stretched myself out for a while. Within just a few minutes the topside watch came back to ask what I was doing and I told him to just leave me alone as I needed some color. It must have been right after lunch, because before too long the warm sunshine combined with a full stomach to put me into a deep sleep.

The next morning was Monday, and we were heading back out to sea. I tried to just man-up and go to work, but my duty station was at the feed pumps, where it was probably 100 degrees F or more. Before long the pain and itching was just driving me crazy, so I finally broke down and asked someone to get the Doc to come and take a look. Having just been busted, I was afraid of being charged with malingering, so I did not want to leave my watch station.

Doc took a quick look and knew I was in deep trouble. This was probably the worst sunburn I've had in all my life, and with my white skin that is saying a lot. He told me not to worry; he would go and mix up some kind of medicinal ointment that would ease the pain. I thanked him and encouraged him not to dilly-dally, as this was getting really painful.

In a few minutes the Doc was back with a bottle of something, and told me to just spread it all over and it should relieve the pain in a few minutes. Then he was off to take care of his other duties. I stripped off my shirt right there and started spreading this stuff all over. It seemed to sting a bit, but I figured that must be the medicine, and it would be feeling better in a few minutes. Oddly enough, as time went on it seemed like the stinging and itching was getting worse. Then the phone rang and it was the Doc; he asked me if I had put the medicine on yet. I told him, "Sure," and he said, "Oh, no! I don't know what to tell you but I made a mistake and put way too much acid in that stuff. You're about to have a chemical peel, and it is probably going to hurt." By this time my arms, neck, shoulders, chest and stomach were really burning.

Before that Maneuvering Watch was over, my skin was peeling off. The pain was excruciating, especially around my nipples. I don't think I've ever felt such intense pain. It didn't help that I spent most of my time in the Engine Room or AMR2, where the temperature was mostly around 100 degrees F. The funny thing was, by the next day most of the skin had peeled off, and it wasn't so bad. In fact, it was the fastest recovery from sunburn I've ever had. I didn't mind so much when people called me "Lobster Man". And the chemical peel worked wonders; to this day I have baby-smooth skin on my chest and stomach, not a wrinkle anywhere and that is, of course, "no-_____".


Unclassified tales from the Cold War.

For more than forty years, the United States and the Soviet Union maintained a state of virtual war, often supporting proxy wars in small countries on the frontiers of their so-called empires. One of the most important fronts in this long war was the "stealth war" that took place under the surface of the oceans. Much of this story has never been told, as many of the missions remain classified to this day.

Recently, there have been books written that tell part of the story; a good example is "Blind Man's Bluff" which was written by two newspaper glory hounds, using declassified information from the Navy, and first-person interviews with some of the men who served in the Silent Service during those times. There have also been fictional accounts by authors like Tom Clancy that have the ring of authenticity, but those of us who were really there know these books only paint a distorted image of what really happened.

I think the time has come to tell some of the tales of our adventures as Cold-Warriors on the "Battlin' BILLY BATES" (aka Redfish) but in order to keep myself and my friend from going to prison for a very long time, I am going to redact enough information to keep this story unclassified. I hope that you find that it brings back some memories, even if it may not keep you on the edge of your seat like a Tom Clancy novel.

This tale takes us back to late 1983, or perhaps only 1984 (the exact date is classified). We were operating somewhere in the Western Pacific Ocean, exactly where I cannot say as that is classified. We had been at sea for a long time, on a mission that ostensibly involved charting the bottom of the ocean and gathering data on weather changes, but that was only a cover story for the real mission, which, of course, remains classified.  What that mission was, must have been very important to the national security of the United States, because the crew of the "BILLY  B." was awarded the Navy Unit Citation for what we did, and each member of the crew received a Navy Expeditionary Medal.

So exactly what were we doing out there?  Well, some things are able to be discussed openly; for example, it's widely known that nuclear submarines stay submerged nearly all of the time to avoid being seen by ships, airplanes or even satellites, so as a result we were mostly driving blind, relying only on the charts of the oceans to visualize the world around us. Also, unlike what's often depicted in the movies, we don't use active sonar, for that would also give away our position, so we're not able to navigate by echo soundings the way that dolphins and whales do.  No, all we could do was listen very carefully and use the information that was available from the sounds we heard to try and figure out what was going on in the sea around us.

Now, like a lot of guys who wind up in submarines, I am naturally very curious and I love a puzzle. In fact, I don't think I've ever met a group of guys who were better at solving puzzles that the guys on submarines. I think that's why I signed up for submarines; it seemed to be the most intellectually challenging and exciting job I could imagine. At first I found the nuclear science to be quite a challenge, but after you finish all the schools and become qualified, the excitement begins to dim. After all, as we like to say at the power plant where I now work, you don't really want to use the nuclear reactor. In other words, the job is designed to be extremely boring, and most of the time that's all it is. So being a naturally curious guy who liked puzzles, I looked elsewhere to satisfy my curiosity. And I found my answer in the Sonar Control Room, or as we called it, the "Sonar Shack".

Now, for a lot of people this room was nothing but a mysterious place filled with computers, on whose monitors were strange patterns of green and black, with three or four geeky dudes wearing headphones. But for those who understood what was going on, this room was usually the center of the universe for the submarine. And I found myself drawn to the Sonar Shack like a fish to water. Even though I was usually working 10 to 12 hours out of every 18 in the crazy submarine 18-hour day, I would spend any spare time in the Sonar Shack. I got to be good friends with a lot of the Sonar guys, and I also learned to be pretty good at solving the sort of puzzles that Sonar techs had to deal with.

As a matter of fact, one of my best buddies in those days was an older Sonar tech that we called "Pappy". He was a first class at the time, but was older than dirt because he had got out of the Navy for a while, worked in some electronics company making sonar equipment, then came back in. Perhaps he enjoyed motorcycles and hard-drinking too much, as that can work against you in the corporate world. Not too much of a problem for a Navy enlisted man, as long as you don't let it affect your work. And he was a good Sonar tech, so he was happy in the Navy. He encouraged me to hang out in

Sonar; perhaps he saw something in me,
who knows? By the time the events in this
story took place, I had been hanging around
in Sonar quite a lot, and in fact had got some
sign-offs on a qual-card for Sonar. But this
is the background and it's time to get back
to the story, leaving out any classified bits,
of course.

Being in that part of the ocean for
that period of time we were specifically
trying to listen for a particular thing, exactly
what that was is classified. Well, we came
across one of those things, and we listened
to it very well for a long time. For quite a
while we went around in circles in the
ocean, not quite staying in one place but
staying close to the thing that we were
listening to hear. We made atomic-clock
time-logged records of what we were
hearing, and tape-recordings so that other
shore-based evaluators could listen to the
same sounds someday. We took careful
note of the bearings of the noises we heard,
and other things that are probably classified.
We filled out logbooks and other documents

that most certainly are classified. And we did a darn good job of it.

How do I know we did a good job? Well, that's the point of this story. After doing this thing for a good long time, we had gathered a lot of information. There were a couple of guys who did not belong to our crew that were going along for the ride on this WestPac patrol, and some of them spent a lot of time in the Sonar Shack. I got to know them pretty well, since I was spending all of my spare time in Sonar. You can't really blame them, I suppose, when they came to believe that I <u>was</u> a Sonar tech. Finally one day the Captain came in to see how things were going when we were involved in what was something that was so highly classified, most of the people on the boat probably still don't know that we did it. His eyes opened as wide as saucers when he saw me in there, and he was furious, demanding to know what the heck I was doing in there. One of these fellows who was our guest stood up for me, saying that I was very good at what I was doing, one of the best he had ever seen, and if I was not a

Sonar tech the Captain should consider changing my job.

Well, that wasn't quite good enough, so I offered that I did in fact have a Top Secret clearance, as I was the one who developed all of the photographs. The Captain then said that was all fine, but I did not need to know what was going on in there, and had better leave. He also gave a very stern lecture to all of the guys in Sonar about information-security, keeping information limited to those with a "need-to-know", and all of that stuff. Finally he told me and everyone else in no uncertain terms that I was to stay the heck out of Sonar whenever anything like this was going on. And I was never to tell anyone about what happened in there.

So that's what an unclassified submarine cold war adventure reads like. Perhaps in another few decades all of this will be declassified, like the World War II stuff was declassified fifty years after that war ended. For now it's kind of like tea made form a used tea bag. You may sort of get the idea, but then again unless you were actually in Sonar with us you really have no idea what I am talking about. Still, if you've read this far I'm grateful to you, as I can assure you that everything in this story is absolutely true, as best as I can remember it after all these years. Yup, it's one of those "no-____" stories, along with such other favorites as:

When we went somewhere.

When we went someplace we can't talk about.

When we heard something scary.

When we felt something really scary.

When something happened that was really bad.

One of these days, we will be able to fill in the blanks. For now, I hope that I've brought back some memories for you readers. It sure was fun!

<u>The "Billy B" earns respect.</u>

This may be one of the strangest "BILLY B." stories in my memory, because it took place about four years after I left the old boat. After spending three years on shore duty with the surface Navy guys down at 32$^{nd}$ Street Naval Base, I came back to finish out my active duty career with one last year on the USS CHICAGO SSN-721.

Now, in 1988 the CHICAGO was really something special, the first of a new generation of modified ("improved") LOS ANGELES class submarines. She was a stretch-hull version, the front end was expanded to include a Vertical Launch Missile System, and the boat had many other upgrades. Basically, she was quieter and much more potent than any previous attack sub, and of course had the latest and greatest sonar. And there were some other special touches that made it almost impossible to detect. Some of these designs were the result of those SPEP trials we did back in 1981 and 1982.

When CHICAGO arrived in San Diego in August 1988, we proceeded to tear up every other boat we went up against. I mean literally every exercise we had a broom flying over the sail on the way back, because we always got a hit with every single torpedo or water slug, and nobody ever even got a fix on us. That boat was so good it was scary. The other San Diego subs were getting tired of being abused.

(For fans of Tom Clancy, the CHICAGO is the real basis for the 'DALLAS' in "The Hunt For Red October", not the HOUSTON as you might think. I learned this when Tom Clancy came to visit our ship. The HOUSTON was actually a very noisy boat, so noisy that the Navy allowed them to film many scenes from the movie on board the HOUSTON. It was no loss to the fleet to have it used for a movie. Enough about that.)

Then in late 1988 we were assigned to go up against the "BILLY B.", at that time under the command of my former Engineer. I warned the guys in Sonar and Fire Control that they might be in for a surprise, but they had just got done wiping up the floor with all the 688 boats and thought an old 637 would be a joke. So I just waited to see what would happen.

We set out Monday morning to conduct "adversary exercises", each boat armed with practice-torpedoes. I think that we had ten shots each. As the week went on, we did manage to get off a few shots, and even a couple of hits, but the CHICAGO's crew was really stunned by how hard it was to find and track that old "BILLY B.". Most surprising of all, when we would sneak in close for the kill, about half the time that old boat would detect us and turn the tables on us with an active sonar blast.

Now, poor old "BILLY B." was at a serious disadvantage here, because CHICAGO had some special stuff that made it impossible to get a sonar return, we were kind of a stealth boat. But we must have been making some noise or something, because one or two times the BATES took a shot at us, and came pretty close to a hit.

We still ended the week with a score of like 8 to 2 in our favor, but the "BILLY B." earned a hell of a lot of respect from the guys on our ship. No other sub had ever detected us, let alone took a shot or made a hit! We had 20 years of research and technology in our favor, had creamed the so-called best boats in the Pacific Fleet, and found our biggest challenge to date in an old 637 class boat named the "Battlin' BILLY B."

There were few times when I was prouder of that old boat, and the men who made it all happen. She was recycled at Puget Sound in October of 2002, but that boat was one of the best in the fleet right up to the end, don't ever let anyone tell you different.

Welcome to the "Horse and Cow Tavern" (in Mare Island, CA).

There was a tradition at the "Horse and Cow" tavern in Vallejo that if you brought in your ship's brow banner on the first weekend in port, the bar would give you a free keg of beer. Of course, CDR Uplinger was former enlisted and knew of such things, so he made it clear that ANYONE who tried to steal the ship's brow banner would be court-martialed, and any topside watch who allowed it to be stolen would also face punishment.

This would strike fear in the hearts of ordinary mortals, but not submariners, (and all those who served with me during my four years on the BATES, know well that I could have that banner hanging over the bar in the Horse and Cow that very evening. We waited patiently for the CO to leave the ship, presumably to conduct some important business with the Mare Island shipyard command personnel. As I remember things, the CO's car had barely turned the corner when I started to cut down that brow banner, to the shock and horror of the topside watch. (He made some kind of comment about shooting me or something, and I don't remember exactly what I said to him, but it wasn't nice). Someone helped me roll it up and we made a quick getaway towards the town of Vallejo with the banner in the back of the car, I'm pretty sure it was Mac's Corvette.

It sure was fun hanging that banner up on the wall of the bar, and I could hear a roar of excitement from the crowd gathered behind me, which I assumed was the arrival of the beer keg. Then I turned around to see who, but the Captain, standing right behind me. Of course, I invited him to have the first beer, the first of many drinks that flowed that night in Vallejo. Indeed, there were those who probably drank so much they can't recall what happened that night, and others who drank so much they did things they WISH they could not remember, but that is a story for another time.

P.S. – For those with a hankering to revisit those glory days, the "Horse and Cow Tavern" still exists. It had moved down to San Diego a few years ago but left for the Seattle area in 2004. They're located just outside the Sub Base in Bangor. You can check out their website or facebook page, if you dare.

FROM: Robert Kell, USS KAMEHAMEHA
SSBN-642(G) –

I remember the new XO that came
aboard during my second patrol. A few
shipmates decided to hi-jack the XO's
stateroom door while he and the CO were
busy elsewhere. He was, to say the least,
rather upset when he discovered that his
door was gone and soon ordered the Soft-
Serve ice cream machine red-tagged, and the
movie of the day would remain, "The Great
White Hope" until his door was returned.
Every Department Head was ordered to
conduct inspections of their area. The door
was well hidden (I am told) in the Missile
Compartment. It remained missing for a
couple of days when the hi-jackers were
able to replace the door on its hinges without
the XO knowing who did it. To his credit,
the XO chalked it up to the "new guy"
initiation, and never pursued the culprits
who had absconded with his door.

FROM: John C. Yuill, QMSN(SS), USS NAUTILUS SSN-571 –

Me and My Old #10 Can.

I heard an ad for Dramamine the other day and it brought back some very unpleasant memories of my bouts with motion sickness. Now, mind you, I did not hold the all-time record for getting seasick while in NAUTILUS. That dubious distinction is reserved for, and is probably still held by a certain CPO know as "Chief Green". He would start turning green at the 1MC announcement to "station the maneuvering watch", prior to getting underway. I, on the other hand, would delay that coloration until number 1 line was taken in.

That brings me back to the wondrous concoction known as Dramamine; it worked for me. In fact, it worked so well that an hour or so before getting underway, or if we were submerged and about to surface, my boss, "Doggie", or one of the other two

Quartermasters, would notify me to take my Dramamine. I kept a stash close by me at all times in case the dreaded surfacing alarm was to be sounded in the next hour or so. I was a bona-fide "Drama-Junkie". One particularly sad tale went like this:

It was late August 1958. We had just gotten underway from New York City following our triumphant return from Portland, England and the North Pole. We had just passed Ambrose Lightship abeam, when the maneuvering watch was secured and the regular underway watch was set. It was just after 2000 and the seas were getting rough due to a large tropical storm just off the Atlantic coast. To my horror, the watch having been set was mine. It had to be a mistake – I hadn't taken my Dramamine. How could I have been so foolish to assume that I wouldn't be on watch until after we crossed the 100-fathom curve and submerged, which would be after midnight, or 2400? Curses!! I reluctantly retrieved my trusty old #10 can and relieved Ron as QMOW. I fought it with all my might but mind over matter wasn't working. I managed to stay my normal color for about 45 minutes but soon turned a pale white, then a lime green. I began filling up "my can" but very soon was as useless as the proverbial bull with mammary glands. "Doggie" was taking Loran readings down by the Radio Shack and very soon one of the other QM's, (I couldn't tell which of the two, nor did I care), had, for all intents and purposes, assumed "my" watch at the chart desk. The navigation center was located in the attack center, a step or two from the ladder that led up to the Bridge. It was customary for the Quartermaster of the Watch, if not busy, to accompany visiting dignitaries to the Bridge if asked. I was, by this time, in a semi-conscious state, sprawled across the chart desk moaning when I heard the familiar voice of Captain Anderson. I looked up at him, and he at me, and then in a soft, almost apologetic voice, he said, "Oh, I was going to ask you to take the Admiral to the Bridge but I'll get someone else". At that moment, Captain Anderson, next to my Father, became my most favorite person. I remember saying, "thank you, sir" but beyond that everything else was a blur. Of course, this tale was added to the many sea sick stories concerning me and to this day, every time one of my shipmates sees me, he inquires after my #10 can. And, oh yes, the irony of ironies, just after my watch was relieved, we submerged to the peace and quiet of the deep.

## Oops – I think we just hit the ice.

I was bored to tears – nothing to do, just sitting there at the helm, with no headway nor sternway on the boat, while the Diving Officer struggled to achieve a hovering trim and neutral buoyancy. It was August 1957 and the NAUTILUS was under the Arctic Ocean, returning from an aborted attempt to reach the North Pole. The team of Ice Watchers had spotted a polynya, (an opening in the sea ice pack), on the upward-pinging sonar. It was decided to attempt a vertical surface into the polynya. With a hovering trim finally achieved, the Auxiliaryman of the Watch began pumping water from the Safety Tank. (A tank located at the center of the boat and kept full of water so that pumping it out produces a positive buoyancy making the boat lighter). The boat slowly began its vertical rise toward the polynya when there was a gentle shudder. Captain William R. Anderson was seated at the periscope in the Attack Center above the Control Room monitoring the cloud-like vision of the approaching sea surface when he suddenly lost vision through the scope. He immediately ordered, "Flood Negative". In that instant I was no longer bored but tensely aware that something extraordinary was happening. The Chief of the Watch (COW) reached past me and operated the lever to flood Negative Tank (a tank with the exact opposite task of Safety Tank). This tank is also at the center of the boat and is kept partially filled with sea water. In the event an emergency dive is required, this tank is flooded and produces negative buoyancy making the boat heavier). After going deep, a subsequent surfacing attempt in another polynya indicated that #1 scope was also damaged so now the sub was optically blind.

The first thing needed was a complete assessment of the damage. We proceeded out from under the ice pack into clear water and surfaced. It was discovered that the damage to the upper portion of the sail was more extensive than first imagined. The top of the sail was crushed bending both periscopes back like broken straws.

A dilemma now presented itself. After fulfilling the Arctic Ocean expedition portion of our cruise, NAUTILUS was to proceed to the Atlantic and participate in the NATO exercise code-named "Strikeback". Damage to both periscopes would preclude our participation in that exercise, resulting in an embarrassment to both NAUTILUS and to the U.S. Navy.

The #2 scope was beyond repair, but one of the LT's suggested to Captain Anderson that the #1 scope might be straightened and made useable. Various crewmembers were assembled for this task. After Herculean attempts with hydraulic jacks in bitter cold conditions, the team managed to straighten out #1 scope, only to discover that in so doing, the scope barrel had cracked at the kink in the bend.

The inside of a periscope operates in a vacuum-environment to ensure that no fogging occurs due to moisture. Another disappointment and challenge now faced the Captain and crew. NAUTILUS was blessed to have every manner of talent and skill available to the ship and so it was to have two qualified stainless steel welders on board. Welding stainless steel is difficult under the best of circumstances, but to do so in a howling wind and frigid cold presented a daunting task. For some twelve hours or so they labored to repair the crack, alternately welding, subsequently applying a pressure test. After every failure they would grind down the weld and repeat the process, again and again until finally a pressure was maintained within the scope.

But a new problem now lay before the boat. How to reinstate a vacuum to the inside of the scope returning it to a usable condition? This time another shipmate came up with a solution. He suggested that a very high vacuum could be achieved within the scope-barrel by rigging a hose from the scope, through the boat, to the engine room where that end of the hose would be attached to main-steam condenser vacuum pumps. It was soon done and in a very short time the periscope was emptied of all air and moisture. A charge of nitrogen was then applied to the scope interior using the vacuum to draw it in. This, at last, insured that the scope was free of all moisture and would provide a clear view.

The whole project required some fifteen or so hours to complete and its success enabled NAUTILUS to not only participate in the NATO exercise as scheduled, but to "kick some butt" while doing it.

I spent some amount of time on the Bridge as a lookout during that incredible repair, and how those men managed to work under those conditions remains a source of amazement to me to this day. It says something about the quality of those I was privileged to serve with in NAUTILUS. It is something I shall always remember, especially when the going seems to be difficult if not impossible.


Personality Plus.

It has long been acknowledged by seamen that their ships are thought to have "personalities", particular characteristics that are a result of the combined influence of both officers and crew. Navy ships are no exception. A submarine's personality in particular, can be more notably defined because of its small size and complement. A ship's personality can vary from time to time depending upon the change in chemistry within the crew. I can only speak to the boat's earlier years when I was fortunate enough to serve in NAUTILUS which was then blessed with a remarkable personality. Since responsibility and accountability start at the top and filter down, I believe that the leadership positions that made up the "well-oiled" submarine command during my time in NAUTILUS resulted in her particularly good personality. To my mind, the three main submarine leadership positions that have the most impact on the ship are the Commanding Officer (CO), Executive Officer (XO), and the Chief of the Boat (COB).

The CO, or skipper, is the supreme boss and has the final say and responsibility as to the vessel's war fighting readiness, safety and well-being.

The XO is his immediate subordinate, second in command and, among many other duties, is responsible for overseeing the overall operation of the boat's various Departments such as Navigation, Weapons, Supply, Communications, Electrical, Operations, and Engineering, etc.

The COB is the most senior enlisted man aboard and is the liaison between the Wardroom and the enlisted crew. He is the XO's right-hand man, so to speak. Among other things, he is responsible for seeing that all ship's hands perform their daily tasks as required. He is the "go to guy" for solving many of the everyday problems on the boat at the enlisted level. The COB also monitors discipline among the enlisted hands and may dispense punishments for any minor offences. If these three key positions are in synchronization, there is harmony and efficiency throughout the boat.

I had the good fortune to serve under the first three skippers, and as such, was able to witness first-hand what it was like to serve with the best of the best and experience this ship's extraordinary personality.

The first skipper, Captain Eugene P. (Dennis) Wilkinson, was gregarious and somewhat flamboyant. He loved NAUTILUS, and the publicity and lime-light that shown on her. He was the perfect representative for the world's first nuclear-powered ship. He never tired of meeting the press and other media to extol the virtues of his fine submarine. He was all business underway and ran the boat with flair and utter confidence.

The XO when I checked aboard in April 1957 was LT Warren R. (Bus)

Cobean, Jr. He was the third person to hold that position.

The COB was Chief Torpedoman Lynus J. (Dutch) Larch and he had relieved Leroy (Pappy) Ingles. In 1957, Commander William R. Anderson took command, and Lt. Cmdr. Frank Adams relieved Mr. Cobean as XO.

Most of my three years, six months, and five days spent in NAUTILUS were under the guidance of Capt. Anderson, XO Adams and Chief Larch. Aside from my own Father, these three men, among others, became the most admired and respected persons to have impacted my life.

CMDR. Anderson's personality, demeanor, and management style was somewhat different from that of Capt. Wilkinson. Anderson was more quiet, introspective, and soft-spoken; a product of his Tennessee up-bringing and honed during WWII, where he survived eleven war patrols in three boats, TARPON SS-175, NARWHAL SS-167, and TRUTTA SS-421. Those experiences, plus later duty in

SARDA SS-488, TANG SS-563, and his
first command WAHOO SS-565, no doubt,
reinforced his ability to resolve any situation
at hand decisively and quickly.

   With respect to confidence, he
"gathered flies with honey rather than
vinegar" and as such, the crew had a great
affinity and admiration for him. He is
probably to this day the truly most humble
man I've ever known. In any situation it
was never about him, but always about the
crew and the ship. It's my feeling that, to a
large degree; it was the other way around. If
we were a good crew and ship, it was
because he was a good skipper.

   The XO, Frank Adams, was a perfect
complement to Anderson's command-style
and their personalities matched perfectly.
He, like Anderson, was also soft-spoken and
low key. They seemed to work together as
one person. Those two officers exuded
confidence in the crew, which was a
remarkable stroke of good fortune for
NAUTILUS, because it made a seamless
chain of command for what was to become
the "mother of all tests".

"Dutch" Larch, as COB, made up the third member of this remarkable triumvirate. If the heart of a submarine is the skipper, and the soul can be found in the XO, then the pulse of the boat has to be the COB. He maintains the beat, or rhythm of the boat. As such, no one did it better than "Dutch" Larch. He, along with other crew members, had seen action during WWII. "Dutch" made six war patrols in BATFISH SS-310, making history during her sixth patrol in the South China Sea, when BATFISH sank 3 Japanese submarines within 75 hours, a feat never duplicated before or since. (Since 1972, BATFISH has been a Museum Boat overlooking the Arkansas River.) For those feats, the boat was awarded the Presidential Unit Citation. (He would later receive another one awarded to NAUTILUS). He was a seasoned submariner and leader when he came to NAUTILUS in 1957. The crew had in those three leaders, the "real deal", and how fortunate we were for that.

Those years, 1954-1959, were without question, NAUTILUS's glory years. Once at sea, one "first" followed another as

NAUTILUS showed her "stuff", demonstrating to the Navy and the world that unlike any other ship that had ever gone to sea, she was "cut from a different bolt of cloth". As part of showing off this "new toy", the Navy spent the early years demonstrating her wonder and prowess to naval commands and all that clambered to visit or view her. It was a time of long, hard work that demanded maximum effort from NAUTILUS and her crew. It was during these times that the remarkable personality of NAUTILUS was forged and flowered. She became a reflection of those who sailed her, due exclusively, I believe, to the leadership qualities of those persons mentioned earlier. Thus the NAUTILUS of my time developed that certain personality that set her apart from other vessels. She had it all. Indeed, she had personality plus.


Piercing the Pole.

There I was, 20 years old, riding around under the Arctic Ocean in the most sophisticated and fantastic ship in the entire world, the nuclear-powered submarine USS NAUTILUS SSN-571. What could be better than that? How could that be happening to me?

The adventure of my life began with my graduation from Submarine School in March, 1957, and my subsequent assignment to NAUTILUS. After a shakedown cruise to Bermuda in April, the boat prepared for a trip to the North Atlantic and the Arctic Ocean, where an unsuccessful attempt was made to gain the geographical North Pole. Several close-calls were had while under the ice, and much was learned from that experience.

Fast forward to the summer of 1958. This time NAUTILUS was on the west coast of the United States, departing Seattle, WA, heading, so the crew thought, back to Panama and on to our homeport at Groton, CT. Instead, sealed-orders for Capt. William R. Anderson were to turn north upon leaving the Strait of Juan de Fuca. To our surprise we were on our way once again in an attempt to gain passage under the Arctic ice to the North Pole.

Unlike the attempt in 1957, I was now "striking" for the rating of Quartermaster and was a member of the Navigation Department. The ship was equipped with a much-improved array of ice-identifying sonar, an advanced gyro-compass, the MK-19, and most importantly, an inertial navigation system once used in a guided-missile, which was the first use ever on a ship. Unlike the gyro-compass which uses Earth's magnetic poles as a reference, thereby becoming very unstable at high latitudes, the inertial navigation system picks a spot in outer space as its reference and is not affected by this condition. It was a very complicated system requiring the almost constant attention of two North American Electronics engineers assisted by two of our own ship's company. It was a "jury-rigged" affair in the Attack Center with a maze of wiring and equipment which looked to me as if a telephone switch box had exploded. How those four guys made any sense of that mess was, and still is, an enigma me. However, they did so and, to everyone's relief, it worked very well.

We submerged in the Pacific just off Swiftsure Lightship and began our journey north. For the first week or so, our QM2 and I stood what is known as "port-and-starboard" watches (alternating watches of set hours – 6 on and 6 off, for example) while the QMC and QM1 feverishly updated all the northern-water charts that had been clandestinely smuggled aboard earlier. This watch routine was a very tiring affair, the only upside being that neither of us had to perform any other duties while in this arrangement.

We soon passed through the Aleutian Islands chain and into the flat and shallow Bering Sea. On June 13, we passed the Pribilof Islands and the following day, skirting the western side of St. Lawrence Island we encountered our first ice. This is when things started to get interesting. The ice became much thicker and more closely-packed than originally anticipated. We squirmed around, going this way and that, trying to find a path under the enormous ice ridges that we were encountering. The ocean bottom in this area was only about

180 feet deep and with recordings of ice-thickness up to 60 feet that left only about 120 feet of navigable water. NAUTILUS took out approximately 50 feet, keel to top of sail, so that in turn left only 70 or so feet of water to maneuver through – 35 feet above the sail and 35 feet below the keel. It was not a comfortable feeling.

We retraced our steps and passed around St. Lawrence Island to the south and began our next passage between that island and the Alaskan shore. This route posed its own set of problems, mainly, extremely shallow water. It meant that NAUTILUS would have to make the run just skimming above the ocean bottom. The water continued to shoal and Capt. Anderson inched the boat ever upward until our keel depth was about 65 feet, placing the top of the sail just under the surface of the sea. We had only approximately 45 feet of water under the keel, not enough room to pass under any ice should the opportunity present itself.

We arrived at the Bering Strait, passed through this watery slit between

Russia and the Alaskan coast at periscope depth, entering the Chukchi Sea. This sea was just as flat and shallow as the Bering Sea so the same degree of alertness was required to maintain safety. After much maneuvering to avoid ice floes, we passed the Arctic Circle and I became a "Bluenose" for the second time.

It was now June 17th and once again I was the Quartermaster of the Watch. There was a lot of ice overhead, so very close attention was being paid to the ice detection equipment and upward-looking sonar's TV monitor. It was just around 2300 (11:00 p.m.) when there was an unusual amount of activity around the ice-detection sonar. Capt. Anderson was immediately summoned from the Wardroom. We had just passed under ice 63 feet thick. Capt. Anderson increased our depth to 140 feet leaving only 20 feet from our keel to the bottom and slowed the boat to just enough to maintain headway. Meanwhile, Sonar reported two massive ice ridges dead ahead over a mile wide. A hard turn was ordered and NAUTILUS began a slow swing away from the huge ice floe, which by this time was directly over us. The needle on the chart recording the ice-thickness kept going down until, finally, it began to recede. We had cleared the ice by a mere 25 feet. Ahead of us still lay another piece of ice even bigger than the last one. Were it not for the humming of machinery all about us, I'm sure that if the proverbial pin were dropped, it could have been heard. We all stood stock still, transfixed, and as the chart-recording pen began another slide down the paper, it almost touched the reference line on the chart. That line represented the top of the sail. Finally the pen became stationary and then began to recede up the paper. We had escaped unscathed again but ahead of us lay even shallower water and much more ice. The handwriting was on the wall – we would have to turn back.

The news was disappointing to say the least. The prospects of returning through the ice to the miserable, shallow, featureless seas to our south, followed by a <u>very</u> long way home, did not conjure up many happy thoughts, especially for the married guys, for whom the way north under the pole was the quickest way home.

After we had retraced our steps to clear water, Capt. Anderson relayed a top secret message to the Pentagon reporting on our situation. More ice was encountered and more maneuvering was required to evade these menacing obstacles. Finally, we received the anxiously awaited message from the Chief of Naval Operations directing NAUTILUS to proceed to the port of Pearl Harbor, HI. Needless to say, this came as quite a pleasant surprise to the crew, with the possible exception of some of those who were married. Be that as it may, we were headed for paradise.

The trip to Hawaii involved quite a bit of preparation as the true nature of our trip was "Top Secret" and any evidence of our excursion up north had to be completely erased. All beards had to be shaved, all letters home, all foul-weather clothing and survival gear, all evidence of any kind which suggested a trip north was to be hidden away and locked up. This included all ship's logs, reports, records and charts showing northern waters, especially Arctic waters. New charts showing false ship's tracks had to be drawn up to show NAUTILUS had been steaming about the mid-Pacific doing general naval operations. All manner of cover stories had to be fabricated and rehearsed. The crew was sworn to secrecy and told to "forget" about what had just befallen us. I'm sure Capt. Anderson, and perhaps others as well, crossed their fingers and prayed that time spent in Hawaii would not loosen anyone's tongue as to our real purpose. As it turned out, he need not have worried.

On the morning of June 28th, NAUTILUS surfaced just off Diamond Head and several of the seaman gang was sent topside to repaint the boat's hull numbers in their appropriate locations (all identifying markings had been painted out before our initial dive upon leaving Seattle). The maneuvering watch was soon stationed and I took my usual place on the Bridge with the Quartermaster's Notebook. At 1000 hours I placed into the log, "Moored

port side to berth Sierra One, U.S.
Submarine Base, Pearl Harbor."

It was quite a sight to behold –
bands, naval and civilian dignitaries, and
best of all, Hawaiian girls, all in traditional
attire, were on the pier to welcome us.

What can I say about Hawaii? One
thing I can tell you is that it was a lot
different then, than it is now. It wasn't even
a "State" for one thing, and for another, it
was a somewhat distant and expensive place
to reach. Though the tourist business was
beginning to boom, there was still a real
distant and exotic feel to the place. There
were no "interstate-type" highways, only
two-lane paved roads and dirt secondary
roads which took one to any number of
beautiful places. I teamed up with my
"sports car" shipmate and together we rented
an MG-A Roadster and drove practically
everywhere one could drive a car. It was a
wonderful and welcome change from Navy-
life at sea. We saw many fantastic sights,
one in particular was a remote water fall,
"Angel Falls"; it was well-back in the jungle
at the foot of the ever pervasive and majestic

mountains. There's probably a four-lane road to it now along with a "Gedunk" stand.

Since I was a fan of jazz, I spent time at the different lounges that presented that genre of music. I remember in particular spending time with a cool drink in hand (the legal age for booze in Hawaii was 18), listening to the modern sounds of "The Four Freshmen", a group very popular at the time. Another fantastic local musical group was "The Martin Denny Band". It was a small aggregation and their music was unusual to say the least. It was composed of all percussion instruments featuring a Vibraphone. It played music in a tropical vein complete with bird calls and all manner of jungle sounds interspersed with the music – very exotic and perfect in a setting such as Hawaii.

One of my regrets while in Hawaii was that I did not take the time to see the other islands. I also wish I had visited the "Royal Hawaiian Hotel, a place steeped in WWII submarine history. I also regret not having taken the launch out to the remains of the Battleship ARIZONA to pay my respects. Youth is so wasted upon the young.

"All good things must come to an end". And so it was with our stay in that beautiful place. The most important event of our stay in Hawaii was that not one single word of our trip's true purpose was leaked by the crew. It was still a secret.

On Tuesday night, July 22nd, the maneuvering watch was stationed and once again NAUTILUS stood out to sea. Out of sight of land and under the cover of darkness, the deck gang once again painted out all identifying hull numbers and we resumed our interrupted covert mission to gain the North Pole.

Our third trip north was pretty much without incident and fanfare with the exception of our grand submarine logging her 40,000th league (120,000 miles). This was twice the distance covered in Jules Verne's fabled novel "20,000 Leagues Under the Sea". Our rider-techs again crouched over the upward-pinging ice detectors while other techs, along with a couple of our ship's company, monitored the inertial navigation equipment.

We finally passed between Yanaska and Herbert Islands in the Aleutians and into the Bering Sea but it was different this time – foggy and sullen. This was probably the most tension-filled time for me thus far during my QM watches. I had to spend a great deal of time on #1 periscope maintaining a diligent watch for anything out of the ordinary. It was not only stressful but <u>incredibly</u> boring. I would hang on the scope handles, peering through the eyepiece, and scan the water ahead to the horizon (if it were visible) for anything that might endanger the boat, such as floating logs, flotsam and jetsam, etc. It was also of very great importance to identify any signs of human presence or ships of any kind.

The seas for the most part were smooth and glassy – nothing to see at all. It is sometimes far easier to be at one's best and sharpest when involved in a lot of activity. To stare endlessly into an eyepiece of a periscope searching for something – anything, was enough to make even the most

wide-awake insomniac fall into a deep
trance after about ten minutes. It required
every ounce of energy to stay focused on
that monotonous job. To make matters
worse, when I took my eye away from the
eyepiece for a quick rest and looked around
the darkened Attack Center, the effect was
dizzying. One eye was dilated and the other
was not. The effect can be described as if
one were to go outside on a bright sunny day
and cover one eye. I felt as though I looked
like the cartoon character "Bill the Cat",
with one huge eye and one little tiny eye.

On July 29th, NAUTILUS slipped
between the Soviet Union and Alaska
through the Bering Strait and once again
into the Chukchi Sea. Several attempts were
made to penetrate the ice as far from shore
as possible but because of the heavy
concentrations it soon became apparent that
NAUTILUS would have to find another
route. The plan then was to skirt the
northern shore of Alaska to about Point
Barrow, where an existing sea valley was
known to lead straight into the Arctic Basin.
This entailed some risk of being detected but

there was no other choice. Finally, on August 1st, Capt. Anderson ordered the helmsman to make his course heading North. Next stop…the North Pole – 1,094 miles dead ahead. I remember standing my watches with an ever-increasing degree of anticipation, but without really knowing what to expect when the moment came.

As we got closer and closer to the pole, the tension throughout the boat increased. We were at 400 feet making over 20 knots. The Crew's Mess was crowded with just about everyone off watch. As the final moment approached, Capt. Anderson addressed the crew via the 1MC concerning what was about to happen, followed by a few moments of silent meditation in dedication to all who had gone before us. Suddenly he was counting down, "4 – 3 – 2 – 1 – MARK! August 3, 1958, time 2315 (11:15 p.m., EDST), for the United States and the United States Navy, the North Pole." We had not only passed over the Pole, but in the words of Tom Curtis, "we pierced the Pole".

At that moment the entire ship erupted with cheers and shouts of joy. A big party followed in the Crews' Mess complete with a visit from Santa Claus. A cake along with a ceremony followed, including the first enlistment at the North Pole by James Sordelet. A contest to name this crossing of the Pole was then announced. The winning name designation was "PANOPO" – Pacific to Atlantic via North Pole. A great time was had by all and it was then that I realized just how fortunate I was. There are tens of thousands of "Shellbacks" throughout the world's history, but I would forever be one of only 116 people to be designated "PANOPO".

Some interesting statistics were noted in Capt. Anderson's subsequent book, "Nautilus 90 North".

1. We had assembled the largest number of men ever at one time at the North Pole, 116.
2. The water temperature at the pole was 32.4 degrees F.
3. The depth of the water at the pole was 13,410 feet.

    4.   Our ice-detection equipment noted the thickness at the pole as 25 feet.

Suddenly it was over, just like Christmas to a child – all that waiting and anticipation was gone, but unlike Christmas, this would never come again. A feeling of "post-celebration blues" settled over me, but it didn't last long. There were watches to stand, equipment to monitor and maintain, and a long way to go before we were safe again in open water.

On August 5th, we completed our transit and surfaced in the Greenland Sea where Capt. Anderson sent the now famous radio message, "NAUTILUS, 90 North".

The skipper was airlifted off the boat via helicopter to nearby Reykjavic, Iceland, and then flown by plane to the U.S. for a meeting with President Dwight D. Eisenhower. We continued on to Portland, England, where to our great surprise, we were greeted by much "pomp and circumstance". We were just happy to see land again and couldn't wait to set foot on it, although it was somewhat of a nuisance at the time for we just wanted to get home. Arriving at the coaling-pier in Portland, I was on the Bridge keeping the Quartermaster's Notebook, the official ship's log; I couldn't believe the sight that greeted us. The quay was full of cheering people along with bands and local dignitaries. We were certainly not prepared to be treated like "rock stars". People everywhere greeted us warmly and asked for autographs. One couldn't buy a drink. There were any number of official notices, proclamations, and ceremonies hailing us as heroes. Gaggles of giggling girls followed us everywhere we went giggling and asking for autographs. It was <u>unbelievable</u>. It was a bit overwhelming to such a young lad as I. It was almost a dream-like and surreal state of mind. We were sorry to leave those new friends upon leaving Portland, but still anxious to get home, but there was yet one more stop along the way. We arrived in New York City to the same adulation as received in England. Upon arriving there we were received by an even more spectacular greeting, with tug and fire boats spraying great plumes of water into the air as they escorted us to our berthing space. This was followed by all manner of tributes and allocates, a luncheon at the Waldorf-Astoria, free tickets to Yankee Stadium where the crew was acknowledged, and of course, the free drinks and requests for autographs were repeated. It was almost too much to bear, but somehow we managed.

All this was topped off by a ticker-tape parade down Wall Street. It was indescribable, like being in an old news reel.

Finally, underway one last time, we stood into the Thames River the one thing everyone wanted by this time was just to get home to Groton. As we slowly stood into the Thames River and passed New London Ledge Light we began to see the multitude of people on the pier at Electric Boat. We arrived at our homeport of Groton once again to a tremendous welcome, but this time by friends and family; and we were greeted by a huge banner reading, "Welcome Home PANOPOs". I never felt such warmth of camaraderie and pride in accomplishing something of substance.

Only time has allowed me to place the event into the context of history and by the sheer stroke of luck, and GOD's holy hand, I was part of it. It was, in the words of our XO, LCDR. Frank Adams, "Fan-Dam-Tastic!" We knew we were home and we were happy. Life was good.

Some memories of my 1958 trans-polar trip in NAUTILUS.

So many years have gone by; it hardly seems possible to me, but make no mistake, these memories are, thankfully, still vivid in my mind.

As a 20-year-old Seaman First Class Quartermaster striker (apprentice), I didn't realize at the time the true significance of what was happening. That came later with maturity. I was much too naïve to realize that the forthcoming trip under the North Pole would become one of the most momentous and important focal points of my life.

At the actual time of the polar crossing, I was off watch and in the Crew's Mess, along with most of the off-watch crew. I recall listening to Capt. Anderson count down to the "Mark" and feeling, "Is this truly happening? Am I really here, a part of this?" After the party, cake, "Santa Claus" and various ceremonies, things returned to normal very quickly. A sort of "after-Christmas blues" settled over most of us, only, unlike Christmas, this moment in time would never come again. It was back to the business of navigating our way back to land from under the Arctic ice.


Stick a fork in me – I'm done.

I hated to see it go – it was such a beautiful place; but the Panama Canal was now astern of NAUTILUS as she stood out into the great expanse of the Pacific Ocean. It was May 4, 1958, and we were beginning our second tour of the west coast.

Captain William R. Anderson decided that since we were so close to the

Equator and, being ahead of our SOA (Speed of Advance – an average speed calculated to arrive at a designated destination), that we should cross that imaginary line in the ocean and give the boat a chance to initiate any "pollywogs" on board into that royal order of the deep as "Shellbacks". Alas, it was not to be.

For some time during the transit from Groton, CT, watch standers in the Engine/Maneuvering Room had been complaining of watery and burning eyes but no cause could be found. It was the Main Propulsion Officer who noticed a small wisp of smoke emanating from around the port main turbine. It was suspected that a small oil leak was responsible. As personnel began to investigate further, the smoke became more prevalent and soon all those in the area began to have trouble seeing and breathing. News of the situation was passed to the Control Room and the announcement was made over the 1MC (the boat's main announcing system), "Fire in the Engine Room". Of all the things that can happen on a submarine, uncontrolled flooding or fire are the most dreaded.

Acrid smoke soon filled the Engine/Maneuvering Room, but no flames were visible. The compartment was sealed off from the rest of the boat with the water-tight doors at either end while watch standers within put on goggles and draped wet towels over their faces in an effort to breathe. Meanwhile, two men donned portable breathing devices and entered the lower level section of the Engine Room to locate the source of the smoke. Capt. Anderson stopped the port turbine, brought the boat to periscope depth, and ordered the snorkel mast raised in an effort to ventilate the boat. It was to no avail – the engineering spaces were becoming uninhabitable.

Realizing that the problem could not be fixed while submerged, Capt. Anderson ordered NAUTILUS to the surface. The boat surfaced into a beautifully bright, calm, tropical sea and the Engine Room hatch to the afterdeck was opened to help evacuate smoke from the compartment. To assist in this, the "Dinky Diesel", a source of emergency propulsion and battery charging on the surface or while snorkeling was "lit off" (started up). The diesel engine took its air supply from the Engine Room and as such would draw the smoke from that compartment very quickly.

By now it was recognized that NAUTILUS had a serious situation on her hands. The smoke was really pouring out of the lower level but by this time the source had finally been identified. Now began the process of removing the smoldering lagging, or insulation, from around the port turbine and passing it topside where it would be thrown overboard. It was a very slow and tedious process and involved heroic and dedicated efforts on the parts of all those involved.

Meanwhile, the remaining members of the crew not involved in fighting the fire were allowed to go topside through the forward or Torpedo Room hatch. Since I fell into that category I went up on deck and, finding such a beautiful summer day, promptly stripped off my shirt to get "some rays" – big mistake. I had not realized that at those latitudes the rays of the sun came almost straight down and did not have the benefit of being filtered somewhat by slanting through more of the atmosphere such as was had at northerly climes. Soon, very soon, I began to feel heat on my body and flipping up my sunglasses realized that I was already red. Get the fork ready – I was done! I looked like a lobster right out of the pot. I whipped my shirt and went below but it was too late. I had the "Mother of all sunburns".

By the next day my entire back was one big blister. Later as the blister began to dry, my back turned into a crusty mass and each and every movement brought excruciating pain. I was completely embarrassed at being so stupid as to place myself in such a situation. The thought of my not being able to pull my weight, especially in light of what my shipmates had just gone through in fighting the fire, was unthinkable. I had to stand my watches, and I did.

In retrospect it was probably foolish and immature of me to take that action, but at the time it seemed like the thing to do. I was indeed fortunate that I did not suffer any infections or other complications that might have placed me on the "Binnacle List" (sick and off duty list) and in a far more precarious position than if I had just gone to the Pharmacist's Mate for treatment. It was a hard lesson learned, and since that day I've never gone out to get a suntan.

As for the fire, it was discovered that after a very long time, the lagging on the turbine had become saturated with oil, and when heated to higher temperatures because of the tropical seas, had ignited and begun to smolder, bursting into flames every time some of it was removed, exposing it to oxygen. Only the heroic efforts of those crew members who fought that smoky blaze saved NAUTILUS from a potentially disastrous situation.

Finally, NAUTILUS resumed her trip, not south to the Equator, but north to San Diego, CA. Instead of becoming a

"Shellback" I remained a lowly "Pollywog",
albeit, a very well-done "Pollywog".


The Air-Expulsion Head.

HEAD – toilet compartment aboard
a vessel; originally at the small tower deck
forward with the most privacy; well defined
on vessels such as Santa Maria, Mayflower,
etc.

This definition as described in
"Royce's Sailing Illustrated" and the
"Navy's Bluejacket Manual".

We all have need for devices such as
these, be it fancy or plain. When we were
tiny tots, we all either went "pee-pee",
"wee-wee", "piddle", or "poop". Now that
we are sophisticated adults, we go take a
"piss", a "whiz", a "leak" a "dump", a
"crap", or "see a man about a dog", a phrase
the meaning of which has always eluded me.
If one is properly polite and politically
correct, one has a "B.M.". In this
electronically enlightened age we might
even be said to "download" our most recent

meal. The most proper and respectable elite among us probably "relieve themselves in the facility".

As youngsters in school, when "nature called" we were required to raise our hand and extend either one or two fingers to indicate the task to be attended to. Why in this world any teacher would ever want this information was way beyond me, but the technique usually worked to get out of class at least once a period.

The venue for all this activity is likewise fondly known by a myriad of names. We go to the "John", to the detriment or amusement of all so named (so named in honor of the toilet's inventor, John Crapper). We also go to the "rest room", where I strongly doubt there is very much restorative rest to be had. We have the "lavatory", (Latin – Lavare, to wash), and the toilet, (French – toile, a room with a bowl-shaped fixture for defecation and urination. This is not to be confused with the French word, toilette, which is the process of grooming oneself). Unfortunately, some visit the toilet without using the lavatory; do not share your popcorn with these types. Often we are said to be "on the throne", in none other than the "throne room". Of course, some disappear for hours in the "library", while those in Great Britain go to the "loo". There are endless names for these facilities, but you get the point. As Shakespeare once said, "A rose by any other name…"

While at Sub School, part of the training involved learning the operation of the boat's sanitary system. The school-boat I studied was the USS BECUNA SS-319. She was a Balao-class variant Perch, laid down 4/29/43, launched 1/30/44, and commissioned, 5/27/44. She made five war patrols during WWII, and is credited with sinking four ships with a total tonnage of 18,600 tons, a respectable war record. By the time I studied her, she had undergone many modifications, being thereafter designated as a "Guppy-1A", but much of her interior layout remained as she was built, including the "heads".

Upon graduation from Sub School on 3/27/57, class # 141, I was assigned to the USS NAUTILUS SSN-571, the world's first nuclear vessel. Most of what I'd learned in Sub School went out #1 torpedo tube. Permit me to jump ahead for a moment to describe, for comparison's sake, the sanitary systems aboard NAUTILUS. They basically worked like this:

The bowl is made of stainless steel with a large rotating plug, or ball valve, in the bottom. (Think of a solid cylinder with a long slot cut through the side). When the slot is opened to the bowl by rotating the cylinder with an upright and long handle, the waste flows through it to a sanitary tank below. Rotating the lever the other way re-closes the valve. This valve was known as the "flapper valve". A small amount of water, through another system, is used to put a water-seal on the plug before and after use. Below the flapper valve is a large gate, or stop valve which seals off the bowl from the sanitary tank. To empty the sanitary tank, done by qualified persons on watch, one would shut the flapper valve, stop valve, and check the inboard vent on the sanitary tank, shut. Now the tanks were ready to be emptied, or blown dry.

Blowing sanitary tanks is usually done once a day and at a fairly shallow depth to minimize the amount of compressed air needed to overcome sea pressure outside the boat and to minimize the venting time after emptying is accomplished. Once all systems are "lined-up" the order is given from the Control Room, "Blow Sanitary Tanks". After they are emptied, the tanks, because they are now full of compressed air, must be vented of that air. This is the not so great part since, being at sea, submerged, the foul air must be vented inside the boat. It's sort of like being locked inside a wooden, "three-holer" out-house after "depositing" a week's worth of corned-beef and cabbage. The venting is done through the large activated-charcoal filters to minimize the smell. Of course, no filter on this earth could be efficient enough to eliminate the entire stench that then wafts throughout the boat until the ventilation system can absorb it. Pretty simple, huh?

Now we will examine the "Air-Expulsion Head" on the "Fleet Type" submarines that served so magnificently during WWII. The primary way to flush the heads was to apply air pressure directly to each "unit" after use, blowing the waste from a small receiver tank overboard. This, on the face of it, may not seem so difficult, but to actually perform this complicated task, one practically had to have a PhD in engineering and physics, plus a thorough knowledge of the sub's "plumbing" system. Any variance from the procedure, or the slightest lapse in total concentration could result in a "face-full" of whatever one just put into the bowl. The other consequence was that one could flood the boat through the toilet. I don't know which was worse.

### Before Deposit.

See that bowl flapper valve "A" is <u>shut,</u> that gate valve "C" in the discharge line is <u>open,</u> and that valve "D" in the water supply line is <u>open</u>.

<u>Open</u> valve "E" next to the bowl to admit necessary water to bowl.

Close valve "D" and "E".

<u>After Deposit.</u>

Pull lever "A".  Release lever "A".

Open valve "G" in the air-supply line.

"Rock" valve "F" lever outboard to charge measuring tank to 10 psi above sea pressure.

Open valve "B" and "rock" air valve "F" inboard to blow waste overboard.

Close valves "B", "C", and "G".

An alternative to "blowing" waste overboard with compressed air was to "pump" it overboard.  The instructions were the same except that instead of opening the air valve, there was a pump handle nearby which required arms like "Popeye the sailor man" to operate.

So it was with the most diabolical device ever conceived, probably by Satan himself, designed to flush human waste into the "green locker".  I was forever thankful that NAUTILUS didn't have one of those constipation-inducing waste disposal contraptions as part of her design.

Now, if you'll pardon me, I have to go use the head.

The North Pole, fifty years later.

"I may never do anything else in my life that anybody outside my own family cares about, but I have done one thing that gives me a place in history."

I was reading a book about the 1928-30 Byrd Expedition to Antarctica when suddenly, these words quoted by an unknown member of that expedition jumped off the page at me. I stared in wonder as they seemed to levitate off the page. It was as if someone had plucked those very sentiments from my brain. I was transfixed. I read and re-read the sentence over and over again, wondering how anyone could have experienced those exact same emotions as I.

The book, "With Byrd at the Bottom of the World", written by Norman D.

Vaughan with Cecil B. Murphey, recounts
the adventures of the very young Vaughan
who, by skills acquired in training sled dogs
in New Hampshire, obtained a position on
that expedition, where Byrd would become
the first person to fly to the South Pole. It
turned out that Vaughan was a key player in
the success of that long and perilous
expedition, although at the time, he felt that
he was just part of the team doing anything
he could and feeling privileged just to be
along on such an adventure. His duties were
to train the almost 100 sled dogs and plan
and coordinate all the logistics involved in
every use of the dogs. The plan was three-
fold. The first part was to transport by dog
sled from the two supply ships, six hundred
and fifty tons of supplies and building
materials, including three airplanes, needed
to construct "Little America", the ice base
from which the expedition would begin.

The second part was to strike out
from "Little America" and lay a cache of
supplies along a southern route to the Queen
Maud Mountains, about half-way to the
South Pole. Once there, he was to be part of

a geological party to explore east and west for evidence of historical and geological importance.

The third part of the plan was to be a sort of life-guard station to rescue Byrd should his plane be forced down at or near the pole.

That Byrd Expedition would later turn out to be the end of the era of primitive exploration with the use of expendable dogs. The final chapter in that form of Arctic and Antarctic exploratory history would be forever closed. Newer forms of exploration and new technology would soon follow and, as fate would have it, I was to be a part of it.

Vaughan, waited some sixty-odd years to write his account noting that "Being twenty-five and not as mature as some of the others, I didn't appreciate at the time the lasting personal significance of membership in the Byrd Expedition. I had not begun to understand that in the years ahead, no matter what else I did, I would point back to the months in the Antarctic as my finest."

These are my very same personal reflections of when, at the age of 20, on August 3, 1958, I was part of the USS NAUTILUS transit under the North Pole, another first in history. As I now look back upon in excess of fifty years during my role as a tender and naïve crewmember in NAUTILUS, I realize that I was not alone in having those same emotions so well expressed by Norman Vaughan. I'm now sure that, to a man, anyone who has ever been blessed with such an experience would, no doubt, feel those very same thoughts.


A day late and a dollar short.

I was so excited. It was 1000 hours, March 27, 1957, and being just shy of my 19th birthday, I had graduated Class 141, U.S. Submarine School, New London, CT. (The Sub Base is actually across the Thames River in Groton, CT). I finished pretty well too as #8 in my class of 44 with a grade point average of 3.68. The best and most amazing part was that I was assigned to the U.S.S. NAUTILUS SSN-571, not only the first atomic sub, but as it was then called, "the world's first ship powered by nuclear power". But before reporting aboard, I departed on March 29th for a ten-day leave to see my family in Bellaire, Texas.

There I had a wonderful time with my parents and two brothers, Charlie and Richard, but all too soon it was time to head back to New London. I read through my orders and decided that I needed to head back on April 7th. Dad drove me to Dallas where we said goodbye at Love Field Airport and I boarded one of the now famous Lockheed Constellations for my flight back to the East Coast (Jet-aircraft were just starting to replace "prop-jobs" in the field of commercial aviation, and I now consider myself very lucky to have flown on perhaps one of the most beautiful airplanes ever designed).

By today's standards, that flight would have been almost intolerable in its number of stops. We made five including the final landing. The first at Shreveport, LA, then on to Jackson, MS, Atlanta, GA, Washington, DC, and finally landing at

Newark, NJ. In time-frame it was "wheels-up" in Dallas at 0800 and "touchdown" in Newark at 1800, actually not too bad considering all the stops along the way.

After visiting my cousin in Irvington, NJ for the evening, I took a bus to New York City and caught the New Haven Railroad train out of Grand Central Station at 0040, bound for New London, CT. It was now April 8th. The train screeched to a stop in New London at 0330. I grabbed my sea bag from a "locker club" across the street and above a pool hall, and took a cab to E.B. (Electric Boat), where NAUTILUS was completing her first reactor core refueling. I passed through the guard shack and descended down the long steep hill, through the "wind tunnel" between two buildings, and found the barge where the NAUTILUS crew was billeted. I found a rack (bunk) and climbed in for some "shut-eye". It had been a long day.

The next morning after quarters, the Chief of the Boat (COB) pulled me aside and said, "Come with me." He took me to the Wardroom where he introduced me to the XO (Executive Officer, or second in command). I began to sweat as he informed me that I was a day late in returning from leave. I should have returned the previous day, April 7th. I had in my inexperience, misread and misunderstood the return date. I had visions of breaking up rocks at the Portsmouth Naval Prison for the rest of my enlistment, but apparently realizing how completely "green" I was, charged it up to extreme youth and let it slide with no punishment. I can tell you this, however, from that time forward my eyes scoured the words off the paper that any orders were written on and therefore always arrived before the assigned time.

Hell hath no fury like a tempestuous sea.

If I close my eyes I can still vividly smell that first rush of salt air coming down the bridge trunk upon surfacing. Some thought it stunk but I liked it. Actually, I loved being on the surface as long as I had taken a dose of Dramamine beforehand. If not, I dreaded running on the surface for I became violently sick.  On those rare occasions when I didn't have time for "my fix" I could usually be found retching into a #10 food can, wishing I were dead.

On this occasion NAUTILUS was on the surface between Scotland and Ireland, in the North Channel, returning with a damaged sail and periscopes from an aborted surfacing attempt under the Arctic ice.  It was the autumn of 1957, and after the portion of our cruise north we were scheduled to participate in a NATO exercise.  We were on the surface because the water in that area was not deep enough to run submerged.

My underway watch duties at that time involved helm and planes watches. Being on the surface negated any duties on the bow or stern planes so the three seamen assigned to these duties would rotate between a one half-hour turn on the helm and a one hour turn on the bridge as lookout.

As it happened, there was a huge gale blowing with seas running twenty to thirty feet or so with monster swells that would almost completely engulf the boat from astern in the following sea. The seas would sweep over us alternately placing us in a trough, leaving us to look up at the wave crests as one would stand in a valley gazing up at the mountains, then pushing us to the crest of one of those swells where it seemed one could see forever. So it was that I found myself on the bridge as the port lookout. On the bridge besides myself and the starboard lookout was the Conning Officer. The bridge hatch was on the latch (shut but not dogged down) because of the heavy seas. It felt so good being up on the bridge where I could keep my bearings and gaze at these magnificent seas, that I volunteered to remain as lookout for my entire four hour watch. That was a big hit with the other two seamen because they didn't want any part of being topside in that storm any longer than they had to be and were content to just alternate between the two of them. To a young kid this was exciting stuff.

At times I thought the boat was diving out from under us as the swells would cover the entire hull leaving only the sail out of the water. On several occasions the swells came up the sail almost to the bridge deck, so high in fact that we lookouts hoisted our feet off the platforms we stood on in anticipation of getting our feet wet.

After one of the swells rolled over us I looked aft and noticed a portion of the afterdeck was missing. I had to scream the observation to the OD in order to be heard over the roaring wind. With each passing swell, the hole got bigger and bigger, even ripping away some ballast tank piping and miscellaneous gear. It's just hard to imagine just what water can do to a metal ship. It was an awesome display of power by the sea when it gets angry; an unforgettable lesson in hydraulics.

We had to put in for temporary repairs alongside a Sub Tender up the Firth of Clyde in the Scottish port of Rothesay.

With repairs made we then proceeded to our assigned duties in the NATO exercise dubbed "Strikeback" as scheduled and with only one periscope and a huge steel patch on our after deck we proceeded to show the world's navies what NAUTILUS could do.


How I almost became fish-food.

NAUTILUS was in Mare Island Naval Shipyard in summer of 1958 during our "tour" of the west coast. It was here that I finally completed my submarine qualification (the 164th person to do so in NAUTILUS) and was promptly tossed over the side into the murky river. I was a happy, happy kid.

It was a very busy time in the Yard with much emphasis on finding and repairing the elusive leak in the port main condenser, (it was never found), and a myriad of other repairs and upkeep items. This included some work inside the sail and a complete paint job of the boat topside. The day before we got underway, it fell to the QM gang to thoroughly inspect the inside of the sail for any loose gear adrift. That, in turn, meant me, the junior man in the Navigation Department. The submarine's sail houses all of the boat's different masts – periscopes, radar, radio, ECM, snorkel, etc. The inside of the sail is a labyrinth of hundreds (it seemed like thousands) of angle braces going every which way imaginable, which support the sail structure, in and around all of the masts. I spent better than an hour crawling and squeezing through this endless maze retrieving all the stuff I could find including shipyard fire extinguishers used during welding repairs. After the Yard made their count they were one short. Time was up and we finally got underway. Once outside the Golden Gate Bridge and into deep water we made a trim dive. Some banging and clunking was heard in the Attack Center but no one knew the cause.

I had the QM watch when we surfaced after the dive. It was normal to make radio transmissions while on the surface so the command came over the 21MC to raise the starboard whip antenna. The comforting squeal of high pressure hydraulic oil coursing through the piping to

the mast was suddenly broken by a loud
bang followed by a roaring sound which
lasted about a half a minute or so. Then
silence. Next came a call over the 1MC for
the Chief Auxiliaryman to lay up to the
bridge. That would be "Big Daddy" who
went flying by me up the ladder to the
bridge, closely followed by other members
of A-Gang. After a few minutes a call came
over the 21MC for QM striker to lay to the
bridge, "on the double". I climbed up the 20
foot bridge ladder to come face to face with
the Chief A-Ganger who was as angry as I
have ever seen a man be. In his hand was
the oily remains of our errant fire
extinguisher. Lost and unseen in the jumble
of angle braces, it had become dislodged
during our trim dive and then jammed near
the starboard whip antenna mast. Upon
raising the mast it severed the hydraulic line
and broke off the extinguisher nozzle which
promptly turned the entire area into some
kind of oily winter wonderland. Not so
wonderful for the Chief Auxiliaryman and
his crew who had to make repairs under
those slippery and filthy conditions. Well,
I'm sure that those present on the bridge can

attest to the fact that as the Chief handed that dripping, slimy mess to me, with the order to lay down to the main deck and heave the beast overboard, every ounce of blood drained from my face. I clambered down the sail ladders with my slippery charge, opened the sail door, and was about to store the thing in the "green locker" when I heard the Chief, livid with rage, holler down to me that if I knew what was good for me, I would follow the damned thing over the side. No one will ever know just how close I came to doing just that. Even facing my boss, "Doggie" afterward was a relief.

How I spent my 21st birthday.

It was April 23, 1959, my 21st birthday, and I had just gotten off the QM mid-watch. NAUTILUS was submerged at about 600 feet somewhere in the Atlantic playing "cat-'n'-mouse" games with three "tin cans" (destroyers). I crawled into my rack in the lower starboard bunk located in the Forward Torpedo Room and immediately drifted off to sleep. It seemed I

had just fallen asleep when I was jarred
awake by the stern command, "Surface,
surface, surface, over the 1MC, the boat's
"public address" system. This was followed
by the usual three blasts of the klaxon alarm.
Now on some submarines, at the
Commanding Officer's discretion, the word
"surface" precedes the sounding of the
klaxon alarm. That was NOT the case with
NAUTILUS. Such a change in procedure
rang an alarm bell in my head and I was
awake and out of my rack in a heartbeat.
The surfacing alarm was closely followed by
the collision alarm and the words, "flooding
in the Engine Room". Now that really got
my attention. I started up the three or four
steps from the bunk room to where the
water-tight door that separates the Forward
Room from the Crew's Mess was located.
Also at that location were the bulkhead
flapper valves, ventilation valves that
separate one water-tight compartment from
another and can be operated from either side
of the bulkhead. One of our Torpedomen
had already secured both by the time I
reached his side. We stood there glancing at
each other, wondering what had happened as

the deafening roar of 3000 pound air rushed into the main ballast tanks. The boat took an ever increasing up-angle until it was close to 45 degrees. We discussed whether we were going up or down, waiting for some tell-tale sense of motion. In the background was chatter from the 21MC, another communication circuit that connected the Forward Room, the Control/Attack Center areas and the engineering spaces. It was clear while listening to that, that the Engine Room was taking on a lot of water. There was apprehension but no fear as we waited to see what would happen next.

During such times it is not unusual for the most bizarre and peculiar thoughts to occur. It certainly did with me. I remember joking that if we failed to surface, I would never get my first legal drink.

Finally, after what seemed an eternity, to our relief, we sensed an upward motion, much like one would feel in an elevator. Well, from the original 600 foot depth to whatever the maximum depth the boat attained during the flooding, (the depth could only be estimated based on the angle of the boat), the sudden positive buoyancy resulted in an ever increasing speed as she raced toward the surface. The three destroyers operating with us, and having been warned of our predicament via "Gertrude", the underwater telephone, promptly peeled off in some direction, hopefully turning away and not toward us. It must have been one hell of a sight to them as we broached from the depths like a whale and then slammed back onto the surface of the ocean.

It was determined that a 4" sea suction flex coupling in the lower level Engine Room had failed, filling the space with an almost atomized spray of water under the intense pressure. Visibility must have been almost impossible under those conditions, but somehow the watch standers in that space managed to quickly locate and secure the stop and sea valves to that coupling.

We were now on the surface, bobbing around while the engineers tried to restart the reactor which had "scrammed" (shut down) automatically upon rigging the boat for collision. Now another thought occurred to me. I was always prone to sea sickness and upon knowing beforehand that we were to surface, I would take Dramamine. Well, it was too late now and the thoughts of barfing into a #10 can had already begun to make my stomach turn (no doubt the power of suggestion). Thankfully, our tired old reactor was started up in about thirty minutes while repairs were made to the coupling and we bid adieu to the surface and dived into our proper element to continue our operations.

One interesting sidebar to this tale is about the power of the human body when it is fed vast amounts of adrenaline. While the engineers were enabling all the systems to restart the reactor (go critical) it was discovered that some of the valves that had been shut by hand during the flooding casualty were secured so tightly that come-a-longs (a cable winching device) was needed to reopen them.

I'm sure that many of the crew, especially those who dealt first hand with the flooding, later reflected on the ramifications of the casualty that befell our fine submarine, but if they did it was done in private for I never heard anyone discuss the incident to any great degree. It was just something that happened – it was dealt with and then it was back to business as usual.

Much later in my life, on April 10, 1963, to be exact, I listened with horror to the radio broadcast of the loss of the USS THRESHER SSN-593, and thought, "there but for the grace of GOD went we". On board that doomed submarine were two of my former shipmates from NAUTILUS. A third shipmate had escaped their fate by remaining home on the day of the fatal cruise departure. But for the heroic efforts of all those who were on watch, NAUTILUS might have met the same fate as THRESHER and subsequently dealt a severe blow to nuclear power.

Since then I mark my calendar every year with the loss dates of all U.S. Submarines and when those days arrive, I pause to reflect on those souls still on "Eternal Patrol" and how much different things could have been for us.

"Lola"

That wasn't her real name, only a nickname. She wasn't "born" with that moniker, but acquired it shortly after she fledged into the U.S. Submarine Fleet with her commissioning on September 30, 1954. Her real name was USS NAUTILUS SSN-571, the world's first atomic powered ship – the "Atom" sub. I say "atomic" because that's the term that was used way back in January 21, 1954, when as the brainchild of then Captain Hyman G. Rickover, she was launched down the ways of the Electric Boat Company in Groton, CT. Eventually the term "atomic" was replaced by "nuclear" to describe the type of power plant that drove this new kind of ship.

Being the new "Queen" of the Submarine Navy, she was lavished upon befitting any real live royalty. Her every whim was met, almost without question. However, the U.S. Navy had budgets to adhere to at every level of command and the submarine fleet was no exception.

However, whatever NAUTILUS wanted or needed, she got, sometimes at the expense of other submarines' budgets. All of a sudden, along came this new-fangled boat with all its "hoop-la" and publicity, getting anything she wanted. That was not well-received among the other subs attached to the Sub Base in New London (Groton), who sometimes had to extort any means to gain equipment for their boats. Soon, NAUTILUS became known around the sub fleet (at least around the Sub Base in New London), as "Lola, after the song in which the lyrics claim, "Whatever Lola wants, Lola gets". It was a somewhat derogatory term, but to NAUTILUS, it mattered not. It could have been rumored that crew members were known to hum the tune while filling out supply requests. Who knows?

As in all life, times change and things never stay as they once were. That was also true of NAUTILUS. As the years progressed after 1960, she matured into the submarine fleet and her assignments changed from the headline grabbing kind into more standard type of submarine operations. Also, as newer and more advanced nuclear subs came off the ways, they grabbed the headlines and notoriety. Slowly but surely NAUTILUS's fame and fortune began to fade into memory as she aged. She was no longer known as "Lola", the submarine that got anything she asked for, but became just another submarine in the fleet that had needs like every other boat. After more than twenty-five years of service she had become an "old lady" who's parts, as they wore out, became increasingly difficult to replace. On March 3, 1980, she was decommissioned from the fleet at Mare Island Naval Shipyard, her future, if any, to be determined.

Eventually, in 1982, she was designated a National Historic Landmark and on July 6, 1985, after an extensive conversion as a museum ship, she triumphantly returned to Groton, CT, the place of her "birth", where she became the showcase of the Submarine Force Library and Museum. As such she will forever remain, "The First and Finest" of the nuclear submarine fleet. But in the hearts and minds of her early crew, she will continue to be fondly remembered as "Lola".


FROM: Bob Marble, TMCS(SS), USS PIPER SS-409 –

Sandpiper.

Back on 7/19/1958, PIPER got underway to check out two newly-installed "goodies". One was the new Magnetic Underwater Log, replacing the old "Pit Log" and a newly-installed depth sounder (Fathometer). After successfully completing the checks and calibrations, we were en-route to the Faroe Islands near Soviet Territory to do things that make "Blind Man's Bluff" believable. Our Chief Radioman, Barney, was COW on the 0400-0800 watch, and the Chief Electrician's Mate, "Dinny", was his relief. PIPER is laying off Wood's End at Provincetown, MA waiting for sunrise to run the "measured mile" to calibrate the new Magnetic Log and check out the new Fathometer. I was up early and passed through COC with coffee in hand, when Barney says, "According to the trace on this new-fangled thing, we're aground". The Conning Tower was manned by Skelton, QM2, taking "fixes" every 15 minutes, logging them and reporting to LT "Willie", the OOD on the bridge and the Operations Officer, LT Rowan. Skelton noticed something wrong immediately. PIPER had stopped swinging in the morning breeze as had been the case earlier. He logged this and reported as before. The OOD acknowledged and the OPS Officer told him "not to sweat it and lay back down on the Conning Tower deck mats, to go back to sleep." Barney was relieved by the COB "Dinny" as COW.

The IC Electrician on watch in COC noticed the inclinometer reading at the COC Emergency Helm, "twas a bubble off, indicating a list. The COW dispatched the off-watch lookout to notify CO LCDR Bowcock, Jr., who was asleep in his stateroom. He came into COC in his shorts to find out what was happening. It was obvious we were aground on a sandbar. The

CO ordered the COW, Dinny, to open all vents, so that the incoming tide would not force the boat any higher on the sandbar. The CO got dressed and practically yanked me out of the "Goat Locker" and says, "Get topside with Chief Dinny and stand by to rig for tow."

The COB got a relief, donned his gear and headed out on deck through the Conning Tower. I followed after summoning a few guys from the "topside gang" to assist. We broke out #2 nylon mooring line and some "heavies" ready to send to a Coast Guard vessel that inevitably would show up as soon as they got the word. Just about then, a Piper Cub type plane (very appropriately designated) flew over with its starboard window down, yelling, "Are you guys stuck in the sand?" It made a few passes and lo and behold, it wasn't long before a trusty Coast Guard cutter showed up, and via radio offered to get PIPER off the sandbar. Our CO dare not refuse his offer. (The name of the cutter was FREDERICK C. LEE, based in Provincetown, MA.)

PIPER was still holding fast on the sandbar as the tide rose and as the water was nearing topside level. Back in the Engine Rooms, the Enginemen were checking the strainers for the diesel seawater cooling and the Electricians in the Maneuvering Room were checking the Main Motor seawater coolant system for sand intrusion.

Via radio, the CO agreed to accept a tow from the cutter, and a 5" nylon hawser was sent by the cutter in its whaleboat, where its eye was placed on a port cleat adjacent to the sail. The procedure was for the PIPER to shut the MBT vents, blow the ship's whistle to signal the cutter to start the tow, and PIPER would "blow and go" Ahead Full on two main engines. When this was executed, the poor little cutter was being dragged along stern-first, with the sea swamping his after decks due to his "cracker box"-shaped stern. He was screaming in his radio to cease the tow, and our CO says, "What did he say?" I could see a little smirk on his face as he took his time to cease the tow. Our CO radioed his thanks to the cutter's Captain and wished him a safe return to port.  The guy must have been mad after he received the message.

Prior to all this excitement, ComSubGruTwo had been notified and Captain Hazzard had embarked in USS SUNBIRD ASR-15, and left New London at 0930, arriving quite sometime later as we remained underway making no headway.  A sort of critique was convened and it was agreed that no apparent damage was sustained to PIPER, so we all headed back to New London, tied up at pier #2 awaiting entry in the marine railway nearby.

A Board of Inquiry was convened after PIPER was thoroughly gone over, and no damage was found, except some sand was found in the strainers as a result of the "blow and go" and Full Ahead on two main engines.  The CO, Bowcock, was relieved of command by LCDR Francis and we got a new XO.

LT Crabtree who came below and caught me in the Goat Locker sucking on a cup of coffee and said, "Congratulations, you're PIPER's new COB, find Chief Dinny

and send him to my stateroom immediately.
I did that, catching his stress on the word
"immediately". When Chief Dinny arrived
at his stateroom, the XO handed him his
service record and orders to another boat
and says to him, "Don't ever ask why."
Chief Dinny went into the Goat Locker
where all the Chiefs were crammed in their
bunks and standing around to find out what
was happening, pushed them out of his way
and stuffed all his belongings (except his
uniforms) into a "fartsack" cover, and left
the boat with me trailing behind with his
uniforms in his Valpack. I never had a
chance to speak to him about all this and
often wondered what the reason was. It's a
good thing I was a curious sort, because I
used to hang around the COC observing
what each man's job was, especially the
COW's duties, whenever I could be spared
in the FTR and ATR. When the XO told me
that I was now the PIPER's new COB, I
almost wet myself when that exploded in my
face. The OOD at the time of the grounding
was LT Willie (son of an Admiral) and the
OPS Officer, LT Rowan, were transferred
and so was the XO. Contrary to all the

newspaper articles, the PIPER did not "run aground", however, a grounding no less. The last I heard about LCDR Bowcock's whereabouts, he was on "Dewline Patrol" in the Atlantic on an LST, a broken man, no doubt. The USS SEAWOLF SSN-575 relieved PIPER, after just returning from a Med cruise. A lot of unhappy campers and their brides were created as a result of their new assignment. A calibration of the new Magnetic Speed Indicator and the new Fathometer was accomplished at a later date far away from Provincetown, MA.

Final Remarks of PIPER'S Third War Patrol.

By LTCDR Edward L. Beach, CO USS PIPER, for her Third War patrol. July 1945 – September 1945.

The Commanding Officer may be pardoned, surely, for feeling a little disappointed at the fact that, after eleven War Patrols in subordinate capacities, he finally achieved command, and entered one of the last areas still considered potentially productive with a ship and crew trained to a high condition of readiness, only to have the war end ten hours after he arrived in the area.

It is, however, with a soul full of emotion that he adds these final remarks to what may well be the last War Patrol of the Submarine War. Having served in Submarines Pacific since the start of the war, since those dark days of 1942 when disaster appeared to be pressing steadily closer and closer, having seen (and been part of) that thin gray wall which held the enemy in check while the nation looked at despair and came raging back – having fought beside men who laughed at futility, who spit in the face of the dragon, who quietly and gaily interposed their puny bodies athwart the course of the Beast – having grieved at those names who inspired us and left their legacy – HARDER, SEAWOLF, WAHOO, TRIGGER, GUDGEON, TANG, BONEFISH, GRAYBACK – he hopes that he may be forgiven for a bit of sentiment.

The realization is growing swiftly
that no more will the warheads announce
our answer to the barbarians; no more will
the loins quiver and spine tingle at the chase;
no more will the heady champagne of
conflict steady our aim; nor will experience
the fierce joy of a sturdy hull, a steady hand
on the helm, four engines roaring a bit more
than their rated full power, of riding our
steel chariot bridge right into the teeth of the
huge foe, tearing out his vitals while in
terror he vainly shoots his guns and
helplessly tries to get away.

Never again the blind groping of the
water mole, listening, always listening – nor
the steaming, sweating, drenching heat, the
decks and bulkheads solid water,
perspiration running down your bare chest
and back, soaking the rags and towels you
vainly throw around you, soaking your
trousers and shoes – while you pay no
attention, act unconcerned (if they only
knew), keep reliefs going to the planes and
steering, keep checking all compartments
after each salvo, keep the soundman on –
He's dead tired but you couldn't get rid of

him anyway – and you listen, and guess, and maneuver, and wait…

And now, the small perspective grows large. It wasn't just one sub against Japan. In that cloudy sky, there are no longer enemy planes, out to get that sub. In those white-capped waves are no longer the periscopes of the foe, but only our own. In these contested waters floats a mighty fleet, but it flies the stars and stripes. On that distant shore there is a great army, but it calls itself "G.I." instead of "Son of Heaven". Suddenly the truth stands as high and broad as the free air we breathe. We were never alone! Japan, poor fool, you never had a chance! The thin gray line never faltered – couldn't falter – as long as we had faith. And never was faith more fully, more gloriously justified. Our thin gray line suddenly exploded with the accumulated wrath of years of toil and patience, became overnight, the gray juggernaut of revenge, and it ground, slowly at first, then faster and faster, more audaciously, finally with breath-taking speed, but always exceedingly fine.

Pearl Harbor, you will never be forgotten. The day of infamy will live in the memories of men who gazed, with shocked eyes, on the pride of our Navy sprawled in the mud. It will never be forgotten by a people who suddenly found that their vaunted steel walls had been betrayed by a complacent public, and all but destroyed by a vicious enemy. But that day welded our country into a force, backed by outraged reason, righteous indignation, and burning shame, which has not rested until the debt has been paid. Yes, Pearl Harbor, you have been amply and truly avenged. And, as we dwell upon this destruction we have wrought upon the perpetrators of the crime, we may well give thanks to Almighty God that, although the price was heavy, we have reaffirmed the faith of our fathers, the founders of this great nation. The flag of our country stands, now more than ever, as a symbol of liberty, and everlasting triumph of a free people against the putrescent hordes of the Beast. Long may it wave on high!

From:  Bob (Bubblehead Bob) Marble
TMCS(SS), USS PIPER SS-409 -

Booster, Booster, Who's Got The Booster?

I was looking through the "PIPER
Shipmates on Eternal Patrol" and decided
that I'm the only one alive to relate this
story.  It has been a well-kept secret until
now.

PIPER got underway from New London and
headed north for its first Cold War deterrent
patrol in September, 1957.  We had tin cans
in all the bilges and all over the Torpedo
Room decks; spuds in the AB hatch trunk
and showers.  We had a full load of MK 14-
3A steam-driven and MK 27 electrical
acoustic torpedoes in both rooms.

As we neared the Texas Tower near
Boston, MA, sonar picked up a contact.  It
wasn't one of ours, so the CO ordered a MK
27 made fully ready to shoot from the FTR.
The TM2 and I worked the Forward Room.
We broke out the Operation Procedures for
the MK 27 and looked at the photos of the
warhead and its components.  Then we got a

MK 142 Exploder mechanism out of its storage and searched for a booster, but could not locate one. I checked the torpedo log for the day we loaded our ammo from the Sub Base, and could not find any boosters on the list. The Torpedo Officer had signed that receipt.

I went to the ATR and asked the TM1 and TM2 if they knew where the boosters were. They never heard of one, until I showed them the photo of one in the MK 27 OP.

A couple of days prior to getting underway, we asked the torpedo shop for some instructions on the MK 27 acoustic torpedo, but they were very busy getting warshots ready for all the boats that were going to sea, and they just told us to check the OP, all the info is in there. None of the torpedo gang had been to school on this new torpedo.

Needless to say, we had to do something fast. We decided to insert the MK 142 Exploder mechanism in the nose cavity of the torpedo, make it fully ready and tube-load it.  We reported "MK 27 loaded in #1 tube" to Control and got a "Control, aye" response on the 7MC.  We now had a secret, and swore not to divulge it to anyone, not even to "Shorty", the COB.

Some time later Sonar lost the contact and we continued on our merry way to the Faroe Islands for our patrol, hoping that if we shoot it, the evidence will go with it.  When we got back to the base in New London, we off-loaded the MK 27's and never heard any more about the missing booster.  We checked with the TM's on the USS SEA ROBIN SS-407, and they didn't have any boosters either.

Blow Negative To The Mark.

Some time ago before I made acting Chief Torpedoman on PIPER, we were out on the briny doing independent operations.  I was running hot coffee to the FTR, passin' through COC as we started to dive.  I held up the delivery, just aft of the air manifold, observing the procedures, carefully, because shortly I'll be on the hydraulic manifold training for COW.

The speed, course, depth and bubble were ordered and then the order, "Blow Negative to the mark" and the Auxiliaryman on watch dutifully did his thing as the COW was watching the Negative Tank liquidometer for signs of water being expelled, when a sort of muffled "bang" occurred near the Negative Tank flood valve operating gear. The COW is not noticing water movement on the liquidometer and as the indicating needle approaches the 8,000 mark, he signals the air manifold operator to secure the blow and attempts to shut the Negative Tank flood valve and reports that Negative has been blown to the mark, but when he puts his hand on the Negative Tank control valve handle, he finds it already in the "shut" position. He says, "Oh ____, I think I blew the flood valve open with high pressure air." Well, that's exactly what he did.

The Diving Officer orders, "Cycle Negative Tank flood valve one time." The COW obeys and the indicator lamp on the

Christmas Tree doesn't show any change.
Negative Tank flood valve is still open (it
sets with sea pressure). The IC Electrician
has informed the CO and he comes charging
into COC, as the bow is rising to the surface.
He says, "I have the Dive, Surface, surface,
surface."

After surfacing and a normal 12-
minute blow with the low-pressure blower,
the COW (Chief of the Auxiliary Gang), his
EN1 and the COB have a chit-chat with the
CO, XO, and Engineering Officer on what
to do. The EN1 says he has spare flood
valve linkages and pins in the Pump Room.
Now to find out who can go over the side
and try to replace the busted stuff in
Negative Tank. Those were the days when
no one on board was a qualified diver. I had
played around with some simple shallow-
water diving gear on a destroyer in WWII,
but that was years ago. The COB had all the
right gear aboard and the knowledge how to
use it, so he volunteered to attempt the job;
and we had over 100 volunteers to assist,
'cause it meant going topside for some sun
and fresh air.

The COB ran an air hose off a 100 psi reducer, tied into the 225 psi air system and took all his gear up through the Conning Tower hatch with a stream of "volunteers" signing in with the Quartermaster in the Conning Tower and me following close behind. He rigged a 21-thread manila safety line to a port cleat near the steps cut into the superstructure side plating and fastened it to his weight belt worn over his dungarees. (Yes, dungarees. We weren't worried about being "politically correct" then). Our "Ship's Diver" then lashed the new linkage, two 12" adjustable open-end wrenches (crescents), diagonal side-cutters (for the cotter pins) to his belt using Marline with slip-knots for easy removal down below; put the new 5/8" diameter pins and cotter pins in a pocket of his homemade diver's belt, turned on his air, checked out his mask and climbed down into the Atlantic Ocean to do his trick in #2 MBT at the bottom centerline of the PIPER's hull.

The adjustments to the linkage were made by the COB satisfactorily the first time due to the fact that the EN1 knew just how to explain the procedure to the COB and knew his stuff. After the COB came back topside and rested awhile, the Negative Tank valve was cycled and the Christmas Tree indication was satisfactory, he went back down and watched for air bubbles around the flood valve seat after the EN1 applied 225 psi air slowly into Negative Tank, and everything was OK.

I spoke with the COB later after his successful attempt in restoring and adjusting the linkage, and he says he had to go into the Negative Tank, partially to remove the damaged stuff, and he got so scared that he pissed himself. We didn't have any "dry suits" at the time, just dungarees or shorts, so no one was the wiser.

No one got chewed-out by the CO, 'cause he was delighted to have his COB back aboard safe and sound and the repair was a success. He went to his stateroom, pulled the curtain shut and said a long prayer of thanks to his Maker.

This is the kind of stuff submariners are made of and I learned a lot from my

COB. (Thanks, Shorty, wherever your last patrol has taken you). Before he was transferred much later on, about using that diving gear and how to take care of it he said, "Don't let anybody use it but yourself if you want to use it in an emergency."

Incidentally, I was one of the 100 volunteers that signed in with the Quartermaster that day, and am glad that I did. Sub guys can really pitch in and help each other out without being "volunteered" – they just "Get With It".

FROM: Philip D. Lecky, EM2(SS), USS PIPER SS-409 –

Cumshaw Paint.

I clearly remember the day we were tied up in New London doing our thing. I was on the Seaman Gang, chipping paint. Chief Marble had two large cans of paint, one in each hand that probably weighed close to 50 pounds each. He started to come aboard the brow, which was not secured properly, and slipped off the pier when the boat shifted. The Chief went down like a rock and was completely submerged, but quickly popped up still holding on to the cans of paint. I was impressed by his strength and tenacity.

At the ship's reunion in 2001, after not seeing Chief Marble in 44 years, I asked him why he did not just let the paint cans go as he was falling. He answered, "I had to do a lot of cumshaw to get that paint, and I was not about to let it go!"


Lung-power.

PIPER was on a Med Run, tied up outboard a Tin Can. Some of the skimmers were asking Ralph Clark about what submarine sailors had to do to qualify. Clark told them that they had to be able to stay underwater, on their own lung-power, for a minimum of five minutes. They were skeptical, so Clark and three of his buddies bet them. Then they dove into the water,

swam into Bow Bouyancy, and then seven
or eight minutes later they swam back up to
the surface, blowing air and sucking wind
like they'd really been holding their breath
for all that time. PIPER sailors win the bet.
Skimmers are amazed.

FROM: Richard Collins, CS3(SS), USS
PIPER SS-409 –

Wonder Boy.

PIPER was operating in Long Island
Sound, practice-firing torpedoes and
retrieving them. We had a new arrival on
board, a Chief Electrician from NAUTILUS
who had just gone to "90-Day Wonder"
school. He had the Conn. We fired aft and
retrieved forward. He forgot to compensate
for the weight shift by pumping water. On
the next dive, we went straight down with
more than a 20 degree bubble. Thank God
we had a good Auxiliaryman on the air
manifold. He got us back up. The "Old
Timers" in the crew stormed the Control

Room; they were hot. We had held on for our lives. I had been holding onto the After Battery ladder and was looking straight ahead at the overhead! So this guy says, "Everything is OK now", and we dive again. Same thing happened! Control blew Negative and everything but the Sanitary Tanks forward. We made it back up, but before we made port, the "Old Timers" had started turning in papers to get the hell off the boat. The old man made sure that "wonder boy" was gone before the last line was secured to the pier. It was pretty scary at the time, but funny to think back on it now.

FROM: Bob Marble, TMC(SS), USS PIPER SS-409 –

The way it really happened –

After reading Richard Collins' story about PIPER's deep-angled dive, now I'll give you my version:

This new Ensign, wearing Silver Dolphins and a former EMC from USS NAUTILUS SSN-571, dove the boat with a not-too-good trim, due to his failure to compensate for the MK 14 torpedo that was fired aft. When he dove the boat and tried to level off after blowing Negative to the mark, he noticed he was heavy forward. He then ordered the trim manifold operator to pump from Forward Trim to After Trim, and the operator acknowledged his order by repeating it. Now, normally the air manifold operator checks to see if there's suction on Forward Trim and venting on After Trim, but, the air manifold operator was making a coffee run at the COC/After WT Door, waiting for his full coffee mugs and not checking his air manifold.

The Diving Officer Ensign, saw he was still heavy forward and slowly losing ground in getting the bow back up, so he ordered the trim manifold operator to continue pumping from Forward Trim tank to After Trim tank, and the trim manifold operator repeated his order again. By now there's a lot of excitement throughout the boat and the air manifold operator is back at his manifold, but not checking it.

The IC Electrician notified the XO, "Jollie Ollie" and he charged into the COC and ordered, "Silence in the Control Room; Diving Officer, I have the dive; Air Manifold operator, check your manifold and report; Trim Manifold operator, secure the trim pump, secure your manifold. Check your manifold line-up and report." With the depth gauges indicating approach to excessive depth, he ordered, "Blow Bow Bouyancy, Blow Negative dry."

After checking his trim manifold line-up, the operator noticed that he had been pumping from After Trim to Forward Trim all the time, and the air manifold operator confirmed this before the trim pump was secured.

RMC Barney drew a mark on the sight glass of the snorkel-whip antenna hydraulic tank, just outside the Radio Shack, at that critical angle for later reference.

TM2 Jimmy, from the south, was crapped-out in a FTR port "pull-out bunk" and woke up during this depth excursion, ran between the torpedo tubes, climbed on the "jeep" seat and was clawing away at the overhead trying to find a way out. He was having a nightmare. The hold-down straps on the torpedo skids were straining in both the Forward and After Torpedo Rooms, but held.

The galley was a friggin' mess, needless to say. Quite a few "brownies" appeared in the crews' shorts after that event. The CO remained in COC and observed the coolest performance he had ever witnessed by any submarine officer, when his XO took the dive. "Ollie" was some sharp cookie.

A "critique" was held in the Wardroom after everything had settled down and the final results were not "published" to the crew at the time, but the ENS did get transferred when PIPER returned to port. Needless to say, that some butt-chewing did occur to the persons responsible for the fiasco. I got shook up just like the rest of

the crew. I don't even remember who the
COW was and I was in COC training to
stand watches in that capacity. When the
XO ordered, "All non-watchstanders clear
out of the Control Room", I high-tailed it to
the FTR to see what was happening there. I
saw a lot of pale faces in the Forward
Battery and the FTR, but none as white as
that TM2 sitting in a bunk shaking like a
palm tree in a Florida hurricane.

A story about the XO.

PIPER made its first "Cold War"
patrol around the Faroe Islands during the
"Jerusalem Crisis" at the end of 1957, and
we carried reel-to-reel tape recorders
monitoring USSR radio traffic whenever the
seas permitted us to get the snorkel whip
antenna up.

RMC(SS) Barney and the XO would
stay up all night listening to the tapes in
Russian; the XO was a "spook".

Sometime later, after PIPER was
back in New London, "Jollie Ollie", as the

XO was nicknamed, was transferred to the Soviet Embassy in Moscow. His family went too and his wife got a job at the U.S. Embassy as a receptionist. One day a young fellow came in and dropped his passport on the counter and says, "I want to renounce my U.S. Citizenship, immediately". The young fellow was Lee Harvey Oswald !

Upon completion of his Moscow tour, "Ollie" was assigned to JFK's staff and on November 22, 1963, he had the duty in the Situation Room at the White House when JFK was shot in Dallas.

The first thing he did was to have the Marines lower the colors to half-mast. Upon receiving confirmation of the Commander-in-Chief's death, he ordered the Cabinet Members' plane to return to Washington immediately. (They were on their way to Pearl Harbor).

Strange coincidence, isn't it? You can find all this good stuff in William Manchester's book, "Death of a President," available in any library.

FROM: Frank Whitty, FTG2(SS), USS PIPER –

Shot and a Beer.

The USS PIPER SS-409 was tied up at the Submarine Base pier in St. Thomas, U.S.V.I. It was in the mid-sixties, and we had just left San Juan. The island of Puerto Rico was once again dealing with the threat of nationalists who had been causing all sorts of hate and discontent. We had to rig med-lights for our stay and post a double topside watch. Although we were now in St. Thomas, we were cautioned to be alert to any potential threats.

It was afternoon and I had the below-decks watch. I got a call from topside that a pleasure craft had been "buzzing the boat" and yelling stuff at the watch. I popped up through the After Room hatch, and sure enough, a boatload of young civilians, probably a draft-dodger among them, was having a grand old time in "daddy's speed boat".

I dropped down into the room and grabbed a six-pack of "medicinal" beer from beneath the skid, which, of course, was packaged at the time in steel, church-key-only cans of that era. I don't recall who the "gunny" was but I rigged the ejector and told whomever it was to "shoot" on my command.

I went back up the ladder and gave the command to launch a test shot. Harkening back to FTA School in Bainbridge, and based on the pressure setting and impact spot of that trial round, I calculated my solution and gave the command to reload and stand by. My head just above the coaming, and on their next approach, I launched my first war-shot. No stable vertical at my disposal, it flew over the target, but the track was good. They never saw it, however, because they went back out into Charlotte Amalie Harbor and began their next approach.

Steady now…I whispered below, in an icy, controlled tone…NOW…SHOOT! I gave the command and watched as the next round landed about twenty yards directly into their path, a modest burst of Caribbean water kicking up as their bow crossed the spot. They sure as hell saw that one! Swerving away in an evasive maneuver, I thought that I'd made our point, but the enemy was arrogant and persisted.

RELOAD! Here they come…Final solution and then…. Stand by…Stand by…SHOOT! Perfect, Excellent, Fantastic, Pissa. It bounced right off their superstructure. I could hear the impact and their alarmed shouts of dismay. You could see them looking over at us, wondering what the hell was happening.

They hove to a few hundred yards away and after pointing their well-manicured fingers and shouting effete threats and infantile obscenities, broke off their lame attack and withdrew to the marina, no doubt, for cocktails and anti-military invective.

Once again, PIPER had won the day. The topside watch was truly impressed. Of course, I regretted the loss of the beer, but a man has to do what a man has to do.

FROM: Arnie Miliefsky EN2(SS), USS PIPER SS-409 –

Beetle Bailey's Ultimate Explosion.

Around 1959, we used to go to the "Submarine Bar" on Bank Street, where it was always crowded. One night, Beetle and I walked into the bar, and inside his Navy jumper was a hot water bottle filled with Campbell's Condensed Vegetable Soup. We squeezed in tightly among the boys at the bar. Beetle hit his chest, which made the vegetable soup look like projectile vomit. Then I took a spoon and ate the soup!

Those who didn't throw up, ran from the bar. His prank cleared out the place, and the rest of the PIPER crew came in to claim the bar.

And now for the big explosion! Beetle Bailey was running a snorkel test in the Forward Engine Room. The word, as usual, was passed, "Do not open the Forward Engine Room Hatch, Snorkel Test in Progress." When it hit three inches of vacuum, Beetle cracked the hatch. Two guys were sitting on the head, and crap went flying! When the snorkel test was completed, they chased Beetle all over the Sub Base. Lucky they never caught him, because he never would have survived.

FROM: Bill "Beetle" Bailey, EN1(SS), USS PIPER SS-409 –

Mascot of the USS PIPER SS-409.

PIPER was in the Philadelphia Naval Shipyard for overhaul and, as always, shipmates get bored and looking for something new, a mascot was brought to the surface. After some discussion, a collection was taken and we ended up with $40.00. We wanted to get a monkey but they were too expensive, so we looked at the alligators and found them to be too nasty – it bit my pencil in two. So we found the snake, "VO". The other shipmate that was in on the adventure was Polovitch. We brought the snake back and I kept him in my locker in the barracks until we found a cage. We had food for VO and it was a rat from the pet store (snakes only eat live things). We then took VO to stay in the Engineman's Cage in the shipyard.

One night Scotty and I took VO to the Acey Deucy Club and turned it loose on the bar and that cleared out the whole place. We then turned it loose at Bingo, two stories up, and they all took off. Subsequently we were both banned from the club for one year (we could never understand why). Next, Satch and I went to Packers Bar in town and turned VO loose on the bar. Primo Darwood, the bartender, took out a .45 gun and threatened me and VO. Our next trip was to the Pink Poodle, a black bar on Broad Street and he cleared out the whole bar. The people were terrified! The only place we were allowed was the AKA Dolphin bar.

Each week we had the Snake vs Rat.
Rat always lost.  Hecklesmiller's job was to
obtain the rats.  The rest was routine until
PIPER was ready to leave Philadelphia.  The
Commanding Officer, V.O. Harkness, told
us if the snake came aboard he would bust
Chief Paris to Fireman and me to Fireman
Recruit.  This left us in a bad spot as to how
we were going to get the snake up to New
London Sub Base.  Mother Burke let me put
VO in a duffle bag and put him in the trunk
of his car.  When we got back to New
London, the snake had died from heat and
carbon monoxide poisoning.  We held a
burial at sea at pier 12, LT. Sutliff delivered
the eulogy.

May "VO" rest in peace.

FROM:  Author Unknown –

Shorty's Blues.

Seems there was going to be an
inspection of the boat.  Shorty wasn't in a

good mood and said to \_\_\_\_-can anything
that was left hanging out.  I can't remember
the TM striker who was in charge of the
"field day".  Anyway, there was a set of
dress blues left hanging up and they ended
up in the "\_\_\_\_-Can".  After inspection,
Shorty couldn't find his dress canvas and
wanted to know if anyone had seen them.
I'm not sure who told him to check the
"dumpster" on the pier.


Doc Bowman.

      If I remember right, Satch and
Pertiko were behind this stunt.  I think that
Doc wanted to be woke up for a card game
around midnight.  Anyway, Satch wanted
this to be a different kind of wake-up call.
Him and Frank went back to "Hogan's
Alley".  Frank picked up a battle lantern and
held it by Doc's feet.  Satch went up by his
head and made a noise like a train blowing
its whistle.  He said, "Doc, get up quick!
You're on the track and the train is coming!"
Doc must have believed him and forgot that
he was sleeping in his bunk.  He hit his head

real hard trying to bail out of that rack.
Satch and Frank ran real fast for the After
Torpedo Room.  I'm not sure if Doc ever
found out who woke him up.


 FROM: Denise Brogan-Kator, nee David E.
Kator, QM2(SS),

USS GRAYBACK LPSS-574 –

[ I received this email in March of 2009 in
response to an email posting for submissions
to this book that I made on one of
facebook's Submarine sites]

Jim,

        See if you enjoy this story as much
as I do, now looking back on it 36 years
later.  I think this is entirely factual, but I
have to confess that some of the details may
be fuzzy or even incorrect after so many
years.

        I was a non-qualified Quartermaster
striker standing one of my first watches
under instruction during sea trials, after a

lengthy overhaul in Yokosuka, Japan. The boat was the USS GRAYBACK LPSS-574. It was sometime in early 1973. We'd been sent to Guam to conduct our sea trials and my supervisor, a QM2(SS), was taking it easy as I was manning the QM station, getting checked out to stand this watch alone. To this day I've yet to figure out why we would be ordered to the Marianas Trench to test whether or not we had hull integrity. We were conducting a routine dive, not our first after the overhaul, when all hell broke loose.

The Seaman manning the stern planes (the main diving planes for this type of diesel-electric submarine), reported to the Diving Officer that he had no control over his dive planes). The DO, a young LTjg on his first watch, ordered him to, "Test the planes." The Seaman did so, first by pulling the stick completely back against his chest, theoretically putting the planes in "full-rise", and then pushing the stick completely forward which should have put the planes into "full-dive". But his indicator remained in the neutral position, showing that the dive planes had not changed position. The DO ordered the stern planesman to turn off the power switch to his planes.

Suddenly, seawater at high pressure started shooting into the Control Room. The Officer of the Deck sounded the Collision Alarm, shutting all watertight hatches and ventilation flappers. I put on the headphones and began keeping a log of events and taking reports from other compartments. At nearly the same time, the DO reported that he was unable to control his depth and the boat was heavy at the bow. The depth indicator started to increase and I began to announce the depth as we passed each 50-foot mark, and as we began to approach the test-depth, each 10 feet. The Officer of the Deck ordered full rise on the bow planes and ordered the Negative Tank pumped to sea. All this time, crew members are trying to locate the source of the water spraying into the Control Room. The OOD ordered the forward ballast tanks blown and the bow raised, slightly, then plunged back down. We were now past our test depth, and we were rapidly approaching crush-depth. At that point, the Captain came in from the Forward Battery (Officer's Quarters), and ordered "Emergency Surface". With all ballast tanks blown, we popped to the surface like a cork.

After an investigation, it turned out that a leak from a gauge behind the dive panel had shorted the stern planes dive indicator; the hydraulics worked just fine. When the Diving Officer ordered the planes-man to turn off the control to his planes, he left them in the "full-dive" position...recall that he was ordered to test them first by placing them in full-rise and then in full-dive. So, we essentially were driving ourselves deep. The leak was nothing more than a loose connection on a gauge, but at sea pressure, it produced what seemed like a lot of water.

After it was all over, I was putting away the headphones and turned to my supervisor. Unlike the rest of us, he had nothing to do during the emergency. Although I was new, I was preoccupied with my job in maintaining the log, taking reports from other compartments, etc.

Consequently, I never had time to be scared. He, on the other hand, was as white as a sheet. I asked if he was all right and he said, "You know, I've been on boats for about ten years and I never thought I'd have to kiss my ass goodbye. Today, I bent over and put a big lip-lock on it!" I'll never forget that quote.

FROM: Kelly Dunn, TM2, USS

GEORGE C. MARSHALL SSBN-654 –

<u>While out on a patrol from Rota in the mid-seventies.</u>

The OOD was one of those officers who was a real "dip-stick". He seemed to really enjoy bossing the rag hats. One of his really annoying habits was for him to take off his "Sperry Boat" shoes and put his feet up on the rail in the CONN. The Quartermaster snuck his shoes to the Mess Decks and compacted them and then gave them the deep-six out of the TDU. He got so mad that he refused to dismiss the watch until his shoes were returned. After about ten minutes, the Skipper came up to Control and relieved the watch, and told the officer that he shouldn't be such an A-hole. I was privy to everything as I was the helmsman on that particular watch! We all laughed for the rest of the patrol; what a hoot!

FROM: Vic Webb –

So, we're down in the Crew's Mess playing Spades, having a good time, when the phone rings. "Jug" answers the phone. We only got to hear one side of the conversation, so I'll fill in the rest:

**Jug:**

"Crew's Mess, what the hell do you want?"

**Other party:**

"Crew's Mess, huh? Do you know who this is?"

**Jug:**

"Nope."

**Other party:**

"It's the XO."

**Jug:**

"Well, hey XO!  Do you know who this is?"

**XO:**

"No."

**Jug:**

"Well, screw you then!"

We rapidly and covertly removed our card game to the Torpedo Room.

FROM: Andre Gerard –

The new Ensign.

We had a new Ensign straight out of Nuke School, and the Naval Academy. Total "Dork", (most were pretty cool, but not this one). He thought that he was GOD's gift to submarines and apparently bought into the drivel that he was fed concerning "Enlisted vs Officer". His quals were made difficult as he tested his rank against our "time on the pond". It all came to a head when one of our MM nukes gave him an easy checkout on some minor system. The officer, by this time a LTjg, went to the Engineer and complained that the MM didn't give him a sufficient checkout on that particular system (you cannot make this stuff up). Well, needless to say, his quals came to an absolute standstill. It got so bad that the Engineer sent him as a "rider" on another boat to finish his quals as EOOW. By the time he got back, he was sufficiently "calibrated" and he actually turned out OK for the rest of his time on board; he was still a "Dork" though.

FROM: Billy Papale –

<u>Favorite "Zero" moment.</u>

I was the ERS and up in Control for "section tracking party. The CO and OOD (who was my ENG zero), were looking over my plot.

CO says to OOD: "OK, ENG, let's head west to dump trash and sanitary tanks and we'll pick up our broadcasts." CO leaves Control.

OOD/ENG: "Very well, sir. Helm, right 10 degrees rudder, steer course 090.

HELM: "Right 10 degrees rudder, steer course 090, aye sir."

Me: "ENG, that's due ea…" ( couldn't finish saying EAST).

OOD/ENG: "Be quiet!"

About 30 seconds later (CO must have seen the compass repeater in his stateroom).

CO: (Storming into Control) "Officer of the Deck!! What the hell are you doing? I said head <u>west</u>. Which way is west?!"

ODD/ENG: "Uh..uh…uh….Helm, shift your rudder. Steer course 270!"

OOD/ENG: (Aside to me a few minutes later) "You gotta back me up if I make a mistake like that!"

What I wanted to say, "Yeah, I gotta back <u>you</u> up? Who went to the bloomin' Naval Academy? Don't they teach compass directions there?"

FROM: David Bridges –

On the only "middie cruise" we had while I was on board, ERS and ERUL watch managed to trick a middie into holding something in a vise, then tightened the vice down on his thumbs. They left him there while others came by and messed with him. Needless to say, the middie was pissed when he was finally released, but got over it when we told him the best thing to do would be to help us get another of his middie buddies in the same trick. He goes and gets another middie, brings him back and tries to get him to hold whatever it was in the vise. The new middie, being smarter than the first, plays dumb and finally gets the first middie to show him what he wants him to do. You guessed it; the vise gets tightened again, trapping the middie for the second time and for more punishment. Very funny!

FROM: Randy Lamance –

ZERO moment.

Standing topside watch, and we have another boat tied up outboard of us. We are all the way at the end of pier 22 in Norfolk. It was a weekend and there was little traffic on the pier, and the other watch-stander and I could see a "newbie O-Ganger" walking down the pier in uniform with his orders and his other crap. He approached the end of the brow and hesitated a couple of minutes, and acted very nervous. He walked smartly across the brow, stopped midway and turned smartly towards the flag and gave a sharp salute and then turned smartly towards us and proceeded. He stopped in front of us and hesitated again. He finally asked very nervously what he had to do to cross over to the outboard boat; he could not recall the proper protocol. I answered in the best smart-butt tone I could muster, "Walk". I'm sure he didn't like my tone, but he was too embarrassed and just hauled butt over to the other boat without saluting the Ensign. Meanwhile, the other watch and I laughed our butts off.


Middies.

We had some Middies on board for a couple of days once, and one of them was put in Forward Crews' Berthing across from an STS1 who snored very loudly and woke up very violently if touched. Nobody liked to give him a wake-up call because he usually swung his arms and tried to grab you. Well, this poor Middie tried to go to sleep and the STS1 was snoring, so the Middie shook him to get him to stop snoring, and the Middie was grabbed and shaken violently and his poor face bounced off the top of the bunk a couple of times before he got away. The poor Middie just climbed back into his rack and sucked it up. When the STS1 got up for his watch, he pulled out his high-dollar flash from his camera and poked the Middie to open his eyes and set off the flash right into the Middie's eyes just to add insult to injury.

FROM: Mike Andrews –

<u>Senior JO's.</u>

I think we've all had senior JO's that thought they were smarter and better than the enlisted. We had one guy who was a total arse, until one mid-watch underway; he was standing a proficiency watch as EOOW and had a habit of putting his feet up and sleeping. The mistake he made was to wear wool socks that mysteriously caught fire. He was livid and threatened Mast for everyone in Maneuvering until the RO told him, "OK, call the ENG and tell him we set your socks on fire while you were asleep!

Antics.

Routing 1250's to the CO requesting fallopian tubes for Sonar.

FROM: Ben Blue –

More Middies.

Ahhhh, middie ops. Hated them, but they were an excellent chance to screw with people who didn't know you. We had one Marine Corps-option middie from Annapolis who was only riding the boat because he had to. He made it very clear he was Corps (dammit), and all this submarine crap did not interest him. Then he proceeded to climb into his assigned bunk and try to sleep the entire three days away. After about two watches, we were in the Crew's Lounge and decided that Jar-Head needed our "tender attentions". I went to his bunk, yanked back the curtain, and shook him awake. When he started to come around, I asked him if he had to pee, then left.

Fast forward about 10 minutes when said middie enters the lounge and asked who woke him up. Nobody confessed until he said (This is no _____ ) "I just wanted to thank him and ask him how he knew I had to pee. You sub guys are smarter than I thought."

FROM: Randy Rafferty –

<u>OOD goof.</u>

We were underway playing rabbit for someone's TRE or POM, and the CO was in the Crew's Mess sitting in on our Divisional Training. The MJ growled and the Captain picked it up. As he listened, his eyes got huge and he calmly put the phone back, got up and ran up the stairs to Control. Five seconds later, you hear, "Battlestations, Torpedo Evasion", the works. The attacking sub had shot a torpedo at us and the OOD called the Captain on the MJ instead of taking all the common sense actions upon himself!

FROM: Larry Smith –

Fuse Pullers.

Our Electricians put in a supply requisition to get their Division Officer his very own, solid-brass fuse pullers with his initials engraved upon them.

FROM: John Caudle, USS TECUMSEH SSBN-628 –

A Big Screwdriver.

It was after hurricane Hugo in Charleston, SC; the T-Cup had a loop apart so we had no reactor. Shore power, of course, was gone, and then our ship's diesel got the cooling water intakes clogged so we lost the diesel. The E-Division Chief hot-wired a shore diesel truck with the huge diesel-generator on the back. They call me (diesel mechanic qualified nuke M-Div guy) to come up and get the diesel going. Of course, it is a big CAT Diesel, and not a Fairbanks-Morse. I'm up there with three E-Division guys helping me try to get this thing started. I'll skip through some of the details since it would be a bit long. We ended up re-wiring the batteries to "get more power". I don't even remember exactly what it was that the Electricians did. Hell, we are nukes so it has to work! We didn't have a disconnect switch to "turn on" power with the batteries, so the E-Div'ers decide a big screwdriver will work. Yeah, I trusted them. So, we had the E-Div officer who we will call Mr. Rick, station himself outside the door to the big box-truck with the CO2 fire extinguisher as a "fire watch". Yes, we used first names most of the time. I was

Petty Officer John. So…I'm in front of the truck where the starting controls are for the diesel. The two Electricians are in the back near the door where the batteries are, and they asked if I'm, "ready to go?" I said, "I guess…hit it." They put that screwdriver down across the poles and sparks started flying about four feet into the air…the batteries are smoking like crazy…then they explode with a deafening BOOM, and a cloud of acid-smoke fills the big box-truck. We are all three coughing and gagging. The only thing I can do is walk toward the light. We all three jump out of the truck looking for LTjg Rick with the fire extinguisher. It's laying on the pier. We are like, "What's this? Where's the LT?" We look down the pier and he's running and looking back at us laughing and yelling "You bastards aren't taking me down with you!" We were all three coughing and laughing our butts off at the LT. He was a real good dude, too. We ended up losing him our next patrol; RIP Lt. Rick, you were a good one.


FROM: Gary Christopher –

## Running a Drill.

We were running a drill in the Torpedo Room and the XO comes to the scene to take charge from the TMC. The XO looks for a place to plug in his EAB. The TMC looks for a place to plug in his EAB. Each plugs into the other's buddy connection and suck their face masks down tight…look at each other in terror when they realize they're on "recirc."!

FROM: The Author –

Back in the pre-glowboat, diesel boat days, the boys from CARP SS-338, which was moored next to  CUTLASS SS-478, snuck over under cover of darkness and changed the L to an E, as payback to their pier-mates who had the night before covertly altered the sign on USS CARP by switching the A and R in their signboard.

FROM: Michael Hatten –

Back in the day, the only communication from home while on a Boomer patrol was a 25-word "Family-Gram". They passed over normal fleet communications, so every boat saw every "Family Gram", and the Radio Shack used to post the good ones. The best one that I ever saw read, "My Thighs Whisper Your Name."

FROM: Lance Daily –

I think it is funny that EVERY single one of us had to pass a psych-screening. Who are the most twisted, sick, and perverted people we know? That's right, each other. Seems like every one of us was able to "sneak" through that psych-screening.

FROM: John Petersen –

It is amazing the sarcastic and funny crap that a bunch of over-intelligent misfits, like us submariners, can come up with while spending long hours on watch punching holes through the ocean. I've never laughed as hard as I did after watch on our Med-cruise sitting in the Crew's Mess. We had some guys that should've become professional comedians.

FROM: Larry Smith –

Our naughahide seat-covers were only comfortable if they were made from the hide of the Southern Hairless Naughas. Fine furniture made from the hide of the Northern Hairy Naughas are much more comfortable, but I think they're on the endangered species list now.

FROM: Byron Isaacs –

We had pulled into Norway for a few days of R&R before heading back home. While in port, naturally, we had to empty the Sanitary Tanks. The truck that was to hold the "waste" and the driver pulled up next to us on the pier. We discussed the actions of what was about to happen. This guy is going to stand on top of the truck, and hold the San hose while we blow Sans. Not my idea of a fun day, but I wasn't having to stand up there. All I had to do was blow the tanks. So once everything was in place, I donned my sound-powered phones and got the "go ahead" from the Topside Watch to start blowing the tanks. So, here we go; I wish I could remember the pressures, but I'll try to make you understand. I start blowing Sans at, let's say, 10 psi (pounds per square inch of pressure). I wait a little while and everything is going good, so acknowledged by the topside. So, instead of waiting, I crept it up to 25. The topside can hear the rush, but says everything is still going good. I crept it up to 40 (whatever pressure was max-blowing), yes, I knew it was over the mark. I thought if things are going so good, then why wait. Then over the sound-powered phones I hear, "Secure Blowing" rather loudly. So, I stop blowing, and notice that sans were empty. Topside was requesting me, so I secured everything and went topside. When I got up there, he was on the other side of the sail, so the truck driver could not see him. He was on his knees laughing and crying. So, naturally, I start laughing at him. He pulls me behind the sail, and when he gets his breath back, he tells me. While we were blowing the tanks, everything was going fine. He knew I was bumping the pressure. He said then all of a sudden the truck driver was screaming. He had been covered by the "waste" leaving the hose. The topside said that he was literally covered and it was dripping off of him. Lucky for him he had brought a change of clothes. I went over to apologize, and he said that when the tanks emptied, it was like a slug shooting out the hose, and a lot of it came back out the hole it was going into. He was not happy, to say the least.

I'm sure my chuckling did not make him feel any better.

FROM: David Bridges –

Liberty in Port Canaveral.

Several of our MS's get pulled for speeding by a State Trooper. They had also been drinking and probably should not have been driving. While getting their paperwork, the trooper notices the ball caps the guys are wearing and asks if they're on "'that submarine that pulled in yesterday?" The cooks answer in the affirmative, and offer him a tour (at 3 a.m.) hoping to get out of a ticket, or worse. The trooper takes them up on the offer, tells them to follow him, and takes off, doing about 80 mph. The cooks keep up, and reach the boat in no time. One cook goes below to get permission from the CDO for a tour, and is told "not only NO, but hell no, it's three o'clock in the morning." The cook explains what will happen if the cop doesn't get a tour, and the

CDO then relents. As he comes aboard, the POOD realizes that the cop is carrying a weapon (of course) and says that he "can't bring it on board." The trooper pulls his weapon, cocks it, takes the safety off, and puts it on the topside log book, telling the POOD that it has a hair-trigger, and not to touch it. He goes below with the cooks, gets a tour of the forward end, and leaves with a few ball caps the MS's snatch off some hooks in berthing. His gun is as he left it, and he leaves. The cooks get a couple of hours' sleep before getting up to cook breakfast.

For some reason, our cooks always had interesting experiences ashore.

AUTHOR'S NOTE: I suspect that he means CS, vice MS; CS is Commissaryman (Ship's Cook).

FROM: Andre Gerard –

Funny! The first time I was ever written up I was PO'd and a little scared. By the time I had been written up the fourth or fifth time, I just took it in stride. I never actually went to Mast. I had a bit of a personality conflict with one of the Chiefs on board whom we affectionately named Ass-Wipe (pronounced Ass-Weep'-Ay, from the "Saturday Night Live" comedy skit). He would write me up for anything that he could come up with such as "insubordination" on more than one occasion – it probably made more the fool of him than me.

FROM: Michael Trudeau –

Blowing Sanitaries Malfunction.

I was in Fremantle, Australia and was new to the boat and we needed to pump Sanitaries. Being junior, I was ordered topside to check for flow. When we started pumping the hose began to shake violently. Over the phones I said to shut the pump off, but it was too late. The connection blew off, sprayed all over me, topside, and down the weapons shipping hatch. It oozed all the way down to the Torpedo Room. Turns out that the pier connection wasn't opened, and the converter from American to Aussie had something like four valves to it. Overall everyone had a crappy time!

FROM: Stephen Ischay ET3(SS) USS STURGEON SSN-637 –

"Request Permission"

We all had one just like him on our respective boats; I am sure of it. Sadly, I don't remember his name but will call him Tanner. He was a nice enough guy, but the type that you wonder if he is really all there. Little bit slow to catch on to things, took everything literally, and did exactly as he was told. He was a rider for just one patrol, but it only took about 2 or 3 watches for the guys in my section to figure out we had a live one with Tanner. We spent the patrol with the usual drills of a NUB – getting a bucket of steam from the Engine Room, putting extra packets of sugar in the Dive's coffee (who hated sugar), and the likes. Interestingly enough he never seemed to catch on and get suspicious of our directions, he just always went on his way with his orders.

On the Maneuvering Watch coming home I was the AEF and like most on the boat I was ready to get home, see the loved ones, have a cold beer and fresh food. By now Tanner had endured months of practical jokes, harsh direction during drills, and was not all that much closer to his fish than when he came aboard. He was the messenger for the watch and I thought I would have one last good practical joke. Coming back to Control after a round, I sent Tanner to the bridge to request permission to blow the DCA. To me, and a few others in Control (which I understood why in just a few short minutes) this was especially funny since the OOD was the Damage Control Assistant and not exactly known for his sense of humor.

Tanner clambered up the ladder to the bridge and I had a good laugh with a couple of my buddies in Control imagining the look on the DCA's face as Tanner made his request. Tanner came down and looked a bit confused, if not confident. When I asked him the OOD's response he simply said that the Captain stated that if the AEF wants to blow the DCA he should come up and ask himself. Turns out that the Captain had gone to the bridge while I was on my rounds and that Tanner had not written his name down on the board as a member of the bridge party. Priceless. So while everyone knew that he was up there, none of my good shipmates felt obliged to tell me and let Tanner carry out the request on my behalf. The Captain had less of a sense of humor than the OOD, but never mentioned it to me, while the OOD/DCA and I surprisingly had a good laugh when we hit the pier.


FROM:  Bill Hughes MS –

I was an MS on the USS TULLIBEE SSN-597. We had been in the shipyards at Portsmouth, NH for a couple of years and were getting ready to depart. Naval Reactors were there interviewing all the Nukes and there was a lot of tension as you might suspect. I had made Lasagna for lunch, and there was a lot of it left over, so I kept it hot for dinner and mid-rats. The odor permeated the barge, and one of the Captains from Naval Reactors came down stairs from the Wardroom begging for some of the pizza that he had been smelling all day long.

I thought for a second and decided it wouldn't be too bad if I gave him a little. Of course, he would have to eat what I had and since I didn't have pizza he would have to be happy with Lasagna, I told him.

"I don't have pizza, but I will be happy to give you a little Lasagna," or I should say I tried to tell him that. I never got the chance before I could tell him I would give him Lasagna, he started shouting, "You have Pizza, I know you have Pizza, I have been smelling that Pizza all

damn day, and I want Pizza.  GIVE ME
PIZZA, NOW!!!

I tried telling him I had Lasagna, but
he wouldn't listen to me, and I got sick of
his mouth.  I just acted nice and let him be a
jerk.  After dinner had been going on for a
while, he came down on the mess decks all
head up ready for a fight.  He saw me
serving Lasagna and about s**t himself.  I
told him, "I would have been happy to serve
you something if you had listened to what I
had to say".  Of course he just walked off in
a little sulk.

FROM: Paul –

We used to ask the Non-Nukes to
"find the power supply to the reactor".

FROM: Steven –

While underway on the USS TINOSA SSN-606, we came up with a great way to clean grease off the diesel. We rigged up a reducer to blow soapy water with LP air. While we were cleaning the mist was making us choke, but this was working so good we manned our EAB's to keep cleaning. Shortly we had to emergency surface and ventilate the boat. The practical joke came later.

There were wars going on between the Air-Regen Room and Torpedo Room, so we rigged up the same reducer to suck peas from a number 10 can and sprayed the occupants of the Torpedo Room. Real funny, until it was time to clean it all up; peas were everywhere and kept appearing days later.

FROM: Gary Christopher – "If the Nukes don't groove, the boat don't move."

FROM: Robert Anderson – The loss of all AC sucked. It gets real freaking dark in a submarine. Then there was the BFPI curve violation in Guam while tied to the pier with a severe storm coming in. A steam leak in ERUL in front of Maneuvering was another one. Then there was the fire in a breaker panel during my first watch as RO. It happened while shifting pumps.

FROM: Robert Melter – Heading back to port in Hawaii during a huge storm at night. The ENG and I in the sail and then we submerged due to the waves. They had to emergency blow to get us back up. Went about 15 feet under. To say the least, we secured the watch leaving everything up there and waited out the storm. Big mess in Control and the CO's Stateroom.

FROM: Jimmy Howell – Doing a stores-load at Wharf "Alpha" in Charleston during the worst thunderstorm in recorded history. My Chief said not to worry about being struck by lightning. We had 36 hours before underway and Group 6 would have time to find my replacement.

FROM: Daniel Hastings – Running a Flooding Drill. Didn't bypass the root valve to maintain a vacuum. Went to reset the Main Steam trip valve and MS-4 opened when the trip valve was reset. Steam piping jumping around, dust flying and a horrible sound coming from below the deck plates which was quickly followed by a large amount of steam, apparently we blew the boot.

I was really scared when doing 9 kts astern and lost control of the dive. We officially achieved a 55 degree down angle while going up; unofficially it must have been more when standing up very easily on the wall of the TDU room of a 637 class without support from the deck and watching coffee pour out of the pot and hitting the deck past the Chief's table.

Then there was discovering a mountain ridge while at test depth and only barely clearing the ground with an emergency blow. All Parker check valves were leaking inboard.

FROM: Mike Hemming

The Diving Alarm Ballet.

As I pass between the controllermen, the oogah, oogah, "Dive!", "Dive!" comes over the speakers and they leap to their sticks and rheostats. The engine shut-down air lever is hit, rheostats spun down, sticks are thrown, as the ballet begins. Generator electricity wanes as the huge storage batteries are called on for power. Sticks pulled to new positions and rheostats spun back up to keep the motors turning. The flurry of intense activity over, minor adjustments made and times logged while listening, always for the sound of water doing something it shouldn't.

As I walk forward at the same time into the Engine Room, the two men in each room do the shut-down dance. Throttles are slapped down, hydraulic levers pulled to the closed position to shut exhaust valves and drains opened by the throttleman. As his oiler spins the inboard exhaust valves the 32 turns to shut it, either the oiler or the throttleman (depending on who is closer) will have yanked the pin holding the great intake air valve open so it falls shut with a loud clang. His inboard exhaust valves shut, the oiler drops below to secure the sea valves that allow the seawater to cool the engines. Then, the throttleman checks everything secure one more time.

In the Control Room, the other area of great activity on a dive, lookouts almost free fall from the Bridge to their diving stations on the bow and stern planes. Quickly the bow planesman rigs-out his planes and both he and the stern planesman set their gear to the

prescribed angles for the dive. Arriving soon
after the planesmen, the OOD, now the
Diving Officer gives the ordered depth to
reach and the angle by which to do it. Then
he checks that all is well and will watch the
planesmen to learn if the trim needs
changing.

The Chief of the Watch having closed the
huge main air induction valve will watch the
Christmas Tree to see that all hull openings
are closed. Then he pulls the vents to flood
the main ballast tanks and watches the depth
to signal the Auxillaryman on the air-
manifold when to blow negative tank to the
mark to stop our descent into the depths.
The manifold operator will hammer open the
valve and then close off the roaring rush of
compressed air, as needed.

By this time, the trim manifold operator will
have arrived from the engine room. After
climbing over the stern planesman he will be
ready to pump and flood seawater to the
tanks. This will trim up the boat to neutral
buoyancy.

In the Conn, the helmsman will have rung
up standard speed so the boat will be driven
under by the screws. The QM of the watch
will dog-down the conning tower hatch
when the OOD announces, " last man down"
from the bridge, while pulling the lanyard to
close it.

There is no music to guide this dance except
calm orders given and acknowledged.
Started in a flurry of activity, it will end by
winding down quietly to a state of relaxed
vigilance by men practiced and confident of
themselves and of one  another. They have
done this graceful and awkward descent into
the depths many times. They do it
as fast as it is safely possible. This is where
they belong, with many feet of sea hiding
the strong steel of the hull. Men asleep in
bunks half-awakened by the raucous alarm
and noisy ballet, drift back into deep sleep,
confident they are at home where they
should be.


Navy Hymn stanzas for Submarines.

Lord God, our power evermore,

Whose arm doth reach the ocean floor,

Dive with our men beneath the sea;

Traverse the depths protectively.

O hear us when we pray, and keep

Them safe from peril in the deep.

(Written by David Miller, 1965 and no
information found on him)


Bless those who serve beneath the deep,

Through lonely hours their vigil keep.

May peace their mission ever be,

Protect each one we ask of thee.

Bless those at home who wait and pray,

For their return by night and day.

(Written by Rev. Gale Williamson, date
unknown and no information found on him)

## *History of the Submariner's Dolphins*

On 13 June 1923, Captain E.J. King,
Commander Submarine Division Three
(later Fleet Admiral and Commander-in-
Chief U.S. Fleet, during WWII), suggested
to the Secretary of the Navy (Bureau of
Navigation) that a distinguishing device for
qualified submariners be adopted. He
submitted a pen-and-ink sketch of his own
showing a shield mounted on the beam ends
of a submarine, with dolphins forward of,
and abaft the conning tower. The suggestion
was strongly endorsed by Commander
Submarine Division Atlantic. Over the next
several months the Bureau of Navigation
(now known as BuPers) solicited additional

designs from several sources. Some combined a submarine with a shark motif. Others showed submarines and dolphins, and still others used a shield design. A Philadelphia firm, which had done work for the Navy in the field of Naval Academy class rings, was approached by the Bureau of Navigation with the request that it design a suitable badge. Two designs were submitted by the firm, and these were combined into a single design. This design was executed in bas-relief in clay. It was a bow view of a submarine, proceeding on the surface, with bow planes rigged for diving, flanked by dolphins in a horizontal position with their heads resting on the upper edge of the bow planes. Today a similar design is used: a dolphin fish flanking the bow and conning tower of a submarine. On 20 March 1924, the Chief of the Bureau of Navigation recommended to the Secretary of the Navy that the design be adopted. The recommendation was accepted by Theodore Roosevelt, Jr., Acting Secretary of the Navy. His acceptance is dated March 1924.

The submarine insignia was to be worn at all times by officers and men qualified in submarine duty attached to submarine units or organizations, ashore and afloat, and to not be worn when not attached.  In 1941 the Uniform Regulations were modified to permit officers and men qualified who were eligible to wear the submarine insignia after they had been assigned to other duties in the naval service, unless such right had been revoked.

The officers' insignia was a bronze, gold-plated metal pin, worn centered above the left breast pocket and above the ribbons and medals,  Enlisted wore the insignia, embroidered in silk, white silk for blue clothing and blue silk for white clothing. This was sewn on the outside of the right sleeve, midway between the wrist and elbow.  The device was two and three-quarters inches long.  In 1943, the Uniform Regulations were modified to provide that "Enlisted men, who are qualified and subsequently promoted to commissioned or warrant ranks, may wear enlisted submarine insignia on the left breast until they qualify as submarine officers, at which time this insignia would be replaced by the officers' submarine pin." In mid-1947, the embroidered device shifted from the sleeve of the enlisted men's jumper to above the left breast pocket. A change to the Uniform Regulations dated 21 September 1950 authorized the embroidered insignia for officers (in addition to the pin-on insignia) and a bronze, silver plated, pin-on insignia for enlisted men (in addition to the embroidered device).

FROM: John W. Long – Ah yes, Guam. My most intense memory of that place coming through the fog of age is me standing topside watch on the USS HADDOCK SSN-621 in 1969 or 1971, next to the tender at the Naval Base. As I stood there holding up the sail and a cup of coffee in my hand, all of a sudden I heard an enormous, unbearable rumble and then an ear-shattering screeching noise. I dropped to the deck with my cup flying to who knows where, and damn near pissed my bells. I looked up and directly above my head I saw what had to be a fully-loaded B-52 Stratofortress appear from the opposite side of the tender at about 1,000 feet and spewing four columns of black smoke as it kicked those eight screamers into overdrive. That was one awesome war machine. Looking at maps today it could have been taking off from Anderson but it would have flown over half the island. The closest airfield was Orote Airfield but according to what I've read, it wasn't used for B-52's during 'Nam. I don't remember the orientation of the tender in relation to NESW.

FROM: Mike Hanlon USS SEA DEVIL SSN-664 –

On the USS SEA DEVIL we were completing a one-year overhaul in Kittery, ME. One of the final things the shipyard was responsible for was to perform a full paint out on the interior of the boat. To

accomplish this monumental task, they
brought in about 50-75 painters from
Philadelphia Shipyard. I was sitting in the
box as SMAW (Shutdown Maneuvering
Area Watch) when the duty A-Ganger
walked past the door. I had noticed that the
flood-control accumulators were low on
pressure and I wanted to have him press
them up while I was back aft. I jumped up
and yelled at him to get his attention, but to
my amazement he ignored me. As I looked
out the door the Engine Room was wall-to-
wall painters, they were all black men . It
looked like a scene from "Zulu Dawn". I
stood at the chain with my head hanging out
yelling, "Hey Kuhn". The Engine Room
became suddenly quiet, the Earth quit
rotating on its axis and all I heard was,
"What the Hell did you say Mutha?" I
broke into a sweat but the A-Ganger just
kept going aft. As I looked at these pissed
off Zulu Warriors waiting to kill the Irish
boy in the box, I shook in fear and yelled
that is his name, look at the stencils on his
pants and shirt! Oh God, don't let them kill
me. "Kuhn, stop and come help me," but
my shipmate just kept walking away. I

surveyed the Maneuvering Area trying to
find a place to hide as the Warriors' anger
and chants became louder. All of a sudden
the back door curtain to Maneuvering flew
open and there was my A-Gang shipmate
laughing his arse off as I sat in the corner
saying the Rosary. We all had a great laugh
over this and for the next few hours painters
would walk by the door and say, "There he
is, we will get you Mutha when you come
outta that box." I think the biggest laugh
was when I got relieved watching my arse
running.

FROM: Roger Ramjet , USS TIGRONE
AGSS-419 -

The first boat I served on was the
USS TIGRONE AGSS-419. My original
orders were for the USS COBBLER SS-344,
but she was up North freezing the water in
her bilges when I received my orders, so I
was sent TAD to the TIGRONE which was

scheduled to make one of her runs to the Azores.

The TIGRONE was actually operated by USN/USL (U.S. Navy/Underwater Sound Lab) and carried an experimental active sonar system called BRASS. We had both BRASS I and BRASS II, and if you've ever seen a picture of the TIGRONE during this time in her long and useful service life, she was a weird-looking boat.

The TIGRONE was the only boat I was ever aboard which made no big deal about going to test depth. When we operated that monster sonar we always went directly to test depth; and following the diving alarm, the diving officer would be given that depth to head for and if the various compartments got rigged for deep by the time we that we got there, good enough, if not, oh well, they would as soon as they could get to it!

I cannot tell you how many watts the BRASS was capable of transmitting into the water, but suffice it to say it far exceeded anything else in anybody's Navy at that time and maybe even today's Navies for all that I know. To give you an idea of the sound level it produced, all hands forward to the Engine Rooms were required to wear Enginemen's hearing protection when it was operating! The overhead of that boat was festooned with Enginemen's earmuffs, hanging from every possible location to be readily available when the word was passed, "Now, rig for BRASS operation!"

There were no torpedo tubes on the TIGRONE at that time. The after room had been turned into a bunk room and held tier after tier of racks for the crew. The Forward Room was dedicated to the sonar system including its very own MG set to power that monster. The Sonarmen stood their watches on a standard AN/BQR-2B passive sonar set which was in a little corner up forward where the tubes used to be. The port half of the Forward Room was all the equipment the civilian USN/USL personnel used to operate the BRASS. It was a very sophisticated system, capable of varying both the amplitude and duration of the pulses it generated. There was a huge "trash can" mounted where the bow should be and inside that huge and cumbersome protrusion was a transducer which looked like a huge log lying on its side atop a round table. The round table could be rotated, thereby presenting the horizontal length of the "log" in whatever direction was desired. In addition to the horizontal training, this transducer "log" was constructed in staves (like a barrel) and the operators could select which staves were to be used, giving them the ability to direct the transmitted beam in whatever direction they would like it to go.

We would go to test depth off the Azores and transmit a pulse in a South-Westerly direction so that it could be received by the USS BAYA SS-318 who would be operating off the Tongue of the Ocean in the Bahamas! Like I said, BRASS put out a lot of power into the water.

Needless to say, our activities drew the attention of the Russians and one of those "fishing boats" bristling with antennae would follow us around, undoubtedly listening to and recording every transmission we made.

Well, one day we were pounding away with the BRASS when one of the civilians asked me where the Russian 'fishing boat' was. I was standing a regular passive sonar watch and I need to explain that whenever the BRASS transmitted a relay in my sonar set would cut out my audio for the duration of the pulse and then cut back in. When the audio returned I could hear the reverberations from the transmission bouncing off the bottom, off waves, off thermal-clines and maybe off the Azores themselves for several minutes, it was deafening!

I reported that the 'fishing boat' was dead astern making 80 rpm's, just enough to keep up with our three-knot submerged speed. "Keep us posted if anything changes." I was told and I sat up to pay closer attention. Pretty soon I noticed a decrease in the amplitude (power) of the transmitted pulses from the BRASS. The same was true of the pulses following that, and so on, until the BRASS was barely making a 'b-e-e-p' for each transmission. "He's picking up speed and closing," I announced to the civilians who were twisting the dials on the BRASS equipment and watching me to see if their efforts were producing the desired results. "Tell us when he's directly overhead," was the request as the pulses became weaker still. Evidently the Russian figured that we had sped up and were leaving him behind, as the very loud transmissions we had been making were now so weak he could hardly hear them. "He's making 220 rpm's and coming right up our stern," I reported. The USN/USL boys made some more adjustments to their equipment, "Is he overhead yet?" they asked. "Almost," I said, wondering what in hell they were going to do. Just then he came out of our baffles and I could hear his diesel engine roaring above the sound of his cavitating propeller blades, as he picked up speed. "He's overhead now, now, now!" I shouted and just then the relay in my audio circuit cut my sound. It didn't matter, I could hear the prolonged blast of a BRASS transmission coming right through our hull; it seemed that it would never end. I didn't realize they could extend the pulse length so long! The operators had turned the transducer table until the "log" was cross-wise to the length of our hull, then they had selected just two top staves so that all that transmitted energy went straight up to the Russian Trawler whose listening equipment was undoubtedly turned up as far as it would go in an effort to hear our previously weak signals over their own ship's noise. You guys know what test depth was in those old boats, so you know just how far away his receiver was from probably a million or more watts being aimed directly at him. We fried his sonar system, cooked it, blew every transistor, toasted every tube. Probably rendered the operator deaf for life. You've heard the old saying, "That noise was ten dB above the threshold of pain" – well can you imagine what sound level BRASS could produce at that short of a distance? It was a wonder we didn't blow a hole in his hull and sink him.

For the next week the only time that "Fishing Trawler" caught up with us was when we surfaced after a day's work. He could still pick us up when we were on the surface with his radar, but he couldn't find us when we were submerged and BRASS was transmitting. After about six or seven days, a second trawler showed up and relieved him. They would follow us, but never got real close to us. Once burned, twice shy.

FROM: a buddy of Paul Monaco's –

Liberty.

Our favorite liberty bars were like no other watering holes or dens of iniquity inhabited by seagoing men. They had to meet strict standards to be in compliance with the acceptable requirement for a sailor's beer-swilling dump. The first and foremost requirement was a crusty old gal serving suds. She had to be able to wrestle King Kong to parade rest, be able to balance a tray with one hand, knock bluejackets out of the way with the other hand, and skillfully navigate through a room full of

milling around drunks. On slow nights she
had to be the kind of gal who would give
you a back scratch with a fly swatter handle
or put her foot on the table so you could
admire her new ankle bracelet some "mook"
brought her back from a Hong Kong liberty.
A good barmaid had to be able to whisper
sweet nothings in your ear like, "Sailor, your
thirteen button flap is twelve buttons short
of a green board." And, "Buy a pack of
Chlorets and chew up the whole thing before
you get within heaving range of any gal you
ever want to see again." And, Hey,
a__holes, I know we have a crowd tonight,
but if any of you guys find the head facilities
fully occupied and start pissing down the
floor drain, you're gonna find yourself
scrubbing the deck with your whitehat!"
They had to be able to admire great tattoos,
look at pictures of ugly buck-toothed kids,
smile, and be able to help haul drunks to
cabs and comfort 19-year-olds who had lost
someone close to them. They could look at
your ship's shoulder patch and tell you the
names of the Skippers and COB's back to
the time you were a Cub Scout. If you came
in after a late night maintenance problem

and fell asleep with a half-eaten Slim-Jim in your hand, they tucked your peacoat around you, put out the cigarette you left burning in the ashtray, and replaced the warm draft you left sitting on the table with a cold one when you woke up. Why? Simply because they were among thc type of people on the face of this Earth that knew what you did, and appreciated what you were doing. And, if you treated them like a decent human being and didn't drive them nuts by playing songs that they hated on the jukebox, they would lean over the back of the booth and park their warm breasts on your neck when they sat two beers in front of you.

Then there is the important table wipe-down guy and glass washer, trash-dumper, deck-swabber, and paper towel replacement officer. The guy had to have baggy tweed pants, a gold tooth and a grin like a 1950 Buick. And a name like "Ramon", "Juan", Pedro", or "Tico." He had to smoke unfiltered Luckies, Camels or Raleighs. He wiped the tables down with a sour wash rag that smelled like a skunk-diaper and said, "How aire choo navee mans tonight?" He was an indispensable man. He is the guy that could borrow Slim-Jims, Beer Nuts and pickled hard boiled eggs from other beer joints. The place had to have walls covered with ship and squadron plaques. The walls were adorned with enlarged unit patches and the dates of previous deployments. A dozen or more old, yellowed photographs of fellows named "Goodtime", "Chicago", "C.W. Hog", "Richard Whisky", "Flaming Hooker Harry", "Big Bird", "Honshu Hank", "Jackson", "Doug the Slug", and "Fat Stanley" decorated any unused space. It had to have the obligatory Michelob, P.B.R., and "Beer Nuts sold here" neon signs. An eight-ball mystery beer tap handle and signs reading, "Your Mother does not work here, so clear away your frickin' trash." "Keep your hands off the barmaid." "Don't throw butts in the urinal." "Barmaid's word is final in settling bets." "Take your fights out in the alley behind the bar!" "Owner reserves the right to waltz your worthless, sorry a__ outside." "Sailors are responsible for riding herd on their ship/squadron drunks." This was typical signage found in classy establishments catering to sophisticated as well as unsophisticated clientele. You had to have a jukebox built along the lines of a Sherman Tank loaded with Hank Williams, Mother May Belle Carter, Johnny Horton, Johnny Cash, and twenty other crooning goobers nobody ever heard of. The damn thing has to have "La Bamba", Herb Alpert's "Lonely Bull" and Johnny Cash's "Don't take your guns to town" in memory of Alameda's barmaid goddess, Thelma. If Thelma is within a twelve-mile radius of where any of those three recordings can be found on a jukebox, it is wise to have a stack of life-insurance applications within reach of the coin slot.

The furniture in a real good liberty bar had to be fabricated from coal mine shoring lumber, and was not fully acceptable until it had 600 cigarette-burns and your ship's number or "FTN" carved into it. The bar had to have a brass foot-rail and at least six Slim-Jim containers, an over-sized glass cookie jar full of Beer Nuts, a jar of pickled hardboiled eggs that could produce rectal gas emissions that could shut-down a

sorority party, and big glass containers full
of something called "Pickled Pig's Feet",
and "Polish Sausage". Only drunk Chiefs
and starving Ethiopians ate pickled pig's
feet and unless the last three feet of your
colon had been manufactured by Midas, you
didn't want to get anywhere near the Polish
Napalm Dogs. No liberty bar was complete
without a couple of hundred faded ship or
airplane pictures, and a "Shut the hell up!"
sign taped on the mirror behind the bar
along with several rather tasteless naked
lady pictures. The pool table felt had to
have at least three strategic rips as a result of
drunken competitors and balls that looked as
if a gorilla baby had teethed on the damned
things. Liberty bars were HOME, and it
didn't matter what country, state, or city you
were in; when you walked into a good
liberty bar, you felt at home. They were
also establishments where 19-year-old kids
received the education available nowhere
else on Earth. You learned how to "tell" and
"listen" to sea stories. You learned about
sex at $25 a pop! – from professional ladies
who taught you things your high school
biology teacher didn't know were

anatomically possible. You learned how to make a two-cushion bank shot and how to toss down a beer and shot of "Sun Torry" known as a "Depth Charge". We were young, and a helluva long way from home. We were pulling down crappy wages for twenty-four hours a day, seven days a week availability and loving the life we lived. We didn't know it at the time, but our association with the men we served with forged us into the men we later became. And a lot of that association took place in bars where we shared the stories accumulated in our, up to then, short lives. We learned about women and that life could be tough on a gal. While many of our classmates were attending college, we were getting an education slicing through the green rolling seas in WestPac or the Med, experiencing the orgasmic rush of a night catapult shot, the heart-pounding drama of the return to the ship with the gut-wrenching arrestment to a pitching deck. The hours of tedium, boring holes in the ocean late at night, experiencing the periodic discomfort of tidal turbulence, marveling at the creation of St. Elmo's Fire, and sometimes having our reverie interrupted with stark terror. But when we came ashore on liberty, we could rub shoulders with some of the finest men we would ever know, in bars that our Mothers would never have approved of, in saloons and cabarets that would live in our memories forever. Long live those liberties in the Med and WestPac; especially Olongapo! They were the greatest teachers about life and how to live it.

FROM: Ted E. Dubay, nuke EM; please look for his book, "Three Knots To Nowhere" –

The curious case of the XO's door.

In mid-1972 the USS HENRY CLAY SSBN-625 is on patrol somewhere in the Pacific. I am in the Log Room working on several items for the crew's newspaper, "The Henry Clay Clarion". While hunched over the desk, I hear a commotion in the passageway outside of the tiny office.

Someone loudly whispers, "Hey! Keep it quiet!"

The sounds intrigued me. By the time that I managed to free myself from the cramped space, nobody was in sight. The only evidence of who made the remark was the muffled shuffling of feet at the after end of the Missile Compartment. Although a curious situation, I shrug my shoulders and return to the previous task.

An hour or so later, another disturbance occurs outside the Log Room. This time, I see the perpetrators. A group of officers armed with flashlights is slowly moving through the compartment. They seem to be searching for something. One of them sees me. We make eye-contact but do not speak. Without appearing obvious, I block the entrance to the room. I don't want officers seeing an item for the up-coming publication. It is for an advice column. Someone wrote, "I heard the pistachios have worms. What should I do?" The response read, "Give them to the officers; they eat them in the dark while watching movies."

Soon the officers' fading voices tell me that they are moving aft.

Later the sound of the on-coming Engineering watch section provides a reminder that it is time for the evening meal. I'm grateful. An entertaining article written by a LT made me lose track of time. It is his latest story in the continuing saga of "Super-Nuc", Ronnie Scrambreaker. He has come a long way since our first encounter, when he proctored our first Basic Engineering Exam in Hawaii. Now he is one of the crew's favorites.

I walk towards the Crew's Mess, and see Greg coming from the opposite direction. He has an impish countenance. I ask, "What's up?" "Haven't you heard? The door to the Executive Officer's stateroom is missing. All of the non-qual officers are out searching for it. So far they've come up empty handed."

I do not mention the odd commotion I detected when working in the Log Room and say, "I saw them in the Missile Compartment. So, that's what they were looking for. It was strange to me at the time, but makes sense now. I'll bet the XO forbade them to get help from the crew. One saw me in the Log Room and didn't say anything. Seems like the XO isn't too upset about his lack of privacy. I wonder how long that'll last."

The next day, the XO's loss of patience begins to emerge. He stretches a blanket across his doorway, and the search intensifies. All available officers join the hunt. Like before, no one can find the elusive quarry.

I overhear a searcher compliment those who hid the door, "I can't think of any more places to look for the door. Whoever stashed it, really knows this submarine!" After the third day of fruitless hunting, the exasperated XO takes drastic action. He places an announcement in the POD (Plan of the Day). It essentially says, "If the door is not returned, people will start losing sleep."

The notice has the desired effect and the thieves return the missing item. They

also send their own message.  The door is
back, but now the XO's mattress is missing!


FROM: Noel T. Wood –

The Human Cannonball.

Our TM2, Ernie, aboard USS
GUDGEON SS-567, was the man that was
launched up and out of the Forward Escape
Trunk when the boat was alongside at the
Pearl Harbor Shipyard.  We were doing a 15
psi air test on the Forward Torpedo Room.
The test was satisfactory and it was time to
bleed the pressure.  I was the Engineer and
was supervising the test from the Forward
Battery.  As we were lining up the Drain
Line to bleed off, the Forward Room
reported they were going to crack the hatch.
As I was looking through the deadlight in
the door to the Torpedo Room and saying,
"Don't crack that hatch" into the XU,
everything I could see through the deadlight
turned to fog and there was a hell of a noise.
The TM2 shot up and out.  A shipmate

working on top of the sail looked up when he heard the noise and saw Ernie above the level of the top of the sail. The torpedo loading skid was rigged and Bill, a Sonarman, was standing security watch topside to keep folks away from the forward hatch. As Ernie was coming down, Bill threw a block into him which prevented Ernie from landing across the skid. As it was, he landed on the tumblehome and rolled on to a work-float tied alongside forward, with bruises and scratches, but nothing broken, thank God. Bill's quick-thinking saved a shipmate from serious injury, or worse. As a footnote, Bill was standing on the hatch shortly before it opened. Good thing he wasn't on it when it blew. It opened with such force that the cast-steel hinges were torn and had to be replaced. The good Lord and all the rulers of the deep were looking over us all that day to keep everyone involved from serious injury.

FROM: Ron Durling –

Re- the preceding story: "Smitty" called me the other night and said he remembered Ernie's adventure because he was on the pier at the time. I don't know why Smitty turned to look, but he saw an object shooting into the air and then coming to down and finally resting on a camel. Smitty was involved in ordering stores and he thought, "Oh no, a bale of rags over the side!"

FROM: Mel Britain –

Re- the same story: It would have killed him except he landed on the topside watch on the way down. He had a peculiar-looking nose after that.

FROM: Phil Cole, RMC(SS) –

Everybody on GRAYBACK had a nickname; also ARCHERFISH, which you had to be single to get aboard; all had nicknames.

Re- the same story: I came aboard USS GUDGEON SS-567 while it was in the shipyard at Pearl Harbor, HI, after graduation from Sub School in 1960. This incident took place just before I came aboard. I remember everyone telling me this story. It was definitely Ernie that it happened to. Ernie ended up with an injury from the accident. He had an exceptionally large set of "cocoanuts". I remember at the Ship's Picnics, after quite a few beers, Ernie would take out his coconuts and swing them around. This article was originally on the GUDGEON Website but the website manager has passed and it is there no more.

FROM: Don E. Adams RMCM(SS) –

The Shrink Interview.

I reported to Basic Enlisted Submarine School in September of 1963, the tragic loss of USS THRESHER SSN-593 was in April of that same year. Part of the process of applying and being accepted for Submarine duty in those days was an evaluation by a psychiatrist. I only remember a couple of questions he asked me during that interview. One was a question about my relationship with my Father, and I only remember the question, not my response, but I will add that my Dad was a good man. The other question was related to the loss of USS THRESHER, and what my thoughts were, and once again, I cannot remember my answer, but I do know I talked about the tragedy of it, but it wasn't a deterrent, and that I still wanted to be in the Submarine Force. The memorable moment was after he concluded the interview, he stood and offered his hand and he said, "I'll never understand what makes guys want to do this, but I know someone has to; I'm just glad it's you and not me."

Patrol Dental Problem.

On patrol on my first boat, USS VON STEUBEN SSBN-632, we had a guy with an abscessed tooth and during the '60's we carried Doctors, MD's, who had indoctrination to the basics of urgent or emergency dental care, but no supporting equipment. We didn't come off line, or break patrol, in those days; no med-evac unless it meant imminent death. So the Doc did a root-canal to drain the tooth and relieve the painful pressure, which by then had caused significant swelling of the guy's cheek. No high-speed drill was to be had, so a standard-issue electric drill (think Black and Decker) was utilized. The HMC(SS) had rigged up a water device to keep the tooth irrigated but the slow speed drill and the tooth smell wafted through the boat's atmosphere. The scar tissue distended his cheek and I had heard he required plastic surgery to correct it. On the very next run, I had a throbbing toothache. The Corpsman diagnosed an abscessed tooth, which turned out to be accurate. I implored him to not make a big deal of it; we would be departing for home in a few days returning from patrol. He gave me some Darvon and they took me in to the dentist ashore aboard the Tug that brought out the Pilot on the way into port at Naval Base, Charleston, SC.

Admiral Passing.

On a more serious note – I was a Senior Chief Petty Officer on the staff of ComSubRon 18. We were embarked on the sub tender at Naval Weapons Station, Charleston. The tender was moored at the end of a very long pier. I had arrived for work that morning and I had passed by a relieving crew; this was an FBM Squadron, two crews for each boat. I heard the sentry advise the entire crew, some 90 or so enlisted, CPO's and officers, that they were to move away from the road and behind a building. The building just happened to be the laundry. I still proceeded to the pier. The sentry then asked me to join the sub crew behind the building because the Admiral, ComSubRonSix, was due to arrive. I declined, and then I heard a communication via walkie-talkie, "This is the Office of the Deck, who is the person with you at your post?" The sentry, and E-3 Seaman, looked to me and I said, "Tell the Officer of the Deck that it is Senior Chief Adams, in the uniform of the day, from Squadron Operations; and ask him if he is asking that I hide behind the laundry while the Admiral passes. The sentry's look beseeched me to not make him ask that, so I relented and told him to simply respond that it was Senior Chief Adams, Squadron Operations. The OD acknowledged, the Admiral passed and the pier opened. I then

went aboard and proceeded to Squadron
Ops.  Soon after, my boss, a Lieutenant
Commander, Squadron Ops Officer, came to
me and advised that he had been contacted
by the tender XO, he had a question for me;
"Did I have a problem with the order (move
behind the laundry), or the circumstance?"  I
responded from sheer anger and frustration
for those guys who had to hide from and
Admiral; "Both!"  He told me that was the
wrong answer and detached me to do an
inspection on a boat alongside.  I never
heard another word about the incident.

## Our IC-man and the perceived phone malfunction.

On watch in the Radio Room, the dial-x
(phone) rings, and Petty Officer Berry
answers.  "Radio, Berry speaking, sir!" a
pause, "Radio, Berry speaking, sir!", then,
"Hello? Hello? Damn!" and he hung up.  I
inquired, "What was that all about?"  Berry
answered, "It was Blair, IC1(SS), and he
was checking out a phone, I was just
messing with him."  Sometime later I took a
message out to the OOD on the CONN, and
I saw that Blair had the phone next to the

Quartermaster's stand taken apart. I
returned to the Radio Room and told Berry,
he decided it was best not to tell Blair.

FROM: Richard Soderholm, CDR. –

The landing party.

USS POMFRET SS-391, Guppy IIA,
circa 1957, we had completed Shipyard
overhaul and returned to San Diego for
refresher training. One scheduled event was
"Land a Shore Party and return". This
involved approaching the San Diego
Amphibious Base seaward side (as opposed
to the Bay Side), about two miles offshore in
the dark, launching the inflatable boat and
sending a team paddling ashore and then
returning to the submarine. The landing
party included one officer and three or four
enlisted. The standard inflatable boat was
equipped with several paddles, no motor. It
was inflated on deck via an air hose from the
Escape Trunk.

The POMFRET First Lieutenant contacted the Amphibious Base and determined they offered training with landing and launching inflatable boats. The entire landing party attended a full day of training and returned saying how good the training was, and they would probably never have been able to launch the boat into the surf without the training. I believe the training was conducted by the UDT'S (Underwater Demolition Team), a predecessor of the SEAL Teams. The actual event was conducted successfully without incident. I was then a LTJG and the ship's Communications Officer. I was not a member of the landing party.

USS BAYA AGSS-318, circa 1959, I reported aboard BAYA at the completion of a shipyard overhaul and the ship returned to San Diego for refresher training. One scheduled event was "Land a Shore Party and Return". I was the BAYA's Weapons Officer, but they already had an assigned boat crew and officer, so I was not a member of the landing party. I advised them of the training and experience of the

POMFRET landing party that I had observed, but they were not interested. They scoffed at the idea of special training. The training event started on schedule, about midnight with the BAYA on the surface off the shore of Coronado and the San Diego Amphibious Base. The landing party was expected to return in about three hours. After three hours there was no sign of the boat, and we began to worry. Finally we received a radio message from the Submarine Flotilla One, the submarine operating authority. The boat crew was ashore at the Amphibious Base but was unable to return in the surf. They had surrendered to the Amphibious Base and requested transportation for them and the boat back to the Submarine Tender.

On patrol aboard USS GEORGE BANCROFT SSBN-643(G) –

Some forward guys got together to develop a "New Weapon". We pooled our rescources and developed he first MK-1, Mod-1 (100 psi) "Marshmallow Blaster". We took (3) BQQ-3 tubes from Sonar, Duct Tape from the Torpedo Room, fashioned a pistol-grip, a damage control plug from the DC Locker, and a length of air hose with an EAB fitting, and for the ammo, (2) bags of miniature marshmallows. We filled the barrel with ammo, crimped the air hose and during the "Half-Way Party", we stepped into the Crew's Mess and BLEW THEM ALL AWAY with our new invention. It's amazing how far marshmallows can fly across the Crew's Mess and what a great "grouping tool" it is.


FROM: "Chucky" Pollack -

The Slot Machine.

While we were in dry-dock in Portsmouth, NH, we were told to go to one of the workshops and pick up a couple of valves that had that "Plasti-sol" rubber-type material applied to their handles. No one knew exactly where the particular shop was,

all we had was a building number. The only
thing anyone knew was that the shop was on
the far end of the Base from where our dry-
dock was located. We went into one shop to
ask directions, but everyone was at lunch
and the shop was vacant. We saw the nickel
slot machine on a workbench and we both
had the exact same idea at the exact same
time. Out the door it went with both of us
carrying it. We went down back alleys and
side streets. I remember we went through
the park that was in the middle of the Base
with this thing. It must have weighed about
150 pounds, because it was all steel and had
just been refinished and repaired with a new
"Plasti-sol" handle. I remember it was a
nut-buster to carry it, and in broad daylight I
can't believe that nobody saw us! We took
it down AMR 1 hatch and directly to the
Crew's Lounge. All of a sudden, there was
a slot machine in the Crew's Lounge and we
just kept our mouths shut when people
began asking where it came from. That was
a profitable patrol!!

The misappropriated STOP sign.

Once we all went to town while we were in Florida during DASO. We were really drunk. I think that our brains cells have finally recovered from that night, at least the ones that weren't killed outright. Whew! We requisitioned a STOP sign on the way back to the ship. Try as we may it was a little hard to bend to get it down the AMR 1 hatch so we tossed it like a Frisbee down the pier. It really flew great but landed embedded in the shore power shack on the pier and we couldn't get it out! The next day at muster it was still stuck there and we just laughed our arses off through our hangovers.

Painting Topside, when...

We were in the shipyard up in Portsmouth, NH for a core change and Poseidon conversion. If you haven't been in dry-dock it can be a pretty hazardous place. Besides all the shipyard workers, we still had to maintain our topside watch and help with the painting and scraping. We had just got topside painted with non-skid and we were making final preparations to feather in the sides with gray primer. Our deck crew was using a 10-gallon paint pot hooked up with 100 psi air and was loaded with gray primer. I was standing the topside watch in my Whites. The painting was going fine until some clumsy Seaman (non-qual) tripped over the paint spraying gun and broke the fitting. It was mayhem as the hose was whipping all around, and people were scrambling to turn off the air when the "Old Man" came out of the sail hatch and stepped right into a whipping hose of gray paint. You can imagine what happened. Luckily no one was hurt and the "Old Man" was laughing so hard looking at the painted "6-Stooges" topside that he peed himself. We were all in shock and covered with paint laughing our arses off! I don't think the Seaman who started it all was seen after that day.

The Navy Chief.

The Chief noticed a new Seaman and barked at him, "Get over here!  What's your name sailor?"

"John," the new Seaman replied.  "Look, I don't know what kind of bleeding-heart pansy crap they're teaching sailors in boot camp these days, but I don't call anyone by his first name," the Chief scowled.  "It breeds familiarity, and that leads to a breakdown in authority.  I refer to my sailors by their last names only, Smith, Jones, Baker, whatever.  And you are to refer to me as 'Chief'.  Do I make myself clear?"  "Aye, Aye, Chief!"  "Now that we've got that straight, what's your last name?"  The Seaman sighed, "Darling, My name is John Darling, Chief."………"Okay, John, here's what I want you to do".

FROM: Jim Dove,

USS TRITON SSN-586 –

Sickness on the High Seas.

Soon after the USS TRITON returned from her circumnavigation of the world in 1960, I was brought aboard as a forward Electrician. My duty station was in the Control Room, watching after the Interior Communications and electrical systems for the non-Engineering areas of the sub. I've got to confess, it was the most exciting and best job I ever had, sitting on that little seat watching the multitude of instrumentation dials and the operational activities in the Control Room and Conning Tower. I was a Firemen Apprentice and was made Fireman, by appointment, nearly immediately after arriving aboard. Three years later, I was EM2(SS) with only a six month's waiting time to take the EM1 test when my four year enlistment was complete. I loved every minute of my time aboard the TRITON except the two times I was very seasick.

We were operating with a task force when we encountered some violent seas in the Cape Hatteras areas while Captain Edward L. Beach was still our Captain. One of the perks to my job was that I could generally go to the Conning Tower to look through the periscope or the Bridge upon request if we were surfaced. I recall the seas were so rough the bow plunged deep into the ocean and water rose far above the topside deck submerging part of the sail. Tremendous waves breaking against the sail soaked everyone topside while they hung on for dear life praying to hear the order, "Clear the Bridge." The sub was like a cork, with the bow rising out of the water before submerging out of sight on its downward plummet beneath the surface until she rose above the sea again.

Most people below had a #10 can between their legs for obvious reasons, and after I returned to my watch post, I too was filling the can with my lunch. It was not pleasant to say the least. Captain Beach, bless his heart, called the duty Radioman to his stateroom and asked him to send the following message to the Task Force Commander: "Request permission to dive!" Just a very short time later the Radioman returned to the Captain's office and reported, "Request denied, Captain Beach."

Then the Captain said, "Send the same message again and do not verify our reception when they reply." Again the Radioman returned to the wardroom and said, "Captain, request denied." At that very moment Captain Beach was heaving in his stateroom sink. When he finished the involuntary action, he dried his mouth and ordered, "Send this message: 'We're diving'".

Within seconds, the diving alarm sounded, the topside watches scurried down the hatch to their assigned duty stations, the Officer of the Deck closed and locked the Bridge hatch, and the Main Ballast Tank vents were opened while we slithered into the ocean depths. Incredibly, a violently seasick crew recovered instantly; the not so empty #10 cans were removed, and we descended to maximum depth. Even then, TRITON was moving 5 degrees on either side of the 0 degree bubble, but the side to side motion was slow and of course, the inclinometer indicating the up and down movement was flat as we maintained our depth.

Seasickness is a terrible disease. One moment death would have been a joy; the next life was just beginning. Thankfully, running submerged, as we nearly always were, provided tranquility.

FROM: Richard Hubbard –

The Ship's Bell.

There are probably five, or more, ship's bell clappers on the bottom of the Thames River. Our troops hated that bell, but I liked it. I always asked them to mount the bell and ring the XO/CO aboard. That would always last for a day or two and then, somehow, the bell "broke". I thought it was funny that they hated the bell so much, so I kept ordering clappers, and they kept tossing them.

FROM: John Kuester, STSC(SS) –

## Showering.

One of the first phrases I remember while serving on the USS SENNET SS-408, in 1959, was from an old salty Chief Engineman.

Our water stills never worked as they should, which caused the crew to wish they could at least take a few more showers.

This old Chief would expound in the Mess Decks: "Any Submarine Sailor that takes a shower is too lazy to scratch."

## Rodger.

I reported aboard my first Submarine, the AMBERJACK SS-219 in 1956 as a new 3rd Class Commissaryman (Cook & Baker).

We were home ported in Key West, Florida and spent a lot of time working out of the Naval Base at Guantanamo Cuba, providing Anti Submarine training for the surface fleet. We would normally finish early Friday and stay tied up in Gitmo all weekend.

But, at least one time during the 6-week deployment we would go to Porto Prince, Haiti for a weekend.

This weekend as we pulled alongside the pier, one of our topside line handlers tossed the "Heavie" Line to the native crowd on the pier. This small line has a small round ball of lead attached to provide enough weight so the line can be projected at a 45 degree angle to fall down a short distance to the pier.

However, after the line reached the pier, someone cut the line and ran off with the lead!

Well, you can imagine how this sat with the Capt. He was standing on the Bridge with a bullhorn in hand trying to get someone on the pier to take the line, pull number one mooring line over and put it over the bollard.

Then someone told him that those on the pier probably only spoke French.

So, the word was passed, "Anyone that speaks French, lay to the Bridge."

And, out of the Forward Engine Room bilge came the cry, "I can speak French!" And out climbed a greasy, dirty, 19 year old Fireman Apprentice named Rodger!

Rodger had only reported aboard the AMBERJACK about 3 weeks earlier. So, as the junior non-qualified Engineman, his duty was in the Forward Engine Room bilges.

Now, remember, the average temperature in this part of the Caribbean is 90 + degrees with the humidity near the same. And above the bilges, were 2 large diesels, running.

During his short time aboard, Rodger had proven to be a good-natured young man, willing to help out any way he could. But, he wasn't the smartest person on board. He was having a terrible chore keeping up with the Qualification timeline that is given to all non-qualified personnel. Rodger went forward through the Mess Hall in the After Battery, into the Control Room and up the ladder to the Bridge. Of course, he left a trail of Engine Room grease behind.

As Rodger reached the Bridge, The Capt. looked at him with amazement, and asked; "Are you sure you can speak French?" To which He replied; "Yes Sir!"

Then the Capt. reluctantly handed him the bullhorn and said; "Tell them to put the line on the cleat." The Capt. Thought the term cleat would be easier to understand than bollard.

So, Rodger took the horn and directed in a loud authoritative voice;

**"PUT ZEE LINE ON ZEE CLEET!"**

The skipper ripped the horn away from Rodger and growled, "Get your ASS back down below!"

Well, the boat erupted in laughter and howls.


As he came through the Mess Hall, I asked him; "what made you do such a dumb thing?" to which he answered; "Boy, it's so hot down there in those bilges, I'd do anything to get out of there even for a little while."

And Rodger wasn't finished!

Sometime later, after we were back in Key West,

I don't remember exactly how long, Rodger struck again!

In those days, smoking in your bunk was allowed as long as you used a cigarette ashtray that hooked to the outer rail of your bunk.

Rodger had a bunk in the After Battery bunking area near a ventilation discharge. And like most young sailors of those days, smoking was thought to be "manly", so of course he smoked.

Well, one evening while finishing a cig in his bunk, he fell asleep and it fell onto one of his dungaree shirts that was lying on the deck under his ashtray and started to smolder. Anybody familiar with diesel submarines knows a fire in the After Battery compartment could be catastrophic! So, after a little while, enough smoke had been generated to cause the warning; "Fire in the After Battery Compartment!" to be broadcast.

You can just imagine the commotion when it was discovered that it was Rodgers shirt, soaked with diesel fuel that had been the cause!

The poor guy was ordered to the Officers Quarters Wardroom to face an array of upset officers, his boss and anybody else that could fit in there.

Everybody was growling things like; "How stupid you were smoking in your bunk with a fuel soaked shirt under your ashtray", and other derogatory statements. Finally, even Rodger had had enough. He stood up and in a loud angry voice he proclaimed;

**"Yes, I started the fire on purpose! You see, I'm a Nymphomaniac!"**

The Wardroom emptied.

I think Rodger only did one hitch, but his memorable experiences live on!

FROM: Charlie Jett –

Some of my shipmates from the USS RAY SSN-653 might remember this one.  It was a hot August afternoon, we pulled the RAY into dry-dock in Newport News.  I was NOT the duty officer (fortunately) and was somewhere off of the boat.  It came time to empty #2 Sanitary, and one of the guys on duty did it.  BUT – he used the at sea procedure and pressurized #2 to 50 pounds.  When he opened the valve, the pressure straightened out the canvas hose, it parted at the dry-dock connection, and flung waste from one end of the dry-dock to the other.  I remember that the shipyard was really pissed about this, and I felt sooooo relieved (for a couple of reasons), that I was nowhere near the shipyard that day.

FROM: Fred Reker –

Cuban Missile Crisis.

I reported aboard early October of '62 with the LTJG. The first question that they asked was "what kind of a car" I drove. When I told them a Porsche Speedster, they groaned, "Not another one." There were two others a red and a gray. The next question was, "What kind of coffee I wanted." I tried to decline but the guy had it under my nose before I could say anything. The Stewards took good care of us. Within a week or two, the Captain had an emergency meeting on the USS SPERRY AS-12, early in the week. He returned and had a Wardroom meeting noting the Cuban Missile Crisis had started and we were the most ready boat in San Diego. We were headed for WestPac at the end of the week. "Get Ready, Pronto."

The XO and the rest of the Wardroom got into high gear.

I had the duty that day and we spent most of the night loading war-shot torpedoes. The Weapons Officer had gobs of paperwork to complete and torpedoes to get ready. The Third Officer and the Ops Officer had lots of planning to do for the deployment. The Communications Officer and others spent long hours getting the pubs up to date. The Supply and Commissary Officer and assistant had the cooks order 90 days worth of stores and they were loaded everywhere. The COB was busy helping organize the working parties. We walked on coffee, sugar and flour tins. The Chief Engineer was busy and I was the AE. We got the Chief to ready the Engine Room, load spares, and take on fuel for the trip. A-Gangers were topping off the air banks, taking on water, etc. The Electrician Chief was occupied with an equalizer battery charge. We could not load torpedoes, run a battery charge and take on fuel all at the same time, so the fuel and battery charge waited until the torpedoes were safely stowed.

The EMO had his gang load spares, and getting the equipment tuned up and ready for the departure. At the end of the week as a last minute check we arranged with the Squadron Engineer to have divers go over the side and check the screws, shafts, rudder, planes, etc. Lo and behold, they found cracks on the port shaft! It was all downhill from there. Another all-nighter off-loading torpedoes, stores, fuel, etc. so we could go into dry-dock at 32$^{nd}$ Street over the weekend. We spent a week in dry-dock with the final conclusion that the cracks which turned out to be on both shafts were superficial. We could have left as previously planned. In the meantime, USS CAIMAN SS-323 took our place and left for WestPac. By the time they got to Pearl at the end of October, the Cuban Missile Crisis was over, and they turned around and came home. Over a year later CAIMAN turned out to be my in-port qualification boat. We went back to Ballast Point and dug a little deeper into the supply system. After a few weeks we found our spare parts were woefully inadequate and the SOAP Overhaul we got during our last overhaul was a mess. So we went from the most ready boat to the least ready boat in a matter of a few weeks.

Shooting San Clemente Island.

In the beginning of '63 shortly after our aborted WestPac trip, we had a week-long exercise to test the weapon systems. We were to fire a war-shot at San Clemente Island. The DivCom got his sea time as he rode us for the big test. The Gun Boss and FTR leading PO had the After Torpedo Room blessed with some "Cloud" coverage. Our FT had all systems running including the DKC. We had a tracking solution, but how could you miss San Clemente Island? The Captain gave the order to fire, and worst of all worlds, the fish did not run. We surfaced and I remember standing on the high sail and saw the torpedo sticking out of #1 tube. So we had a war-shot stuck in the tube and no one knew if it was armed or not. We tried to force it out of the tube, but nothing worked. So, in desperation, the Captain had us inflate the life raft and connect it to the nose of the torpedo. The diver got it done; we backed down hard and got the torpedo out of the tube and hanging from the life raft. Now what? The easiest thing was to puncture the life raft and let the torpedo and raft sink to the bottom. So the RM1, who had recently won the Navy-wide Marksman Competition got the rifle and started shooting holes in the raft. This took all day. At night the raft was still floating and it still was the next morning too. The Captain decided to bring the bow alongside the raft and cut the fish loose. I was standing 1 in 3 watches in training and had the 4-8 watch while most of this was going on. Going alongside a war-shot was a delicate operation. We slowly, ever so slowly, maneuvered alongside the raft and got ready to have a diver cut the fish loose. At the last minute the raft sunk by itself. Later in the week we tried again to fire from tubes forward and could not. We finally managed to fire a fish from the tubes aft. It was not a great week, especially with DivCom on board.

The lead Commissaryman was injured just before we were to leave for WestPac. A CS2(SS) was waiting on the pier for us in Pearl. He was a great baker but used twice as much flour and we almost ran out. One of our CS2's was a great "ice sculptor" and we also had a star running back from Nebraska.

When I first stood in-port watch, we had just come in from a week at sea and I was learning the routine of submarine operations including a lecture of the importance of "Rig for Red" at sunset. I was fresh out of OCS and Sub School with no sea experience so everything was new. We were tied up in San Diego and it was the weekend, so not many shipmates were on board. At sunset I told the IC Electrician to "Rig for Red". He came back with, "Rig for red in-port?" I said "Yes", and he said, "OK, if you really want to." After seeing the reaction of the crew, I realized my mistake and retracted the order. But after that I became known as "Rig for Red Reker!".

FROM: Bill Noe, USS SEA OWL SS-405 –

Back in 1969, aboard the SEA OWL SS-405 (DBF), there was a cooling coil in the Pump Room beneath the Control Room. On the side of the duct was a panel and we only used the top and bottom bolt to secure the panel as we would stash beer in the duct and use it as a cooler. Someone, (we suspected officers), discovered our stash and helped themselves. So I took bolts the same size, cut the heads off them and glued them on the panel in position so it looked like all 18 bolts were in use. After that we never lost anymore beer!


POEM by Unknown:

Long ago I was a sailor,

I sailed the Ocean blue.

I knew the bars from Singapore,

To the coastline of Peru.


I knew well the sting of salt spray,

The taste of Spanish wine.

The beauty of the Orient,

Yes, all these things were mine.


But I wear a different hat now,

Jeans and T-shirts too.

My sailing days were long ago,

With that life I am through.


But somewhere deep inside of me,

The sailor lives there still.

He longs to go to sea again,

But knows he never will.


My love, my life, is here at home,

And I will leave here never.

Though mind and body stay ashore,

My heart's at sea forever.

Shipover Prayer by Unknown:

Our Father who art in Washington

Please dear Father let me stay.

Do not drive me now away

Wipe away my scalding tears

And let me stay for thirty years.


Please forgive me all my past

And things that happened at the mast

Do not my request refuse

And let me stay another cruise.


USS CONSTITUTION "Old Ironsides"

"Old Ironsides", as a combat vessel, carried 48,600 gallons of fresh water for her crew of 475 officers and men. This was sufficient to last six months of sustained operations at sea. She carried no evaporators, ie. Fresh water distillers.

However, let it be noted that according to her ship's log, "On July 27, 1798, the USS CONSTITUTION sailed from Boston with a full complement of 475 officers and men, 48,600 gallons of fresh water, 7,400 cannon shot, 11,600 pounds of black powder, and 79,400 gallons of rum." Her mission: "To destroy and harass English shipping."

Making Jamaica on 6 October, she took on 826 pounds of flour and 68,300 gallons of rum.

Then she headed for the Azores and arriving there 12 November, she provisioned with 550 pounds of beef and 64,300 gallons of Portuguese wine.

On 18 November, she set sail for England. In the ensuing days she defeated

five British men-of-war and captured and
scuttled 12 English merchant ships,
salvaging only the rum on board of each.

By 26 January, her powder and shot
were exhausted.  Nevertheless, although
unarmed, she made a night raid up the Firth
of Clyde in Scotland.  Her landing party
captured a whiskey distillery and transferred
40,000 gallons of single malt Scotch aboard
by dawn.  Then she headed home.  She
arrived in Boston on 20 February 1799, with
no cannon shot, no food, no powder, no rum,
no wine, no whiskey, and 38,600 gallons of
water.  GO NAVY!!

FROM: Steven L. Schmidt,

CAPT. USN(R) –

Submariner's Toast by Unknown:

(as remembered from USS INDIANAPOLIS
SSN-697.)

He's a lover, he's a fighter,

He's a submarine rider.

He smokes, he jokes, and he chews ropes.

He makes love to various forms of livestock.

Hog style, dog style, any style.

No muff too tough, no thigh too high,

He craves hair pie.

Submariners once, submariners twice.

Holy jumping Jesus Christ.

We go up, we go down;

We don't even ____ around.

Ooohhh-gaa, ooohhh-gaa,

Dive, Dive, Dive!!!

FROM: Karl H. Betz –

Foreign Ports.

We got the word to "Stay out of the Red-Light district" in Amsterdam.  So we just followed the Chiefs Quarters straight there, and we both found that the Wardroom was already there.

FROM: Matt Tudor, ET2(SS) –

I was a Nav ET and one morning while we were leaving port, about an hour into the Maneuvering Watch, the CO was on the Bridge. He called down for the messenger, and the messenger was not in the Control Room, so the COW (Chief of the Watch) asked me to grab some coffee and go to the Bridge with it. While complaining all the way to the Crew's Mess, I got to the bottom of the Bridge Trunk ladder with a full cup of coffee. I was sure to spill this all over me, so I took a big mouthful and then proceeded up the ladder. Just below the access grating, I spit the coffee back into the cup and handed it to the Captain. After we dove, the Captain informed the Navigator that no one had ever gotten a full cup of coffee to the Bridge before. I got called by

the COW to run coffee to the Captain.
Stupid me! So it was about the sixth time
doing this as I was spitting coffee into his
cup, he was looking down and saw me.
OOPS! He started yelling and told me to,
"Get to Control!" After securing the Bridge,
the Navigator was summoned to the
Captain's Stateroom, where he got his butt
chewed pretty badly. The Nav called me
into ESM but instead of ripping me a new
one, he laughed and told me that was the
funniest thing he had seen. I never had to
run coffee for anyone again.

FROM: Henry Shomber, SKC(SS) –

CPO coffee cups.

We were not allowed to have alcohol
on board; our favorite drink was coffee. It
was standard practice in the Chief's berthing
where we had a small table with seats on
either side. A place to relax, it had a
constant pot of coffee brewing in the coffee-
maker and we had a board with pegs on it to

stow our personal cups/mugs, usually non-
Navy issue. Many of the Chiefs would not
wash the cup, only rinse it out with fresh
water and hang it up. This would cause a
build-up of coffee stain in the cup which
many Chiefs claimed gave it "flavoring".
As the junior Chief it was my responsibility
to ensure that coffee was hot and ready to
drink at anytime. The only problem was
that a lot of the Chiefs would not "stow"
their cups and leave them laying around,
which all submariners know is not a good
idea due to rapid changes in depth at any
moment. This would cause several "non-
nuclear" spills in the "Chief's Mess" (Chiefs
on U.S. Subs ate with the crew, at a separate
table in the Mess Decks). Only the Officers
had a "Wardroom/Officers' Mess". I
became upset about cleaning up their
messes. I told them, as well as posted a
notice, that if I found any coffee cups
"adrift", I would clean and properly "stow"
them. Well, it so happened that the COB's
coffee cup became the first "victim". He
must not have washed it since he bought it.
It was totally black inside. I scrubbed it
spotless and hung it on its peg (which was,

respectfully, at the top of the board), and went back to work thinking nothing of the matter. The next thing I know, the "Messenger of the Watch" came to my "office" and informed me that the COB wanted me in Control. He was on watch as the Diving Officer at the time. Being the LCPO SK though, there was a part that needed to be issued right away. I finally got to Control and asked the COB "What's up?" He went ballistic and started shouting, "What the hell did you do to my cup?" I stared at him for a moment and calmly replied, "COB, I just wanted to make sure your cup did not get broken and wanted to make sure it was clean for you." He looked at me in silence for about 30 seconds and said, "Get the Hell out of Control!" It was almost two weeks before the COB spoke to me again, but guess what…ALL the Chiefs' cups were properly "stowed for sea" from that point forward.

Bootcamp Sunglasses.

This is about the time when I had first joined the U.S. Navy. It happened in boot camp, Naval Recruit Training Center,

Great Lakes, (commonly known as "Great Mistakes"), Illinois. It was July of 1964 (one of the hottest months in the USA). When I was younger I had to wear sunglasses whenever exposed to intense sunlight, or I would get severe migraine headaches (it did not keep me out of the Navy, thank God). During my first day in boot camp it was hotter than Hell. My feet felt like they were on fire while on the "grinder", especially while standing at attention. I was standing in formation with "shades on", and the Company Commander (CC) came past me, stopped and did a quick about face. He got in my face, literally one inch from my nose and commenced yelling, "What the Hell do you think you are doing, Mr. Hollywood? Who gave you permission to wear those _____ shades?" As I tried to explain he kept spit-yelling and got madder and madder. I thought he was going to suffer a stroke. Finally he stopped and looked me straight into the eyes and said, "Get your _____ ass to sick bay and you'd better have a _____ chit in your little d__kskinners which allows you to wear those, or your ass is grass, and I am a lawn mower!" I literally ran to the sick bay and explained why I was wearing sunglasses. The eye doctor looked at my eyes and ran some tests. I returned with the chit in hand, but the CC (a Chief Gunner's Mate) gave me s__t the rest of the time I was there. Did a lot of push-ups, but still wore my shades. As you may guess, my nickname during bootcamp was "Mr. Hollywood."

FROM: William Bain –

Reactor's Interview.

At my Naval Reactors interview, one of the Engineers was trying to prep us for our interviews. An example was, "If you're floating in a canoe, in a swimming pool, and you drop a bowling ball out of the canoe into the pool, what happens to the water level in the pool?" I asked what color the bowling ball was; they picked me anyway.

FROM: Chuck Juoni –

On a Trident in the Torpedo Room, one of my guys set up a spray bottle by the ladder and ran a string to it from the front of the room. Whenever someone came down they would pull the string and spray the guy. He would point to the opposite side of the room and say, "He went that way." The goal was to see how many times he could get the guy to run around in a circle.

FROM: Douglas Kelley

WWII not to the Emperor.

Inscribed on a torpedo warhead in USS GURNARD SS-254's Forward Torpedo Room. This was GURNARD's third war patrol (East China Sea). She was out of Pearl Harbor 6 September 1943. The patrol ended 28 October 1943:

"To the most exalted son of heaven.  May this elevate you a little higher!"

FROM: Glenn Roesener –

Skimmer bubble pop.

      There I was, in a bar in Halifax. Surface squids – turned out to be fellow Sonarmen.  All pumped up and celebrating their "win" over us in the preceding game. After hearing my fill of how awesome their Sonar and Helo-Sonar technique was, I slid my stool over to their table, introduced myself, and congratulated them.  I then went on to explain the ridiculous constraints put on us, and the ultimate failure that they had achieved.  They had, by our best guess, shot a fishing trawler about 20 nautical miles away from us.  We knew this, because we were in their wake, actually between them and their towed array, when they called their shot.

I felt a little bad for a minute. They all looked like the confused puppy that always brings back the wrong stick. I bought them a round, and went back to my mates. Hardest thing I've ever done – holding out breaking down into tears of laughter until they were out of sight. My Sonar crew didn't help, they kept making snarky, hilariously conspiratory comments across the table to each other, but we made it…sort of.

FROM: Brian Walker  -

One day while at breakfast we were serving sticky buns (Cinnamon Rolls) to the crew. On a submarine, how we used to do it was put a certain amount out for the on-coming watch, and the rest for those who were relieved. We had this FTCS(SS) who wanted more sticky buns at the CPO table as an on-coming watch stander. The GWC told the FTCS(SS) that there were no more sticky buns for the on-coming watch and that he had to save some for those that were relieved. The FTCS(SS) then gave the GWC a "direct order" to put more sticky buns on the table. The GWC then said that we have a sticky bun quota around here and it is my job to make sure everyone gets a sticky bun and not just the greedy people. Well, the FTCS(SS) then racked-out the MSC(SS) and told him about the situation. Needless to say, the MSC(SS) was none too happy to get racked-out at 0545 about some sticky buns. The corrective action by the MSC(SS) was this: the sticky buns were issued out and the GWC had to verify each recipient of a sticky bun against the sailing list every time they were served. The MSC(SS) also gave the FTCS(SS) a chewing (as rumor has it) for racking-him-out.


FROM: Gary Vernon, TM2(SS), Storekeeper of Nathanael Greene Base-USSVI –

Venting Number One Sanitary Tank.

I was TM2(SS) stationed on board the USS ARGONAUT SS-475. I qualified on ARGONAUT in 1963, and served into the early months of 1964. I returned for a second tour on her in 1967, and was a member of the decommissioning crew in 1968. She was a great boat and I enjoyed memorable trips on her; but there is one incident I will never forget.

About once a year, if memory serves correctly, a pressure test is required on the torpedo tubes. This involves the support of the tender personnel. They bring the test equipment aboard, hook it all up, pressurize the Torpedo Room, and record any leakage from the tubes.

The pressure test takes all day to perform. At the conclusion, the test equipment is disconnected, and the Torpedo Room is vented. This entails cracking the watertight door to the Forward Battery compartment, as well as the lower and upper escape trunk hatches. Eventually the bulkhead flapper can be opened once the pressure is reduced. It does take a while for the pressure to completely dissipate. Once that happens, then the watertight door can be fully opened, and the lower and upper escape trunk hatches opened.

As it turns out, after the pressure had been vented, one of the junior officers, and I cannot remember exactly which one it was, although I have my suspicion, but so far no one has come forward to admit to it, had to use the officer's head. Well, he entered and performed his number two business, and then proceeded to flush the bowl in the normal fashion. When he did so there was a loud noise and he opened the head door, stumbled out with poop, paper, and wet, and with a big grin asked, "Who did it?" He was not too happy at all. He went to his stateroom to change clothes and clean up. While the poor old steward was ordered to go and clean up the mess.

Well, as those who served on the fleet boats know, the Number One Sanitary tank is located in the Torpedo Room. Number One Sanitary supports the Officer's

Head and shower. The tank vents outboard into the Torpedo Room.

By now you probably know where this is going. The inboard tank vent was secured as part of the set-up procedure for pressurizing the Torpedo Room. However, because the Sanitary Tank is inside the Torpedo Room, it will incur a slight build-up of pressure as well. At the completion of the test and when the room was being vented, the inboard vent on the Sanitary Tank was forgotten, and subsequently not vented. Therefore, when the officer attempted to flush the bowl he received a face full.

It was this TM's job to vent the room, and I absolutely forgot the inboard Sanitary Tank vent. I received a verbal tongue lashing from the leading TM, as well as the Gunnery Officer. It is an incident that I don't think I will ever forget. But I really want to identify the officer who was unfortunate to be on the receiving end of this screw-up on my part. I owe him a beer. That's the least that I can do.

FROM: "seen on line."

<u>TIANS</u>  (This is a no-s _ _ _ _ _ er).

A certain 637 class Fast Attack was extremely low on toilet paper a few days before getting underway.  The Captain was all in the Chop's arse.  The SK's found several NSN's and ordered more, but there was none available locally.  Finally, the SK1 went to the tender, found the NSN for TP onboard and ordered plenty for the up-coming run.  Then more TP showed up and Supply found more room.  Then, more TP showed up and Supply had it stowed in the outboards.  Then, the day prior to departure, two pallets of TP was loaded topside.  The Chop was freaking out.  He was a newlywed and had promised his bride a last night out on the town.  The SK1 had duty and told the Chop to go ahead with his plans for the evening, and that he would handle it.   The Chop knew the CO would be up in his arse if there was any TP topside tomorrow and there was no place to stow it. The SK1 assured the Chop that he would take care of it and <u>told</u> him to leave. The Chop left but he was still worried. He couldn't enjoy himself on the date, but tried to show his bride a good time. He even called the boat and the SK1 assured him that it was being taken care of. The Chop couldn't sleep and showed up at zero-dark-thirty to find empty cardboard boxes on the pallets. He asked the SK1, what he did to get rid of the TP and SK1 said, "I told you that I would take care of it."

The SK1 had spread a rumor that there was not enough TP for this run and everyone that heard the rumor had grabbed a few rolls and put them in their bunks.

FROM: a challenge for everyone on the facebook page to recall their RAT name.

<u>Spit Rat</u>.

Wife spit beer all over the guys during a night out in New London. We tricked her into racing to drink a full pint to the bottom; ¾ of the way down, she realized we hadn't even started and were just sitting there looking at her. So, when you laugh, it has to go somewhere and she was dubbed "Spit" in remembrance of that event.

Other of the RAT's were:

Chief

Big Daddy

Retard

Recon

Punk

Gnarly

Short

Sewer

Cell

Low-Rent

Prep

Sly

Trash

Reverend

Bilge

Cheap

Disco

Silent

Puke.

FROM: Ralph Jennings –

We had an A-Ganger nicknamed "Mongo". He cross-threaded a 4" union by taking a 36" pipe wrench and a come-along to tighten it until we got back into port. The tender crew wondered how a 4" union got cross-threaded as they cut it out to install a new one.

FROM: Joe Kronzer, CDR, USS
ARCHERFISH SS-311 –

In June of 1957, having completed
Submarine School, I was ordered to USS
ARCHERFISH SS-311, as part of the new
crew to reactivate that proud ship.
ARCHERFISH was part of a group of
"moth-balled" WWII Fleet Submarines
moored in the Thames River just above the
Submarine Base, and was famous for having
sunk the Japanese aircraft carrier
SHINANO, the largest warship sunk during
WWII. While undergoing activation
overhaul, ARCHERFISH was dry-docked in
a marine railway at the Thames Shipyard
across the river from the Sub Base.

Our new Wardroom was small, only
six officers. Except for me, all of the officers
were experienced and qualified in
submarines. The CO was CDR Beck; I was
assigned as Supply Officer. My initial job
was to inventory all the equipment and spare

parts onboard, and obtain any missing items. Sometimes, missing items could be ordered (requisitioned) through the Navy Supply System. Other times had to be obtained through more devious methods. My sailors and I were not above doing a little "midnight requisitioning". No, we were not really stealing! We simply borrowed stuff from other submarines in the area.

By September of 1957, we had ARCHERFISH ready to go and, after a successful sea trial period, and a brief commissioning ceremony at the Sub Base, we were on our way to Key West to rejoin the Submarine Force as part of SubRonFour. In those days, Key West was still a small "backwater" town. The north end of the main street (Duval Street) consisted mostly of bars and strip-joints. Any serious shopping had to be done at the Sears catalog office or by making the four-hour trip up the Key Highway to Miami.

ARCHERFISH spent about half the time doing "daily ops" in the Key West operating areas, mostly providing "target services" to the Anti-Submarine Warfare

(ASW) School. Operating out of Key West was fun and with deep water close-by we would get underway about 7 a.m., be in our operating area by 8 a.m., submerge and provide a full day's services to ASW School students learning their ASW skills, and then be back in port by 6 p.m. Frequently after tying-up, we would make a bee-line for the O-Club, where we were joined by the wives for cocktails and dinner.

Not so much fun was the time spent away from Key West. Most of our away trips were down to Guantanamo Bay, Cuba ("Gitmo") where we provided ASW services to destroyers undergoing their periodic "refresher" training. We made several of these trips during my time in ARCHERFISH, each lasting about two months.

The trips to Gitmo were sometimes referred to as "rum runs". In Gitmo, one could buy a gallon of Bacardi white rum for $1.00. The dark rum sold for $1.10 a gallon. Although U.S. Customs regulations allowed a limit of 2 gallons per person, most submarine crews returned with more. There were a lot of good hiding places on a submarine. Besides, the Customs Agents that boarded us upon arrival in Key West generally would have a cup of coffee in the Wardroom, ask a few questions and depart. On occasion, however, Customs would do a thorough inspection of the boat. Somehow the Sub Base people would be alerted to this, and would send a warning message to the boat. This happened to ARCHERFISH on one of the returns from Gitmo, and the word was put out to all hands to bring all excess liquor to the Forward Torpedo Room. This being done, the "contraband" bottles of booze were loaded into one of the empty torpedo tubes, the tube was flooded, outer door opened, and the tube fired. "WHOOSH", out went many gallon bottles of Bacardi rum to the bottom of Key West entrance channel. I often wondered how much booze rested on the bottom of Key West channel.

In addition to our Gitmo deployments, we made a three-month trip to the South Atlantic to survey the ocean bottom. ARCHERFISH was instrumented with gear designed to measure the Earth's gravity, and we would run "full-on-four" with the dinky "on float" (about 21 knots) for 50 miles, submerge, level off and get our measurements. This trip included a February stop in Racife, Brazil during Mardi Gras week. This oceanographic survey mission was the first of many that ARCHERFISH would conduct later as an AGSS.

I should also mention that, on two occasions, ARCHERFISH and all the other ships in Key West had to get underway to ride-out a hurricane. It is always safer for ships to ride-out a hurricane at sea than to risk being dashed against a dock or being blown aground. Of course, the wives and families were left ashore, and Navy personnel were always on-call to assist families as needed.

Being a fleetboat, without a snorkel, riding-out a hurricane in heavy seas while remaining surfaced meant keeping the upper Conning Tower hatch shut, while the Chief of the Watch (COW) would shut and open the Main Induction upon command from the

OOD on the Bridge. Of course, the OOD and Lookout were tied-down to keep them from being washed overboard.

Another interesting time during my tour was when ARCHEFISH "went Hollywood". The submarine movie, "Operation Petticoat" starring Cary Grant, Tony Curtis, and Dina Merrill was filmed in Key West. ARCHERFISH and the USS BALAO SS-285, were two WWII BALAO class fleet submarines stationed in Key West selected for use in the movie. Other than getting to know the actors, the advantage of being the boat used for the movie was that we would remain in port for about a month while certain scenes were filmed. We all thought that ARCHERFISH would be used for the movie, however, at the last minute, BALAO was selected and ARCHERFISH ended up taking BALAO's assignments, including another trip to Gitmo.

Throughout my tours on "the boats" (I served on a total of five), there never was a lack of excitement. As the saying goes, "Submariners spend hours of boredom interrupted by moments of sheer terror".

And two things happened to me while I was on the ARCHERFISH that fit the "sheer terror" category.

When coming down the ladder from the Bridge into the Conning Tower while submerging, the OOD pulls and hangs on the lanyard attached to the Bridge Hatch while the Quartermaster on watch quickly climbs the ladder and turns the hatch-wheel to tightly seal the hatch dogs.

Clearing the Bridge must be done precisely and quickly, because within about 20 seconds the submarine bow would be under and water would be rushing up to the Bridge deck level. Although frowned upon, some OOD's found it amusing to linger on the Bridge for a short period after sounding the Diving Alarm to hear the ballast tanks hiss as they vented air and watch the bow slip beneath the waves. I admit to having been one of those foolish people, and it never ceased to make me smile.

On these "full-on-four" 21-knot dives, I was OOD on the Bridge when the Captain ordered us to submerge. Following procedure, I gave the order, "Clear the Bridge, Clear the Bridge", and as the lookouts were heading down the hatch, I sounded the Diving Alarm and followed them down, pulling the hatch lanyard shut as I came down the ladder into the Conning Tower. This time, however, the hatch latching "dogs" had become misaligned, which prevented the hatch from being fully closed. Realizing what was happening, and that in a few seconds we would have water pouring through the partially-open upper hatch, I ordered the lower Conning Tower hatch shut to isolate the Conning Tower from the rest of the boat and at the same time reached over my left shoulder and pulled the Surfacing Alarm lever three times (ooogahhh, ooogahhh, ooogahhh).

As soon as the Surfacing Alarm sounded, the Chief of the Watch in the Control Room shut the ballast tank vents and initiated a high-pressure air blow of ballast tanks to head us back toward the surface. The rapid response on the part of everyone averted what could have been a bad situation, and we stopped our dive in time to avoid taking on a significant amount of water. The Captain gave me a "well-done", which I needed later when things went really bad.

Every submariner has been in a situation where he and his boat came close to becoming one of those "failed to return and presumed lost" statistic, and my next ARCHERFISH story involves the most frightening event I experienced in all my years on submarines. I still shudder when I think about it today. It happened while we were operating submerged in deep water off of Key West.

Upon clearing the Bridge, as OOD, and commencing a dive, I dropped down into the Conning Tower, shutting the Bridge hatch on the way, and reported "last man down, hatch secure" to the Conning Officer. I then dropped down the ladder into the Control Room to take over as Diving Officer. The Conning Tower sits just above the Control Room and the Conning Officer can look down through the lower Conning Tower hatch at the Diving Officer directly below. As Diving Officer, I was responsible to keep the boat at ordered depth and properly trimmed, while the Conning Officer had tactical maneuvering and safe navigation responsibility.

During this particular dive, I was not yet Submarine Qualified, and my performance was being observed by the Captain. Upon submerging to periscope depth (60 feet keel depth), and having achieved a neutral buoyancy trim, I was ordered to take the boat to 200 feet (I should explain that we had two depth gauges – one used above 165 feet called the shallow gauge and a deep depth gauge that was monitored at deeper depths. Both depth gauges used sea-pressure to indicate depth. When going below 165 feet, the shallow depth gauge was shut off, and the deep depth gauge was used to establish depth). As we submerged below 165 feet, I gave the order to "secure the shallow gauge". The sailor who controlled the Bow Planes was responsible to secure the shallow gauge. To do this he had to reach behind the diving control panel and, by feel, find the correct valve to turn clockwise to the shut position.

In this instance, instead of turning shut the shallow gauge sea-pressure stop valve, the sailor erroneously shut the sea pressure master stop valve, thereby shutting off both the shallow and deep depth gauges. This occurred at the same time I was leveling the boat off to settle at my 200-foot ordered depth. With the sea-pressure master valve shut, the deep gauge no longer registered correct depth, but remained stuck at an indicated depth of 195 feet.

So, there I was, with a depth gauge that was telling us we were at 195 feet when my ordered depth was 200 feet, and with the Captain behind me observing my skill (or lack thereof) as Diving Officer. Neither the Captain nor I realized that our depth gauge was stuck at 195 feet, so the Captain queried, "Mr. Kronzer, what is your ordered depth?", to which I replied, "200 feet, sir." The Captain then ordered, "Well, get down to ordered depth," so I began to take the depth-keeping steps I learned at Sub School. First, I ordered a steeper down angle on the boat and nothing happened. The gauge still read 195 feet. Next I ordered a bit more speed, and still no change in depth. At this point I felt that the boat had become lighter due to a change in water temperature, which is not unusual because the water gets colder and more dense as one goes deeper, causing a submarine to become more buoyant, so I began flooding water into our Trim Tanks to make the boat heavier.

Now, here's where the frightening part of this story comes in. Remember, that the Captain was standing directly behind me and both of us were focused on the Control Room depth gauge while I was attempting (erroneously) to get the boat to descend to 200 feet. The Conning Officer was looking down at us from the Conning Tower while observing his own Conning Tower depth gauge that was reading depth correctly. Although the Conning Officer was watching us go deeper than 200 feet and even 300 feet, he kept silent, believing that with the Captain standing behind me everything must be OK. Finally, as we were descending below 400 feet, the Conning Officer frantically alerted us, "Sir, you know we're passing test depth." (A submarine has two warning depths: "Test Depth" and "Crush Depth". At crush depth sea-pressure will cause the hull to implode. Test depth was 412 feet and crush depth was 600 feet). Upon hearing the Conning Officer's warning, I immediately ordered, "Full rise on the planes, all back full" and "blow all main ballast tanks." At about the same time, flooding reports came in from the Forward Torpedo Room and the Maneuvering Room as equipment normally secured when rigged for deep submergence gave way to sea-pressure. Fortunately our well-trained crew knew exactly what to do and brought the flooding under control before we took on too much water, and we surfaced without further trouble.

Although happy we got out of this, I was sure I would soon get orders to some cargo ship as their Laundry and Morale Officer. However, my good Captain never said a word to me or gave me a bad fitness report, and when we analyzed what happened, we figured that we were near crush depth by the time we were able to stop our descent and head for the surface. Thank

God for the Portsmouth Naval Shipyard submarine designers and builders. I still shudder today when I think about this event.

I should mention here that the years 1957-1958 were interesting years to be stationed in Key West. Castro had taken over Cuba and was establishing a Communist regime under Russian sponsorship. Key West was only 90 miles from Havana, so we were able to get Cuban TV stations. For several months after Castro took over, we could watch Castro's political opponents being executed by firing squad live on TV. Gruesome scenes meant to have an impact on anyone in Cuba thinking about a counter-revolution. The United States increased the Marine Corps garrison at Gitmo, locked the gates, and, ignoring Castro's threats, hung on to our training base there. Castro cut off all fresh water supplies to Gitmo, so the U.S. brought down and installed a fresh water distilling plant on the base. Havana and Santiago, once favorite Navy ports of call in Cuba were closed, but we could still buy Bacardi rum at the Gitmo package store.

FROM: Joseph Morales –

<u>An evening at sea</u>.

I was stationed on the USS
CASIMIR PULASKI SSBN-633(B), in A-
Division in the late 70's and early '80's. We
had just done a day of exercises with USS
JOHN HANCOCK DD-981, during a torpex
(torpedo exercise) in the Caribbean. We had
done really well and the crew was pretty
happy about how we had been able to "sink"
this big tin can without ever being detected.
On the surface as we headed into port, as an
MMFN(SU), I was a lookout during the
mid-watch. With me on the Bridge was the
Weapons Officer who was a pretty cool guy.
It was dark with the whole sky sprinkled
with stars. The breeze coming over the
Bridge was pleasantly cool on this beautiful
summer evening. Suddenly a pod of
dolphins appeared at our bow riding the
pressure-wave generated by the boat's
plowing through the water. Every so often

there would be an explosion of light as the dolphins jumping in and out of the water stirred up bioluminescence from the strong cavitation generated by their tail thrusts. It was one of the most magical moments I'd ever spent at sea. Here we were on the surface of a mighty warship, seemingly being escorted back to port by the very symbol of the Submarine Force. All too soon our watch reliefs were calling for us to trade places. This was perhaps the only time that I never wanted to be relieved from a watch!

FROM: Don Haseley, USS CAVALLA SS-244 –

It was early 1945 and we had just completed our 4th war patrol and were coming into port at Fremantle, Australia. Our hotel was the King Edward in Perth.

As we docked we were all lined up on deck in the aft section and the officers were lined up forward of the sail. First came aboard the top brass which was Admiral (Uncle Charlie) Lockwood, and then a lady following him. I was back there with all the guys when one of the officers comes back to all of us with this lady. She says, "Who is Don Haseley?" Of course, I said, "I am, ma'am" to which she said, "Come with me." I didn't know if I was going to jail or what, but all the guys were laughing at me being hauled off the sub. We went inside this building alongside the dock, and she said, "Sit down." Boy was I scared. We had just completed another patrol and were ready to celebrate, big time. Then the lady said, "Your Father, meaning my Dad, had written a letter to the Secretary of the Navy complaining to him, how come his other son (my brother who was in Africa with the Army Air Corps) writes letters almost every day, and here was his other son in the Navy who wrote only about one letter every 2 months. Then, she said, "You start talking and I will write your Father a letter of whatever you say. When it was all over, I headed back to the sub and boy did those guys unload on me. I tried to tell my parents that I was able to write all I wanted to, but there is no Post Office in the South China Sea while out on patrol. After the war, I came home on leave and explained to my Dad all about it. He just said, "Write more often."

After the war was over, the CAVALLA was at the peace treaty signing in Tokyo Bay. We started back to Pearl, then through the Panama Canal and up the east coast. The Chief of the Deck Crew, of which I was a part, came around and asked each one of us, "Will you have any family, etc., waiting at the dock when we pull in?" I said, "No." I had no girlfriend and my parents lived in Niagara Falls, NY, so I let it all pass. As we got close to New London, the Chief said, "we picked you to man the Deck Watch, meaning all personnel coming aboard the sub had to ask permission to board, and then salute the flag. After all the top brass from Washington had come aboard they all shook hands with the whole crew, except for me, I had the Gangway Watch. Then the Captain came back to the whole crew and said, "You are all excused to go ashore and visit your loved ones." I was stuck with the Gangway Watch. The Captain was gone and all the crew was ashore, and I had the honor of watching the boat while everybody else was ashore. Who needs that kind of honor?

AUTHOR'S NOTE: Don Haseley has been presented a model of USS CAVALLA SS-244 by USSVI Past Commander of Chesapeake Base and of Nathanael Greene Base, as have five other WWII Submariners. Thanks for your honoring these WWII Boatsailor Heroes from all of your USSVI brothers, John.

FROM: Anonymous –

Things weren't going well for a pair of third class petty officer submarine sailors living in the barracks in Groton, CT. They were "dink" in quals, and there was an equal amount of animosity between them and the COB. They had heard that a dirt-bag frocked PO3 as TM2 had stolen a TMSN's deceased-wife's wedding ring. The

Command refused to take action and threatened to charge the E-3 with some bogus UCMJ charge (defamation of character) of the PO2. The two sailors felt that they had to do something. Their moods were as bitter as mid-watch coffee.

It was a Friday in early October of 1984, in Groton. The weather was comfortable and seasonable. The sailors wore their light jackets as they left the boat and walked off the pier for the start of a typical Friday night in the barracks before Saturday duty.

A pile of one-gallon cans of black and white paint was sitting right there on the pier. There were also several paint rollers. One sailor looked at the other and said, "Follow my lead and act normal." These young and angry men each grabbed a gallon of paint, (one black and one white) and a pair of rollers. The rollers went under the jackets and the paint cans swung nonchalantly as the sailors walked off the pier.

Two years earlier, these sailors and their submarine arrived in Groton after an overhaul on the west coast. These two sub sailors had been told many stories of the BOHICA Rock (Bend Over Here It Comes Again). The stories were all basically the same. The Rock would get painted by the ship's in-port crew members. The act was meant to greet submariners as they return to Groton after long and extended deployments. The Rock would be painted with the returning submarine's hull number. It was meant as a morale-builder and a ritual that welcomed the sailors home. The young sailors were told that their boat would be honored in that fashion. It wasn't. Over the past two years, these men never heard a single verified story of any submarine being honored with the traditions of old. These sailors felt the tradition would soon be forgotten and left to die in a Navy that was becoming _too_ politically correct. The death of a salty tradition bothered these two sailors and they vowed to resurrect the tradition at the risk of being disciplined.

The paint and rollers got tossed in the trunk of one of the sailors' cars, and these young men waited for sunset. At the appointed hour, these two men left the Sub Base, drove through town, across the bridge, took the first exit and drove past the Coast Guard Academy. They looked for the first road that would take them down to the river, and directly across from the Sub Base. They found the road, turned right, drove down the hill, crossed the railroad track, and found a place to park. It was a dark night. They had two gallons of government paint, two rollers, attitudes and a flashlight. The area was wooded and without houses. With flashlight, screwdriver and swinging paint cans in hand, the two trekked through the woods to find the river's edge. After several excursions to the river bank and back into the woods, they found a huge flat rock that was directly across the river from their submarine's pier. It had some non-descript graffiti painted on it. Those markings were invisible to all personnel across the river. The sub sailors agreed that it was probably not the correct BOHICA Rock, but it would do.

Pouring from the cans and rolling paint on the rock, the sub sailors made letters and numbers that were ten feet high and four feet wide; black letters with a white background. Without speaking, they worked quietly and quickly. They regularly looked over their shoulders to see if there was any abnormal activity indicating they had been discovered. The deed took less than fifteen minutes. No spotlights, no speedboats, no high-speed tug boat pushing a barge down the Thames River. It had taken longer to find the rock than to paint it. A full gallon of white and another of black did the job. "BOHICA 591" covered this rock. When they finished, they took a moment, stood at the bottom of the rock, between the paint and the river and admired their work. A single high-five completed the shoreline activities. These men threw their paint cans and rollers in the river and walked back to the car. Prior to going back to the Sub Base, they stopped and had a single beer in an undisclosed Groton biker bar.

The next morning, Saturday at 7:00, one of the sailors left the barracks and walked down to the boat. There was a fog lying low on the river and all seemed normal. The far side of the Thames River and its rocky bank was concealed. Around 8:30, the fog started to lift. The sub sailor came topside and walked to the aft hatch. He was amazed at the size and magnitude of visibility of their previous night's work. The sailor went back inside and called his buddy and partner in crime. The sailor told his cohort to keep his mouth shut and not say a word about the previous night's caper.

What these two young men didn't know and weren't told was that very weekend was followed by Columbus Day on Monday. They didn't realize that Columbus Day is a federal holiday and is anointed as the birthday of the U.S. Navy. They weren't told that the Navy tradition was to have Columbus Day/Navy's Birthday events and to open the Groton Submarine Base for families, veterans, and civilians to tour the submarines. These sailors only knew that they would not have a Friday night off

together for at least a month and November
was going to be colder and they were
scheduled to go to sea on Wednesday.

The CO was informed that we
weren't going to sea until "That Rock" got
painted over. The COB tried to take a flat-
bottomed skiff across the Thames River. He
swamped it and had to return to our side,
twice I'm told. On Thursday the COB took
a couple of strikers and drove across the
river but couldn't find it. On Friday they
drove across again, found it, painted it with
white paint and by Saturday morning the
black paint had bled through. They had to
go back and repaint it on Monday. Tuesday
we waited to see if the sign would reappear.
Wednesday, we went to sea.

The amusing thing is what the
command did inside the boat. There was a
long Officer's Call, as well as a long Chief's
Call that Tuesday, followed by, "The
Command wants to know who did it and
they will be punished." No one spoke up.
Then the junior officers were told to find
out, and still no response.

Then the Chiefs were told to find out, to
which there was still only silence. Only two
people knew and they also knew that the
command wanted to make an example of
them. Now, the PO1's were told to find out
who the villains were, and no one uttered a
word. We went to sea, and one of the
Chief's stayed in and did a barracks
inspection, but all evidence of black or white
paint on anything had already been
jettisoned, and thusly we escaped
prosecution.

A month later, the Mother of the TM
Seaman sent our CO a mold of the special,
custom-made ring that was stolen, which
had been fabricated by her local town
jeweler. The TMSN made TM3 and the
frocked TM3 went to Captain's Mast for
theft. He was summarily demoted to
Seaman and was made to serve under the
man from whom he had stolen the ring.

Someone stole across the river, and
twice after our escapade, repainted the Rock
with "BOHICA 591". It wasn't me, but I
suspected that it was my former partner in
crime with a different partner. Again, we

got the very same response from the
command.  I was under suspicion, but
because I had the duty and was on board
they had to look elsewhere.  Again, no one
'fessed-up' to the deed.  Over time, I had
noticed that other boats had marked the
Rock, but never to the outstanding degree
that we did on the Friday night before
Columbus Day with an "Open Base" all
weekend.

That was 29 years ago.  My memory
may be flawed but I believe that was my one
and only display of civil disobedience, and I
expect the statue of limitations has been
played out by now.

FROM: Thomas Neff –

Man Overboard.

When I was on USS THEODORE
ROOSEVELT SSBN-600(G), circa 1969,
we had a young Seaman named Harry Trask.
While transiting out of Holy Loch, or

possibly Charleston after a missile load-out, Trask was the lookout on the Bridge with the OOD, a LCDR. As part of his duties as OOD, the LCDR was asking Trask various questions related to his lookout duties. When he asked what Trask would do if the OOD fell overboard on the starboard side, Trask responded without batting an eye, "Control – Bridge; this is Trask, I have the Deck and the Conn."

He was immediately relieved of his lookout duties and became an instant hero to the crew.

FROM: Keith "Scarpa" Bloomfield, Her Majesty's Australian Submarine Force –

Excerpts from "The Bull Horn", the S-57, HMAS OXLEY's ship's newspaper

Vol. II, No. 4, Tuesday the 44th to Sydney.

Registered at the C.P.O. OXFAN for transmission by hand as wastepaper.

## UP PERISCOPE.

The inclusion of this paragraph depends upon exercise commitments, and as the name implies, we have to be at a certain depth to obtain UP PERISCOPE material. Monday's meager yield was basically the same that was printed in Sunday's BULL HORN. The proximity of other gray counties precluded the gleaning of further outside news today.

## LORD MAYOR DISPLAYS TALENTS – by Tom Crier

OXFAN Monday – On one of his periodic strolls through the county today, the Lord Mayor took time off from meeting people to assist one of the electrical wizards in his dilemma. Said electrical wizard had dismantled an intricate piece of essential machinery to analyze the contents and, due to the great length of time involved in the analysis, was having great difficulty in reassembling same. Enter the Lord Mayor, "What then is this Chinese puzzle you have here, my man?" On being apprised of the nature of the problem, and the difficulties involved, the Lord Mayor requested that he be permitted to try his hand, and LO…within the short space of ten minutes had reassembled the part and demonstrated that it now worked perfectly. Word has it that the Lord Mayor is to be presented with the coveted badge of The Electrical Wizard's Association, the electric flash defined with crossed fingers.

CHUFFYPUFFIN Monday – Ty, the Great White Hunter, has made representations to the Lord Mayor about his choice of parking spots. Ty says he is, "suffering great indignity," in that the Lord Mayor will insist on parking where there are no fish. Ty has volunteered to go with the County Councilors next time they are seeking a parking lot, and by dint of his great experience in such manner of things, point out the spots where the fish are sure to be biting.

LAST Sunday – While swimming off Pulau Tiomen, Ty revealed why he has had only limited success with the fish. Even when he goes down among them and meets them on even terms, he can only manage to capture one little fish, and then with the aid of a bloody great spear.

STOKE CITY Monday – A prominent member of this small community today volunteered to do a standing 2-5 in the OXFAN generating station.  When interviewed Mr. Oggie explained that, "his conscience had been giving him a hard time because he has a better job than the Chief Pokey."  Other members of the community suspect coercion; they say that, "Mr. Oggie is being penalized for his four wins in one night in the gambling casino of which the Chief Pokey is co-proprietor," but Mr. Oggie, displaying missing fingernails and whip wounds, insists that he "Is a volunteer."

FORRARDSVILLE Monday – This large community was tonight seething with indignation over the apparent foul play indulged in by one of its trusted members.  It is suspected that M. Terry leChef is in the pay of the gambling kings, after his FIVE wins out of 8 houses at the casino tonight. Mr. leChef insists that his winnings, (44 dollars in all) were purely a matter of luck, but other members suspect the darkest of foul play.

Results of Games Played:

1. In 73 members      Polto
2. In 78 members      leChef
3. In 75 members      Boong
4. In 81 members      leChef
5. In 74 members      leChef
6. In 69 members      leChef
7. In 64 members      leChef
8. In 73 members      N. Felsch.

The gambling casino is open most nights and times of games are well-promulgated. The proprietors would like to see a good attendance every night; you never know, you may rub against leChef on your way through, or be approached by the proprietors with an offer. Snowball now stands at 65 dollars in 55 members.

There is someone on board who can stand in W/T office and use trap 2.

OXFAN Monday – In an impressive ceremony here yesterday, the office of Beer Caterer extraordinaire was officially handed over to Chief Pokey.  We join with all other members of the community in extending a hearty welcome to the new purveyor of intoxicating beverages and wish him a long and happy term in office.  We also extend our thanks to the retiring Beer Caterer for his long and arduous service in the office.

FORRARDSVILLE Monday – Excited admirers are still congratulating Louie the Slug on his quick action yesterday when he utilized the high-powered speedboat when he rushed a pregnant Malay woman from the shore to the infirmary in the county of MELBOURNE.  Louie counts himself fortunate that he didn't have to administer to the woman during the trip, but he admits that the throttle was wide-open all the way, and he spent the whole trip on his knees.

Meanwhile, in Carriagetown, the Laird is contemplating legal action against Louie the Slug for alleged medical malpractice.  The Laird claims that as it is his job to look after all the medical problems, Louie the Slug unjustifiably usurped his position. However, it has been learned in this office that the Laird is somewhat mollified by the fact that Fingers allowed him to operate on one of his priceless digits early Tuesday.

LATEST ON THE POP SCENE – The newest rage in the world of Pop is the song that is sweeping the county, "DUCK DIDN'T MAKE THOSE LITTLE GREEN APPLES."

OXFAN Tuesday – High Court action is pending following an assassination attempt early today. At 0930 this a.m., a cloud of near-lethal gas was detected in all areas of OXFAN. The perpetrator of this event, Action Cookie, claims he was only, "peeling onions at the time," but evidence has been brought that his account was somewhat red in color and he is trying to asphyxiate the citizens to make ends meet.

A.C. was not available for comment, that worthy citizen being at the time, chained to the garbage disposal unit.

FORRARDSVILLE Tuesday – Serious injury was averted today in the large labor camp north of here, when Scarpa the Broom narrowly escaped death as a high-powered grease gun exploded with a force equal to one damp squib. No one was injured in the accident, which could have been a major catastrophe.

OXFAN Tuesday – There is great consternation in the primary generating station at the news that Nick the Snakecharmer has lost a deadly Cottonmouth from his collection down in the pit. Nick is inconsolable and the engine-drivers can all be viewed hanging from pipes and fittings and casting anxious glances to and fro while Nick is wandering around the station calling, "Here, Cotty." It is feared that the snake may have escaped from the station, so anyone finding anything resembling a snake is advised to treat it with the utmost caution. This does not apply in bathrooms where all snakes sighted can be classified as not dangerous, at least temporarily.

SNIPPET – It may not be commonly known by members of the county that the island we have just left was the site of the filming of the musical "South Pacific." In fact, the Islanders still call the island to the south, "Bali Hai."

WATER – All members are congratulated on the sharp decline in water consumption in the county. Total used yesterday was 326 gallons.

SHORT VERSE – (Contribution) –

There was a high member, who couldn't remember,

If his muscles were working, or not.

He bought a contraption to recover his action,

Drinking "Kai" to speed up the lot.

Attending the fore-ends, accompanied by knee-bends,

He tackles it all with a grin.

And considers the tussles, that will help his poor muscles,

A God-send, and worth all the gin.

## LETTER TO THE EDITOR

Sir,

If you call that scurrilous rag of yours the "BULL HORN", how come the paper is not a good deal stiffer?   – S. Forrardsville.

Dear S.,

This is not the original paper we intended to use. We did have a supply of used cement bags but the inhabitants of Stoke City misappropriated them to use as toilet paper. We trust that further issues will meet with your approval.  – Ed.

Dear Doctor,

Is it true that self-gratification in sea water is hazardous to your health?    – B. B. Forrardsville.

Dear B.B.,

Not to mine, sonny; I don't do it in sea water.  – Doc.

ADVERTISEMENTS

S  A L E:

Monster sale of government surplus; date to be fixed.

1.  TASMANIA – Being sold as the government considers the cost of keeping it afloat and attached to Australia is too great.
2.  MYER EMPORIUM BOWL – It is found that due to it constantly being out of doors, the soup made in it tastes similar to water from the Yarra.
3.  CENTER PYLON, SYDNEY HARBOUR BRIDGE – Due to the increase in traffic in the harbor, this gift from the Imperial Japanese Government has of late proved a navigational hazard and is to be removed.

    4.   AYERS ROCK – The government considers that this rock, (built at great expense by our early settlers for protection against flash-floods), is not getting enough use to warrant its upkeep. The Govt. is also incensed at the vandals who drew funny pictures on it.

Removal of all articles is by the buyer, and the full cost is to be borne by the buyer.

LOST

    From Chufpuffham – One green bush-hat. Owner places great emotional value upon this article, as it is the same one he wore when he campaigned for the Suffragettes. Finder, please return to Rabbit.

TEXT FOR TODAY

From the book of Ruth, Chapter 2:

    …And her mother-in-law said unto her, "Where hast thou gleaned today? And where wroughtest thou? Blest be he that did take knowledge of thee." And she showed her mother-in-law with whom she had wrought, and said, "The man's name with whom I wrought today is Boas."

QUESTION

Where is the emergency stop for the L.P. Blower?

What kind of power supply does the 189 use?

Where is the air pick-up unit for S.I.R.S.?

HATCHED, MATCHED AND DESPATCHED

To Jock and Marjorie Wilson: A son, born Monday 1st June, 1970. Both well. Congratulations Jock.

E & E ELECTRICAL MAINTENANCE AND REPAIR FIRM

All electrical equipment repaired

24-hour service

Contact Motor Rock

All prices reasonable or jobs done for special favours

APOLOGY

The proprietors of the Gambling Joint apologize for the erratic frequency of their games, and for the obvious rigging of the games.

FROM THE EDITOR

The Editor apologizes for the absence of the BULL HORN from some yesterday, but would like to point out that YOU WERE WARNED, and the Ed. Is basically a LAZY BASTARD.

LATE NEWS

Later.

FROM: William Hadley –

STORIES ABOUT LEO:

Intelligence-Gathering Mission.

On this special intelligence-gathering mission, the CIC compartment had been placed completely off limits to the entire crew except for those required to operate both the standard boat's equipment as well as all the additional special systems that I had installed. Most of the crew kept trying to ascertain what was going on in this compartment during the entire trip. We had this one Chief cook by the name of Leo, who just mothered the living hell out of the crew. He wanted to know what was going on in there also. Since submariners like to play jokes on others, both the Skipper and the Special Mission O-in-C agreed to allow us to play a joke on the cook. Therefore, we prepared a bunch of charts with shapes of women, a large number of centerfold pictures from PLAYBOY and other idiotic things. Then we went deep, sanitized the compartment with all this material, and had Leo visit the compartment. We had him take an oath that he would not reveal what he saw and, of course, we let a number of other crewmen know what he had seen. It was funny how he tried to keep his promise.

Hamburger vs. Steak.

Before we departed on this trip, Leo had ordered a large quantity of hamburger from local supply channels. When he opened one case to inspect it, he flipped his wig. Instead of it being 70% meat and 30% fat, it was a very pale pink indicating it contained more fat than meat. I was asked to take color pictures of this meat, which I did. He then went to the Base and began raising holy hell, charging the supply department with fraud and etc. We suddenly had a stream of government officials coming on board and inspecting this meat. The bottom line was that every bit of the hamburger was replaced with top of the line steak cuts of meat. Thus on the trip, we had steak for breakfast, steak for lunch and steak for supper instead of hamburger. Finally, the crew began to request hamburger for a meal in place of the steak. One day as I walked by the galley, I heard Leo crying his heart out. There he was crying as he took a nice beautiful steak and drops it in the meat-grinder, muttering how awful it was to convert steak into hamburger.

Tastes Like Crap.

Another incident with Leo was his weakness to criticism. He would routinely come out of the galley at the noon and evening meal and ask for comments. Some would tell him it tasted like crap; it was really OK, and etc. Well, a number of the Chiefs decided to refrain from making any comment whatsoever on the quality or quantity of each meal. When the crew noticed that this "no comment" action was getting under his skin, just about everyone quickly joined in. It got so bad that Leo would even go up to the Wardroom trying to get some comments about his meals. The more he failed to receive any comments, the more he would be in the mess deck bugging the crew for their input. Finally, he asked the Chief of the Boat at this one meal how the meal was. The COB replied with, "It tastes like CRAP!" and resumed eating his meal. Leo became so excited that he went up to the Skipper's Stateroom and yelled at the Skipper, "The crew says the food tastes like CRAP", and travelled through the boat telling everyone he came in contact with for the next few minutes the same phrase.

<u>To Combat Boredom</u>.

On these trips we would try to come up with anything to combat boredom. I talked Leo into letting me make a huge batch of fudge for the crew this one evening. Everything was going fine until it came to adding the butter to the fudge, and put the mixer on high speed. I began talking with others about eating the fudge and not paying very much attention to the mixer. Suddenly we smelled smoke and heard this mixer grinding to a halt. I quickly shut the mixer off and tried to remove the beater from the fudge. It seems that it had hardened in the huge mixing bowl and required me taking any object available to break or chip the fudge out. About this time Leo came in to begin making donuts for breakfast, and got very upset with me. He grabbed a huge knife and yelled that he was going to carve out my heart. Away we went, running forward and aft through the boat with him chasing me screaming how I ruined his mixer. As we ran through the officers' passageway for the third or fourth time, the Skipper came out of his stateroom and stopped us. I received a harsh lecture about a lack of attention to what I was doing and Leo for losing his temper.

Leo's Sausage.

Leo was a real mother-type to us. He ordered a large quantity of different seasoning and sausage casing. Instead of throwing away all the trimmings from the meat prepared for meals, he saved it. Then this one day I watched him make sausage with all this stuff. It didn't look very appetizing at the time and he didn't make too much. Well the meal at which he served this home-made sausage created a lot of friction between watch being relieved and those not on watch. It seems that those in the first call meal-seating ate most of the sausage, because it was so damn good. Leo asked for a couple of volunteers to help him make the next batch of sausage, since he estimated it would take about 150 pounds to satisfy the crew. Instead of a couple, he had half the crew ready to assist. That is when I learned a little about making sausage.

How Intelligence Gathering Was Altered.

During the trip, we recorded more than 1,800 miles of magnetic tape which took NSA more than three years to process. The information acquired on this trip changed the entire submarine intelligence gathering operation in a major way. Where, before we would periodically order submarines into the area to collect data, it was now to maintain a constant presence. During the winter we utilized diesel submarines and nuclear with vast amounts of specialized equipment during the Spring and Summer.

Sanitary Tanks.

It seems one very consistent activity on every boat at sea is that sanitary tanks are emptied either just before or while serving a meal. It is in some ways simple and others very complex. The sanitary tanks are within the pressure hull and vent inside the boat via charcoal filters. Typically, these filters will work reasonably well if the air travelling through is allowed to absorb the smell. Unfortunately, sanitary tanks are emptied by first sealing all the openings within the pressure hull, open the discharge valve located at the bottom of the tank and applying air pressure consisting of either 225 psi or 400 psi for the TRITON. This pressure differential is sufficient to expel all the waste to sea. The next problem is once the discharge valve is shut, the tank is now filled with air at pressures as much as 400 psi if emptied below periscope depth. If this air pressure were vented at a sufficiently slow rate to allow the filter system to function properly, it would take several hours before the commodes, urinals, sinks and wash-basins could be used. So they simply open the valve to the filters full-bore with very limited effect by the activated charcoal filters.

Almost every Submariner has personally, or knows of another, who experienced the unpleasant condition of being exposed to the results of an improperly secured sanitary tank for discharge. I remember one time when an RD3 on watch in the CIC compartment received orders from the Control Room to blow the officer's sanitary tank. So he posted the sign in the Officer's Head that it was secured for blowing. Most people know that you can still sit on the commode or use a wash basin while this is happening, just that you cannot open the flapper valve on the commode or empty the basin. The Skipper noticed the sign and was going to take a short quick shower and the water would collect in the bottom of the shower stall. The RD3 was supposed to follow normal safety procedures, which required that once all valves emptying into the tank are closed, a slug of air is applied in the tank to see if air pressure increases. If it does then you know every valve has been properly shut. Instead, he simply opened the discharge valve and tried to apply air pressure to the top of the tank. However, once he opened the discharge valve, any space left in the tank was quickly filled with seawater and then pushed feces back up through the drain system. Suddenly everyone in the CIC, Radio Room, and

Control Room heard the Skipper screaming, "SECURE THE BLOW." There he was stomping forward from the officer's head with feces dripping down his face. The standard rule is whoever is responsible for this kind of a mess is the person to clean it up. So this RD3 was relieved of his watch so he could spend the next 6 to 8 hours cleaning up the officer's head, including all the piping in the overhead.

The Tables Are Turned.

I was acting-COB on this one specific trip and decided to play a joke on this unfortunate RD3 by telling him that he was going to appear at Captain's Mast for this deed. So, this poor kid got his dress shoes out and began polishing them, along with "squaring away" his dress blues, in preparation to appear before the Skipper. After one day, I figured to tell him that it was all a joke. However, the Skipper got wind of what I was doing and decided to turn it against me. He called me into the Wardroom and asked me if the RD3 had his uniform ready, for he was to hold Mast that afternoon. I tried to pretend that he was just

cleaning his uniform and realized he knew.
I then tried to explain to the Captain that the
kid really didn't mean it, and etc. The more
I tried to talk him out of it the more he was
insisting on seeing this sailor properly
punished. So, I informed the kid that he was
to appear before the Captain at 1300 in the
Crew's Mess. I remarked to other Chiefs
that I felt badly about a practical joke that
now turned serious.

That afternoon, at 1300, the Skipper
was there with the Yeoman, Executive
Officer, the kid's Division Officer and a
large group of other enlisted as I escorted
the 3rd class into the Crew's Mess. I was
really feeling very low about what I seemed
to have caused. There I was trying to defend
the kid, while both the Skipper and XO
continually rejected my explanations or
excuses for the sailor. Then the Skipper
stated he was prepared to render judgment.
He stated that his punishment was that he
was to receive a 72-hour liberty upon return
to port for sh___ing on the Captain. Both
the kid and I didn't quite grasp what he said
and the RD3 simply replied, "SIR?" Then

the Skipper smiled, told him he was being promised a 72-hour liberty upon return to port. This was his way to foil my effort at a practical joke. I apologized quickly and verbally at this time, being quite relieved that I was not responsible for hardship on someone else. Then again, the Captain had a record for turning practical jokes against those who tried to invoke them.

[That kid had a great sea story to tell, but nobody probably ever believed it!]

Petticoat Cruise.

One trip we went on was a petticoat cruise out of Norfolk, VA. It seems that Captain Beach obtained permission to take his son on this trip to and out of Norfolk as he was to be relieved of command immediately afterwards. Thus, once we arrived in Norfolk, I was informed that I was to be the personal escort for Admiral Grenfell's family on his petticoat cruise. She was quite a lady, in many ways. If a naval officer's wife does have influence in the ultimate promotional aspects, then she surely should be recognized for it. I really enjoyed escorting her and her family through the boat. At one point in this cruise, we were in the Control Room area as they began the process of coming to the surface. Standing close-by was this Commander. Thus, as the Skipper gave the order to come to 120 feet and I did not say anything, he asked me, "Why stop at 120 feet instead of going right up to the surface?" For that reason I assumed that he was a surface-type and I got sort of cute in my response.

So I stated that we routinely stop at 120 feet for several reasons. First, to listen and see if there are any surface vessels nearby, and second, permit the Diving Officer the opportunities to ensure he has a zero trim on the boat. I stated that going from 120 feet to the surface is the most dangerous period for any submarine as it is essentially blind. If there is any vessel nearby, we could accidentally ram the ship before realizing he was there. About this time the Skipper gave the order to shut the lower Conning Tower hatch. So that, my reply was, to ensure that only the Conning Tower could be flooded in the event a surface vessel rams us. He again asked, "What about the Commanding Officer." My reply was there is really no one of great importance if the Conning Tower is flooded as the boat would still be safe. Once we surfaced and settled down to operating on the surface, all the visitors in the Control Room began moving on to other locations. Then one of the crew asked me whether, "I knew who the Commander was that I was talking to?" I told him no. He replied he was to be our Skipper upon return to New London. Ouch!

Busted.

Later, I was assigned the role of phone-talker on the lower sail deck when the Commander came up. I remarked that he played "dirty pool" by asking me all those questions. It really put me in a bad light. Commander Morin replied that he felt someone should explain the process and I did it in a very fun way. My response was again, "Ouch!" He remarked that he was going to keep his eye on me. During the remainder of my time on the TRITON, Captain Morin would hassle, challenge, motivate and support every member of the crew. In fact, they took great pride in receiving a reprimand from the Skipper. He had a talent for motivating crew members to strive for excellence and never held honest mistakes against anyone.

"Married Man's Turns".

I remember one time after we finished our assigned mission that Captain Morin included in one series of orders the statement, "Make married man's turns". One of the planesmen asked the Skipper what he meant by married man's turns. The Skipper quickly turned to me in my role as Chief of the Watch and asked me, "Is he kidding?" I replied, "No, Sir." We never made married man's turns nor did we head straight for the "barn", but arranged for our arrival always between 1000 and 1600 to ensure everyone will notice us. So the Skipper had me explain the meaning as he headed for his stateroom. In case the reader does not know, it was standard regulation relative to fuel-economy for all ships not to ring up speeds greater that Standard Turns on the screws. (typically 15 knots). Married man turns involved the unofficially adding a few extra turns (faster speed) than recorded in the ship's log. One time on the way back from a long mission, upon each change of the watch, the throttleman would add a couple of turns. Finally, the Skipper came into the Control Room while I had the watch and noticed that we were travelling at almost 25 knots while the official log recorded that we were making turns for standard speed of 15 knots. He finally called the Engine Room to back-off most of the extra turns, but did not raise hell with anyone for this. He stated that he wanted married man's turns not newlywed turns.

New Mission Equipment.

Our first major mission under Captain Morin was up off the coast of Russia to monitor their nuclear testing program. My job was to install as much special equipment that I could within the boat. As part of this preparation, I had to make several trips to NAVAL SECURITY GROUP HEADQUARTERS, and the NATIONAL SECURITY AGENCY, as well as to a number of OPNAV offices.

Some of the people developing or assembling the necessary items of equipment for me refused to consult with me prior to actual shipment of equipment to the boat. When the Skipper saw what I had to bring aboard, he flipped his wig and took me with him to Washington on one very short trip. Finally, I was able to inject reason and common sense into what at first was total chaos. At one point they insisted that I install a Model -28 Teletype printer instead of my suggestion of a Model-14. So I got them over the barrel by giving me a direct order to install this unit. I didn't tell them what I would do to enable me to get it on board until afterwards. I actually cut the unit into two pieces and bolted them together once I got it installed on board. Later, they asked me how did I get it on board, and I heard a long period of silence when I told them what I had done. At one of my meetings at Naval Security Group Headquarters with NSA officials present, I made a statement that no one there was prepared to handle the volume of data that will come from this trip. After the meeting, I was cautioned that I had made a very bad statement and it could hurt my career and reputation. My reply was that I couldn't even come up with what I believe would be a reasonable estimate of our potential success. I had to make another trip to Washington about six months after we returned from this trip and stopped by a couple of the branches involved in analysis of data from this one trip. They had to expand their staff by three-fold in order to process what they perceived as the most critical material and estimated that it would take three years to complete going over all the tapes. They advised me of the many meetings now being held by top officials to expand the submarine effort far beyond what had been currently approved.

Critical Equipment.

One item that was critical in their program was an AN/SRD-7A HF-Radio Direction Finder system that had been modified for submarine-use. This system had been installed on one previous submarine in the Pacific, so I was told, and that it didn't work. It had quickly flooded once they reached the northern waters off of

Russia. We also experienced typical actions by those civilians who disliked being forced to bypass their bureaucratic rules, as they put every possible obstacle in the way. That is what happened with this system. It was to be installed while we were located at Electric Boat, our builder, that had cranes capable of servicing our 19 odd masts. It did not arrive until we had moved alongside our tender with its cranes being too short in length to properly pull the designated VHF/UHF antenna and replace it with this antenna.

Antennae Problems.

We informed the Skipper of the antenna problem. Finally we received feedback from NSA regarding the critical need for this system. We had a heated discussion on how we could do it ourselves without crane-service. The RM1 and I figured out how we could accomplish this task in the few days remaining before we left on the mission. It just about killed both of us, but fortunately we were lucky. This antenna weighed over six-hundred pounds with additional unknown weight associated with the RF and power cables that were attached to the antenna base. We had to first remove the old VHF/UHF antenna, which we discovered had become corroded to the mast and we bent two huge steel bars breaking it loose. Then we had to feed both cables carefully down through the inside of the mast and then lift the antenna up through the steel grid-work within the sail without the aid of any crane. We barely finished attaching the antenna to the mast, adjusted the slack in the cabling to allow hoisting and lowering the mast, and fed them through watertight fittings then we got underway. Instead of manning my normal maneuvering watch station, Bud and I finished the internal wiring of the cabling to the display unit. As we left Point Alpha, the Skipper came down into the Radio Room to check on how we were doing on the job. When I replied that, "…we were in the process of finishing the check-out of the equipment," his remark was that, "I surely do like to schedule completion of projects for the very last minute." It was his way of rendering us praise. Both Bud and I had received quite a few bruises during this effort and finally checked in with sickbay to obtain some necessary bandages and ointment. Later the Skipper found out about this and gave us hell for risking our health, as we were more important than any equipment.

## DF plotting for position.

On this trip, I was able to demonstrate my DF plotting skill in tracking our position using only this AN/SRD-7A system. Initially they believed it was nothing but "black magic" as I would plot four or five bearings of known Russian radio stations and instead of dissecting one point, create a triangular area, yet I would indicate our position at a very precise location within these areas. My positions on a number of occasions were verified via star-shots through the 8-B periscope. I finally held class on how to weigh the reliability of different bearings taken and their relation and weight in the plotting process. During this trip, the crew began to realize how much I knew on a variety of subjects unbeknownst to them.

## H-bomb monitoring.

At one point, this telemetry magnetic tape recorder lost its accurate 60-cycle power supply with no spare parts available on board. Since our power-plant produced very stable 60-cycle power, I simply bypassed this one feature. Very early in the trip the Time Code generator used to track tape-speed failed. I jury-rigged another source of output signal and both tested and documented it for reference by NSA analysis later. It seemed that every time I turned around, we had a problem with a specific item of equipment. I was consistently lucky in developing jury-rigged solutions that kept the systems functioning. During this trip, we monitored the first Russian 50-Megaton H-bomb test up close. They had detonated the bomb on the island of Novaya Zemlya in the Barents Sea. We had a spot estimated at approximately 15 miles away. In preparation for this detonation, the Captain ordered the boat rigged for flooding which essentially seals and isolates each compartment from the others just in case we are subjected to flooding.

## The Frozen Sail.

By this time, I had my own theory regarding failures of submarine antennas. At one point during this mission, we lost the stub-antenna on the 8-B periscope and two other antennae to flooding. I was able to convince the Skipper to move sufficiently away to allow us to surface and repair the antenna. Therefore, we went further north toward the actual North Pole and popped up through the ice in a very cold and pitch-black night. Then both Radiomen that volunteered to assist me were briefed by the Skipper to high-tail it back whenever he gave the order to dive, because if we didn't move fast, we just may have to die in the water. My inspection of the periscope antenna convinced me that my theory was correct, as I found I could tighten the mounting screws even more. This theory was that metal contracts when very cold and expands when warm, just enough to allow water to leak past the "O-Ring" seals. So I used alcohol to dry-out the fitting and tightened the screws like they should be. On future missions I had a number of the

Skippers surface after a few days being submerged in very cold water in order to re-tighten all the fittings on their antennae. Those who followed my advice did not experience any flooded antennae during their entire missions. While working on the last antenna which was located just adjacent to the AN/BPS-4 Radar slot in the top of the sail, we heard word passed on the bridge speaker of an aircraft radar signal being detected. I ordered my assistant to go back while I finished buttoning up the antenna. A short time later I heard the report that the signal-strength was now in sector-scan, meaning that we had been detected. The Skipper ordered everyone below and I acknowledged his order to go below, but when I tried to get up, I discovered my pants were frozen to the metal sail. Suddenly, when I heard the vents open and water begin filling the ballast tanks, fear now became real, and somehow I got up and was able to travel across the top of the sail structure filled with numerous openings for antenna masts. The top of our sail was covered with a sheet of ice which made moving on top of it even more dangerous. Somehow, with

God's assistance, I was able to land in the small bridge opening and the Skipper backed-off to permit me to go down first. Since we didn't have much time, I simply dropped the 15 feet to the lower bridge deck, moved over to the hatch and dropped down another 15 feet or so into the Conning Tower compartment. I landed in a heap and my feet began hurting from these two 15-foot drops to land upon steel decking. I just barely crawled out of the way before the Skipper came rushing down along with many gallons of sea water before the hatch was finally sealed. Once we were fully underwater and I was able to move without hurting, I descended slowly, and painfully, into the Control Room. Before I reached the Control Room deck, everyone there began to apparently be laughing at me. I quickly discovered that I had left the seat of my pants frozen to the top of the sail. Once everything settled down, the Skipper authorized everyone who was topside to receive a ration of medicinal brandy. The two lookouts were prepared to decline theirs until I asked them for their ration. So, I eventually drank about 8-ounces of booze on

an empty stomach in about 30 minutes.
About an hour later, feeling three-sheets-to-
the –wind, I knocked on the Skipper's cabin
door and suggested that we repeat the
surfacing process again.  He simply ordered
me into my bunk instead.

German Beer.

My co-worker at Headquarters had
been stationed in Bremerhaven and heard
that we were going to pull into that port of
call on one of my business trips to DC.  He
gave me the names of a couple of friends
and asked me to stop by and visit with them.
Once the problem with the RD2 had been
taken care of, as much as I could, I went into
town and visited them, and I really enjoyed
the visit.  One of their friends was in the
German Navy and I met him on one visit.
He, in turn, invited me to his vessel, which
was a coastal-minesweeper.  He was the
Executive Officer and of equal enlisted rank
as myself.  I spent one full evening on their
vessel drinking beer and eating German
dishes.  I told them how much I loved
German beer, which had more of a flavor or
taste than our own.  When I finally tried to

leave to go back to my boat, they would not let me go unless I took five or six cases with me! I tried to explain that we could not have booze on our vessels and finally acceded to their wishes. This German naval vehicle dropped me off at my boat and unloaded the beer. I sat down and asked everyone coming back from liberty to help me drink it up. At one point in time, the Skipper came back and asked why we were sitting on the pier drinking beer. I told him the German hosts refused to accept an answer of NO, and can't bring it aboard. The Skipper replied, "Bring it on board and keep it locked in my SupRad spaces until we return to the States. Once we returned, a number of the Operations Department personnel came over to my place to help me finish drinking up this German beer.

Captain Beach's Last Patrol.

We made a trip to San Juan and St. Thomas during the 1961 Springboard Exercise as the last trip under Captain Beach. This one was a total disaster for the crew and our morale. As more of our senior personnel were transferred to other boats under-construction, they were replaced with younger and inexperienced men. There was this one young sailor who was married and continually used every trick to have someone else stand his watches in port. When we departed on the six or seven week SpringboardEx, he tried to be transferred temporarily to the Squadron staff, using the excuse that he needed to be close to his wife. That request was denied. Later, when we pulled into San Juan for about a five-day period, he spent every hour possible on liberty, drinking and chasing the local women. One of our tasks before coming into port was to conduct a photoreconnaissance of a designated portion of the coastline. During this five-day period, I located a photo lab and was granted approval for me to develop and print the film there instead of on board. I didn't have sufficient time to complete it before the boat would go to sea for another week. The Skipper had me stay in port along with a few other crew members that were granted leave while I finished the project. We received an outstanding rating on this photo exercise and I later noticed it mounted in the Deputy

Commander Submarine Force Atlantic office in New London when I began working directly for DepComSubLant. He had it mounted like a wallpaper trim touching the ceiling and almost completely traversed the perimeter of the room. When Admiral Ramage discovered it was my handiwork, he had me in to describe in finite-detail how I did it and was able to merge the almost one hundred 8"x10" pictures into one continuously wide panoramic picture. I later learned this kid tried to get approval to remain in port here like he did in New London. When he was turned down, he jumped-ship. Several of us noticed him in the Enlisted Club the first night and assumed that he was granted leave. The next day we received a dispatch for us to locate him and have him turned over to the Shore Patrol. So we went hunting, found him, and turned him over to the Shore Patrol. The next thing I knew, he ran out on them as well. I figured that since we found him once, that we had done their job for them. When the boat returned, I found out what happened on board. It seems that no one really knew he had jumped-ship until it was time for him to stand his watch. This was after the boat had submerged. At first everyone assumed he was washed overboard upon diving when they could not find him anywhere. [What happened to muster on the pier prior to departure for Departments to ensure full crew?] When I reported to the Skipper that we had located him and he was turned over to the Shore Patrol, he thanked us. Then he wanted to know where he was. Once he was informed of what the kid did, he became upset. For two days he had groups searching for him and the sailor actually tried to run away from one group before being caught. We figured that once we got to sea and the CO held Captain's Mast, the kid would have the book thrown at him. However, once at sea, he gave the kid two-weeks' restriction and authorized leave upon our return to home port to settle his affairs. The restriction period was to be applied while at sea and was nothing since everyone was restricted while at sea. [Sometimes in situations such as this, we later learn that the person was the son of an Admiral or a Senator, but not this time.]

## Liberty.

A couple of weeks later we were scheduled to pull into St. Thomas, a small island of about 15,000 people. We were informed that about a week before, other elements of Operation Springboard had pulled liberty and caused all kinds of hell. You can't turn loose a few thousand sailors in a town with only a few bars and many private Yacht Clubs with very rich residents. Therefore, we were informed that only 1/3 of the crew could go on liberty each day until 2200, with Chiefs allowed returning by midnight and officers excused remaining overnight. This did not set well with the crew and it really hit the breaking-point when we discovered we were to tie up at a very isolated pier located at the Underwater Demolition Team training facility. A number of the crew suggested to the Skipper that we would prefer to remain at sea rather than to be tied up to a pier for four or five days. Apparently, Captain Beach wanted to socialize with the local governmental officials like he did in San Juan.

## Movie Stars In San Juan.

While in San Juan, we were not allowed to bring anyone on board for a visit or unclassified tour. This included crew members from a diesel boat moored at the same quay. Yet we noticed the officers would bring down casual guests they met at the various resort hotels. RM1 "Bud" requested authorization to escort some close friends through the boat who happened to be entertaining at one of the local hotels. He was turned down and came storming through the mess decks cursing when over the 1MC the topside watch passed the word that two well-known movie stars were requesting to see RM1 Bud. Both Captain Beach and the Duty Officer quickly changed their decision regarding Bud's request. Therefore, I was able to meet Tony Martin and his wife while they had a cup of coffee in the mess decks with many of the crew. The officers had invited them up to the Wardroom to which they declined. They arranged for a large number of the enlisted crew to attend one of their shows at the hotel as their guests, not one officer was given and invitation. The conduct by the Captain and his officers really pissed off the crew and it became worse upon arriving at St. Thomas.

<u>Ball game and rum and waters.</u>

Since we were the only vessel moored at this pier, it was like being at sea only with the ability to go topside. We witnessed the officers bring casual guests on board for coffee and personal tours through the boat, yet were denied the same privilege. During this period tied up at this pier, I both witnessed and was a key-player in a scene quite similar to the one in the movie "Mr. Roberts". I had always believed that the scene about the crew's first liberty in months was nothing but a wild dream by a few screenplay writers. Now I realized that it could very well manifest itself as a very accurate description of such a liberty during WWII. The day it started, the UDT outfit stationed on the island challenged us to a Beer Ball Game. Since I was the ship's photographer, I loaded up with lots of film and flash bulbs for the 4"x5" Press-Camera and went to take pictures of this game. By the time I had arrived, they were already into the second inning. I noticed that they began to run out of beer at the bases, and began using Rum instead. Finally, I felt it would be wise by the fourth inning to leave, as everyone would be ready to kill me if I continued to take pictures of what was going on. Between the hot sun, rum, and being in a foul mood, the crew really went overboard on their conduct. So, I went into town to capture some of the scenery on film. It was such a crappy town, the handful of bars were run-down shacks manned by natives trying to rip everyone off. Therefore, I walked down along the water front where a number of Yacht Clubs were with hundreds of ocean-going yachts either tied up to piers or anchored-out in the harbor. I went into this one club and took a few pictures of the vessels tied up and decided to have a rum & water before moving on. There was this club-manager, which after a few minutes of listening to him, realized he was queer as a three-dollar-bill! He allowed me to remain while it was a private club type of bar and I was able to talk with a large number of club members. Many of the men seem to either have wives 20 to 30 years younger or just a female companion living on board their seagoing yacht. It seemed that everyone was very interested in my submarine and our recent "Around the World" trip. I spent the entire afternoon and evening drinking rum and water and without any solid food being ingested. By the time my liberty was up, I was totally smashed and had difficulty in walking, let alone going back to the boat. One couple there that also had a car offered to drive me back to the boat.

The return to the boat.

I remember when seeing the movie "Mr. Roberts", that the scene where the crew began returning from their first liberty in many months, that I felt they had really stretched the truth. However, after our visit to St. Thomas, I had to admit it could have been very likely. I do not remember much of what I shall describe while it was occurring. Through subsequent weeks at sea and talks with others, this is a reasonable and factual description of the events of that day.

Many of the crew involved in the ball game that afternoon had passed out

either on the beach or adjacent to the ball
field and finally came to.  Here they were so
drunk that some of them could only crawl on
their hands and knees towards the gangway
to get back on board the boat.  On the pier
were several groups of sailors trying to stand
up while also trying to hit the other person.
The distance between the "so-called"
fighters was sufficient to drive a truck
through!  On board the boat, several sailors
had passed out and were draped over the
lifeline, usually in place whenever in port.
Aft of the sail was one of our Corpsmen
chasing the Duty Officer with a branch from
a palm tree, trying to goose him in the butt.
Another Corpsman was trying to push crew
members passed out lying on deck off into
the water while the topside watch tried to
keep him from doing it.  I came staggering
down the pier swinging my 4"x5" Press
Camera like a flag and having difficulty
climbing on board the boat. Below decks, in
the Attack Center, was a pile of sailors
passed out and stacked like cord-wood just
aft of the periscope well.  The below-decks
watch would determine where a sailor in this
pile was bunked, and then carry him

fireman-style forward or aft to his rack. A few of the crewmen would pass out trying to lower themselves via the Attack Center hatch, and land in a heap on the steel deck waiting for the below-decks watch to stack them in the pile. The Attack Center was located immediately above the Mess Deck where those not asleep yet, though full of so-called "tiger piss" held court. Captain Beach decided to bring down to the boat for a social visit, a group of Catholic Nuns at this moment in time!!

Taking photos on the surface.

Well, the next day we got underway and headed for sea. The Captain had received permission to fire a Mark 14 torpedo at a designated location on another island. Instead of having the boat submerge for launching the torpedo, he deliberately remained on the surface. A submarine is a miserable type of vessel on the surface, especially when the crew has a miserable hangover. You see, submarines have a very smooth outer surface with no rolling chocks to reduce the tendency to rolling port and starboard even in a calm sea-state. The rolling typically is in the range of 25 degrees off of vertical in a very fast rate, not like the slow rolls experienced on surface ships. I was given the task of taking the 4"x5" Press Camera, brace myself up at the bow, and take pictures of the launch sequence. That was not only my most uncomfortable task, but also the first time I almost slipped and fell overboard. I finally had to use a safety-line tied to my safety belt and life preserver to provide some degree of confidence. Between my dry-heaves and the steep rolling by the boat, I was able to complete my task of picture-taking.

The recovering crew.

Down below, there was a serious shortage of #10 food cans. There were cans located at just about every watch station that would permit the sailor from having to go all the way to the head and up-chuck his last meal. Finally, just before the evening meal, Captain Beach gave the order to submerge. The next afternoon, he called for an officers and chiefs meeting in the Crew's Mess. At this meeting, he proceeded to belittle us for our conduct on the last night in port. Then one of the chiefs who had served with Beach during WWII, made the statement that, "If anyone owes an apology, then it is the Captain to the crew!" Everyone was dumbfounded by this impertinent remark, and he continued before even the Captain could respond. He quietly, but forcefully, reminded the Skipper that it is commonly accepted policy that after 2200 is reserved as taps for the crew, and not for entertaining visitors. It was also poor planning on the Skipper's part to bring nuns aboard for a visit at the time that liberty was expiring for all hands. No one using good taste would intrude on people during the period that they are normally asleep. Captain Beach became very red in the face, tightened his lips and stormed off to his stateroom without any further word.

Eating down to the deck.

Everyone on board knew that we were going on a long shakedown cruise early in January of 1960. Over the next 30 days, you would hear two or three times a day over the 1MC for "All hands to lay topside to handle stores". The cooks were

charged with bringing enough food on board
to last at least 120 days. The ET and Radio
gangs had to ensure they had enough
supplies and repair parts to last for 120 days,
also. Each Division spent 10 to 12 hour
days ordering, receiving and finding storage
locations for their supplies and spare parts.
Eventually, we had at least one layer of
cases of #10 canned-goods throughout the
deck surfaces in every compartment. Thus,
we did not only literally, but also actually,
ate our way back down to the deck in all
compartments during our 84-day trip. The
cooks kept records on which compartment
deck contained what food items, and as gaps
appeared in the floor-plan of canned-goods,
working parties were dispatched to regroup
them in other compartments for safety's
sake. By the end of the second month into
the trip, most of these canned-goods used by
the crew had essentially consumed the "false
deck". Thusly, during the trip, we actually
ate our way through the compartments.

Preparing to get underway.

About a week before we left, a
number of unique equipments came onboard

and was installed in the Control Room, CIC, the Forward Reactor compartment, and my SupRad compartment. One such item we labeled as the "monkey in the cage". Another was a continuous depth-recorder to measure the depth of the ocean as we traveled around the world. There was a huge shipment of green cans about the diameter of a #10 can, and three times as long, loaded on board and stored in both Reactor Compartments. Most of us didn't know what they contained until we got underway. They were called "oxygen canisters", which when burned in a special device, produced far more oxygen than it consumed by burning.

Getting underway.

We were led to believe that we were going to pull liberty in Europe, and several other interesting places during this three-month trip. No one realized, other than a few officers, what our trip was really about. The day we departed, all our families were there to watch us get underway. I was happy that Marilyn was not pregnant at the time, as I didn't want to worry like some of

the other men did about their wives.  Once
we arrived in deep water, we "pulled the
plug" and headed in a southerly direction
instead of turning eastward.  After 24 hours,
the rumors were going wild as to where we
were actually going.  Finally, Captain Beach
spoke on the 1MC and gave us a run-down
on our trip of going around the world in 80
days.  We were to head for St. Peter's and
St. Paul's rocks in the middle of the Atlantic
Ocean, just north of the Equator.  Then we
were to travel around Cape Horn, past Easter
Island, past the Equator into the North
Pacific Ocean to Guam, then to the
Philippines, where Magellan was killed and
down through the Strait of Bali into the
Indian Ocean, and then around the Cape of
Good Hope.  We returned to St. Peter's
Rock, then past the Azores to come off the
coast of Spain near Cadiz, and finally a
straight-shot back to the States off the coast
of Delaware.  This trip would consist of
95% boredom and 5% pure terror.

<u>My mission aboard.</u>

My mission on this trip was to
conduct communication tests with some

unique VHF equipment that would become
critical items in communicating with Fleet
Ballistic Missile boats in the future.
Another task was to assist in documenting
the entire trip on film, both in movie and
still photos.  Thus, I now knew the reason
for all these different cameras and the film
they required.  In between these tasks, I had
to stand my watches as Chief of the Watch
under instruction, continue my qualification
effort towards earning my Dolphins and,
along with the rest of the crew,  as a guinea
pig in monitoring physical effects of long-
term submergence under Dr. Stark.

Photographic mission.

Our photographic efforts improved
as the trip progressed due to on the job
training and learning from our mistakes.  We
relied upon the still photographic pictures
that I developed on board to ascertain our
exposure and focus problems via the
periscope, or confined spaces involved in
our shooting and in the use of artificial
lighting.  Over a two-month period we
became outstanding experts in periscope-
photography within the Navy.  This was

subsequently verified on later trips where photo-reconnaissance of a specific location was required. One of my tasks on this photographic team was to ensure that any photographs were taken properly and identified as classified or unclassified. The objective was to make sure that the majority were unclassified and could be quickly released to the media upon request. Some people would ask me, "Where are the pictures of" myself? I would simply point out that I was the person taking the pictures, and could not be in the pictures.

Headed for the Equator.

As we headed for St. Peter's Rock and the Equator, all the Shellbacks would assemble in the CIC Compartment and plan the ceremony of crossing the Equator. While they were doing that, we pollywogs were also developing our own plan. We located every set of barber clippers on board and hid them. As the Shellbacks would make their tools to use on us, we would steal them in the middle of the night. Various pollywogs would place shaving cream around a Shellback's mouth and place a quarter in his hand. Then someone would get on the 1MC, laugh and say, "The little gray fox has struck." Captain Beach got up one night and tried to open his door after one of these "gray fox" announcements and had difficulty opening it. One pollywog had covered the doorknob with grease, making it very difficult to grasp and turn the round knob. By the time we arrive at the Equator, the handful of Shellbacks onboard were in a very nervous state from all of our harassment. Twice, one First Class and I were almost caught red-handed setting up a Shellback for a harassment trick. We even had one pollywog using a fraudulent Shellback Card attend all their meetings and afterwards brief us on their plans. We pollywogs almost succeeded in taking over the boat for the crossing, but a number of us paid the price with extra special attention and care by the Shellbacks.

The Ocean Depths.

The first few weeks of the trip were totally uneventful. As we travelled down towards Cape Horn, our depth recorder began indicating a very steep rise in the ocean floor from the typical 4,000 to 6,000 foot depth, to 300 feet and suddenly, sometimes less than a hundred feet. We had discovered an uncharted seamount peak that rose almost 6,000 feet from the ocean floor to just under 200 feet from the surface. If we did not have this depth recorder continuously recording the profile of the ocean floor, we could very well have run right smack into it at our standard cruising speed of 15 knots, (and TRITON could go very fast when she wanted to; at the time she was the fastest submarine in the U.S. Navy. She had two complete nuclear power plants, one for each propulsion shaft).

Very rough seas.

While in the South Atlantic, at one point, we experienced a storm that must have been of real major strength. While at our cruising depth of 400 feet, we were tossed almost like being on the surface, rolling sharply left and right and even had some difficulty in maintaining a constant depth. The Skipper decided to come close to the surface and as we neared 200 feet, the boat really became too difficult to hold depth, so we went back down. Those who had much more experience in boats remarked that they had never experienced _that_ much turbulence at _that_ depth before, and figured that this storm above must be at least a state-11 sea. No surface ship could ever survive in that kind of storm. As we neared Cape Horn, our Chief Radarman developed kidney stones so badly, that we had to reverse course and meet with one of our Navy cruisers near the La Plata River and Montevideo, Uruguay.

Emergency Medical Evac.

It took us a couple of days running at flank speed, and when we arrived it was dark and had to maintain at least two miles distance from the other ship. Otherwise the ship's magnetic field could possibly alter the readings derived from our own "monkey in the cage device". By this time I was much more knowledgeable about submarine activity. When the Skipper asked if I wanted to film our effort to transfer Chief Poole to the Navy Cruiser, I thanked him and said no. What we were to attempt was very dangerous. We were to broach the boat with only the sail sticking up out of the water and the main decks awash. The Chief of the Watch would have to respond very quickly if we hit a patch of the ocean containing fresh water from the river, for if we did, we would sink like a rock and those people connected to the main deck with safety lines would be pulled underwater. They were successful in getting the ailing Chief into the Cruiser's motor launch with only a few seconds being pulled underwater as part of the process and then we resumed our trip.

Cape Horn.

Once we reached Cape Horn, Captain Beach cruised back and forth and allowed every crewmember that desired to look at this miserable point on Earth. Then I fully understood why it took sailing ships weeks to beat a tack around the Horn. There was a stiff and constant current from the Pacific to the Atlantic Oceans. Add to this current the high wind and huge waves beating them that a square-rigger had to overcome. Our own planesmen had a lot of difficulty just maintaining periscope depth while we cruised at 15 knots. We even had ice collect in our bilges although we maintained the compartments at 68-72 degrees. The salt-water temperature outside the hull was 26 to 27 degrees. Oh, how those poor sailors of yore must have suffered during the trip from the Atlantic to the Pacific Oceans.

Reaching the Rock.

Once we reached St. Peter and St. Paul Rock, we headed northeast to the Azores. I took about one hundred periscope pictures of the island's coastline at a distance of only one mile from shore. I was able to enlarge some of the pictures enough to clearly show people on the beaches enjoying the sun and water. From that point we headed directly for the coast of Spain and the city of Cadiz. There was an old sea story of Admiral Nelson's arm floating in the water ever since his great battle against the Spanish Armada. According to this story, the first person on a vessel to see this floating petrified arm will have unusual luck in the future. Well, we had one very naïve young sailor who was conned into believing this story and spent hours over a period of several days manning the periscope looking for the Admiral's arm. Of course, this permitted the regular Conning Tower crew much-needed rest from the strain of constantly searching the horizon for possible objects to avoid. You would easily know who had just finished a watch in the Conning Tower while we traveled at periscope depth. They had a tendency to list to one side or the other from hanging on the handles and rotating the scope in 360-degree arcs.

Shrinks come aboard.

About this time a group of us planned to pull some skits for the benefit of a group of medical personnel scheduled to come onboard off Rota/Cadiz, and ride the boat home. We understood they were to begin to evaluate the effects of being submerged for almost ninety days during one continuous period. One Doctor was willing to join us in this endeavor. Basically, those who would not be on watch at the time these officials would come on board were told to assemble in the Control

Room and Mess Decks. Immediately upon their arrival, everyone would pretend to display homosexual mannerisms or other unusual conduct. Several, including our riding Doctor, were going to try and kiss several of these medical types as part of the greeting process. Well, it seems that the Captain got wind of our plans, and instead of our normal watches, everyone but our riding Doctor suddenly was assigned an underway watch during the time period they were to arrive on board. Our riding Doctor did not have the courage to pull it off alone. I honestly doubt that any one of us would have had the courage to go it alone.

The Doc trumps us.

Our psychiatric doctor rider was quite a character. When we discovered who and what his function was, the crew decided to work him over. Several Chiefs began to act as if they were homosexual in his presence. Then others would discuss about supposedly having sex parties where they swapped wives. Still others began to express other strange behavior in his presence. When they noticed it was actually affecting his conduct, they really began to develop additional tricks and abnormal social behavior skits in his presence. However, he apparently overheard a couple of sailors rehearse their little skit and things suddenly changed.  The doctor would eat most of his meals with the crew, and this one time he entered the mess hall and went over to the Chief's table.  Sitting there was one of the major players in these skits.  The doctor went up to him using a feminine style voice, remarked how glad he was to see him, and planted a big kiss on his cheek.  The Chief sat there for a few seconds in total shock, turned white as a sheet, jumped up and ran back to the Chief's Quarters instead of finishing his meal.  That's when we knew that the game was over.

The personal certificate of accomplishment.

Another aspect of this trip, which Captain Beach did not address in his official log or his book, was his hang-up over sensual mermaids typically adorning such certificates as for the Shellback.  The crew kept trying to draw up a special and very unique certificate that each crewmember would be entitled to.  Never before or since has any vessel traveled around the world in one continuous trip, conducting the trip totally submerged, or at an average speed of 15 knots, while travelling in the North and South Atlantic, the North and South Pacific, the Indian Oceans and around Cape Horn and not be detected by anyone during the entire trip.  The crew finally gave up in developing this certificate where no mermaids could adorn its borders.

Adjusting to submerged longevity.

Later I was to learn some of the effects from our 84-day submerged trip. About sixty days into the trip, the crew began to develop a tendency towards symptoms of being cross-eyed because the farthest distance most of us could focus on was less than 27 feet.  Another was an inability to adjust to severe changes in light, since we were only used to the amount given off by light bulbs.  NASA was about ready to make a serious decision on the space capsule to be used in outer space.  The engineering problems and cost associated with installing windows was far more than that for installing a periscope type device. The Astronauts wanted windows and were losing the fight because of the associated costs, until the data compiled from our trip was circulated in the scientific community. This trip validated their justification for demanding the installation of windows.

World-wide communications.

One of my mission tasks on this trip was to test communication systems to be used by our Fleet Ballistic Missile Submarines. This system was to be reliable enough for sending missile launching instructions to those boats on deterrent patrols. I was able to ascertain and validate several key problems and devise temporary solutions while at sea. Later they came up with a permanent solution within a couple of months after our return based upon my efforts.

USS SEAWOLF comes home.

While the boat was initially being outfitted at one of the piers at Electric Boat, we were told that the USS SEAWOLF SSN-

575 was going to pull in on the opposite side. I heard that they were coming back from a special mission up north off the Russian coast in my conversations with DepComSubLant's Intelligence Officer. They finally arrived very late in the day, just before dark. I saw one of our CT's who rode this boat and remarked to him that we will be ready soon for him to go with us. His response at the moment shocked me. He stated that this was his 13th and last trip as he finally got the message. Later, after the crew's families had departed, I happened to look over at the Seawolf and noticed a number of holes in the superstructure, and sail that had been covered with cardboard and painted black. It seems the reason why they were so late was that they had remained out to sea long enough to conceal all this damage from public view. This was my first indication that the other side will go to any length to conceal or deny knowledge from us.

In the North Atlantic.

The next mission we went on involved final testing of these

communications systems in the areas of the North Atlantic where the FBM boats were scheduled to operate in. These locations were assigned a Top Secret classification and all navigation repeaters were taped-over except for CIC. CIC was even restricted to only the RD's and ET's who were normally assigned to that compartment. Many of the crew knew that I had total freedom throughout the boat and some felt that I was a member of ONI instead of being a Communications Technician. Fortunately, on this trip, our one and only liberty port was Bremerhaven, Germany. After about forty days running around in the far North Atlantic, we pulled in for ten days liberty.

Into Bremerhaven, Germany.

The day we arrived in port the sun came out and remained out every day until the day that we departed for home. There were thousands along the shore of the river as we came up into the Bremerhaven harbor. The German government put us in this one quay that could be blocked off with nets and isolated from the public. We received about the same level of security as the President of the United States in that they had divers inspecting the underwater areas for possible bombs, limpet mines, etc. They had installed three levels of perimeter guards on the shore side of our berthing area. Each controlled by a separate element of the German government. We had a Naval Security Group Activity (USN-40) located in the area and they were informed of my presence on the TRITON. Immediately after all the official protocols were complete between the boat and the German officials, the local Military Police Commander informed us that all MP's had received orders to assist us and ensure we have an outstanding visit.

German girls on bikes.

The Captain agreed to allow single sailors to arrange with married ones to stand their watches while in port. Several single guys went into the town of Bremerhaven to the red light district called "court martial square", and arranged a package deal with the madam. They paid one huge fee, which entitled them to all the booze and sex they could handle. I guess the madam didn't realize what our submarine sailors were like. As others learned of this package deal, they began to work on their own package deals with the madam.  It was funny in a way; the price that the first two guys paid essentially remained the price for future deals even though the number of days was increasingly shorter.  They were drinking the place dry and trying to wear out the women.  Most of the women at this time did not wear any underwear whatsoever.  Add to this the fact that there were no ladies' style bikes, only a man's style.  Thus, as they would pedal down the street, it would be quite common for the wind to lift up their dresses above the waist and clearly expose their true and natural hair color.  The only people that noticed this was American submarine sailors.  I, for one, walked into several lamp posts while watching beautiful German girls riding their bikes past me.

Untrustworthy Communists.

One interesting fact we learned was that the Communists had spread rumors that we were the second or third crew to man the TRITON since all others died from radiation. They were shocked to learn from us how long we had been stationed on board the boat. Many of the local residents wanted to visit our boat, but the only ones who could were the VIP's from the local towns and governments.

Security Violation.

One young RD2, who worked in CIC, knew exactly where we had been in the North Atlantic. He was overheard by a couple of CT's in a bar in town talking about our mission. Apparently these two sailors were involved in monitoring all shipping activity in our area for possible detection by the Russians. So they heard him talking, and subsequently notified their SSO. I received word for me to come to NavSecGru-40 as they had some information that I should receive. When I arrived, I was briefed about this security violation and informed them that I would notify Captain Beach. I high-tailed it back to the boat and left word with the Duty Officer that I needed to speak with the Captain as soon as he came on board. When he arrived, I briefed him on the security violation and on my own, drafted a rough message to be sent back to Washington. He told me that he would take care of it immediately upon return to the States, and for me to shred the rough draft message. I tried to convince him to send the message immediately, but to no avail.

## Security Breach and Captain Beach.

Immediately upon returning to New London, there on the pier were several officials from ONI waiting to come on board. We no sooner had the brow over and I had secured from my maneuvering watch station, than I heard over the 1MC for me to report to CIC. There was the young sailor, two ONI agents, the Captain and XO, the OPS and COMM Officers. The two agents quickly asked me if I had been informed of the security violation. I replied, "Yes." The next pertinent question was why didn't I advise the Captain to notify Washington immediately? I looked directly at Captain Beach and I realized that he had screwed up, but I was not going to take the blame for him. So, I told them that I had urged him to notify Washington and he informed me that he would take care of it. I was given a set of orders and a .45 cal. sidearm to escort the young sailor under armed guard to the Pentagon. I was given a few minutes to tell Marilyn that I had to go to D.C., and didn't know when I would be back. As soon as I arrive and knew, I would notify her via phone.

Escorting the Prisoner.

This trip was quite an experience for me. I escorted the poor kid there and advised him to simply tell the truth. I warned him that if he lies, it would only make the problem worse for him. I told him that he was in deep crap and he'd better be prepared for the worst; that way, if it turns out better, you will feel better. Upon reporting to ONI with my prisoner, they marched him off to another office and I didn't see him again until three days later when I escorted him back to New London. While I waited for them to be finished with him, they gave me a rough going over as well. They kept demanding to know why I didn't send the message myself. I kept telling them, I was only an enlisted man and had no authority whatsoever to authorize, let alone send, such a message. Then they would ask such questions as my being a CT, "didn't I know that notification of security breaches should be reported immediately?" I would acknowledge that, but kept trying to make them understand Naval Regulations strictly governed my position on a naval vessel. If there was ever a possibility of being involved in such a breach of security again, I was prepared to go to the limit to ensure no one could ever imply that I had failed in my duty. The young sailor returned to the boat with me and was transferred over the weekend.

German Party attended.

The Saturday before our departure from Germany, the entire crew was invited to a party at the local Germany Naval Club. We had just about every German Government official, military personnel, as well as American personnel there at the party. I had a conversation with one old man working in the club and he asked if he could buy my TRITON tie clasp. He was a German submariner from WWI era. When I gave it to him as a gift, he broke down in tears. Meanwhile, the rest of the crew was having a ball, spread throughout the hall with large groups of local citizens. Suddenly, one woman asked if she could have a sailor's USS TRITON SSR-586 shoulder patch and he responded with a, "Yes." Within just a few minutes, every sailor in dress blues had his shoulder patch removed and those with the Flat hat lost their TRITON ribbon. Upon our return to the States, it was difficult for the crew to assemble on deck in a complete uniform, because of missing patches, etc. Those who didn't have spare uniform patches on other clothing, either borrowed from those standing below decks watches or simply remained below.

Power Failure.

Coffee is the stuff that gets a sailor working, as I learned quickly at this command. One day we had an electrical power failure in our building, involving one power distribution panel. This panel provided power to all the AC receptacles in the various offices and shop areas. Thus, no coffee pots would work. So the Chief's had a group of Seamen holding coffee pots in the air while others applied blow-torches to their bottoms until the coffee was ready. Before any white hats got a chance to taste the finished product, every Chief and officer got their first cup of coffee. Once some of the men had their first cup of coffee, then they turned their attention to repair the breaker panel.

Hot seats.

I remember another incident on the ship that in retrospect was very funny. The naval ships at this time had their heads constructed such that you had a pipe pouring water in a long trough at one end with a row of seats and a drain at the lower end. Some guys would periodically sit in the first seat and take a large wad of toilet paper in a bundle, light it and place it in the trough's water flow. As the burning paper floated under an occupied seat, the sailor would experience a very sudden hot seat as it moved along down to the drain end as it opened out to the ocean.

Man Overboard.

Another time I noticed a sailor who had gone to use the head and in dropping his trousers, his wallet fell into the trough and washed down the drain before he could recover it. He quickly ran on deck and jumped over the side where the drain emptied into the ocean. Of course, they yelled, "Man Overboard" and he got verbal hell for it. But he had just been paid and felt it was well-worth the hassle to recover not only his money, but also his ID card. I was able to watch this from an excellent position. I was over the side lashing our mooring lines together and installing rat-guards when he decided to jump over the side.

Enlisted Resourcefulness.

The next incident that stuck in my mind occurred upon returning from liberty while anchored in Long Beach Harbor. Upon returning late at night from liberty, there was this one third-class petty officer totally drunk carrying two fifths of whiskey. Once we reached the ship, he somehow was able to climb up the ladder while holding on to the two bottles. Upon reaching the Quarterdeck, the OOD, (who was a young Ensign), stopped him and informed him that he could not bring the whiskey on board. The Ensign, trying to be a nice guy, told him that he was going to turn his back, and wanted to hear two splashes, and upon turning back around did not want to see this sailor still on the Quarterdeck. So the OOD turned his back and after a few seconds there were two splashes and the petty officer tip-toed down below in his stocking-covered feet. He had simply taken his shoes off and threw them over the side. None of us said a word to the OOD about what we had seen happen. Of course, the petty officer threw away a good pair of shoes costing him about $2.50 at the Small Stores at that time, and rumor later had it that he sold one bottle for $35 and kept the rest for himself. This was my first experience of how resourceful an enlisted man can be in beating the system, so to speak. Over the years, I was either involved in, or became aware of, many more incidents designed to overcome the system. Most officers worth their salt knew this and relied on these enlisted men to accomplish what might be considered extremely difficult or impossible tasks. I think that is one reason why so many Limited Duty Officers were more successful in accomplishing very difficult tasks than those who received their commissions via NROTC or the Naval Academy.

<u>1959 Submarine School, New London.</u>

I remember as I drove into the Submarine Base for training duty, I noticed a large group of civilians standing near one of the boat piers. Of course I didn't think too much of it at the time. A couple of days later while touring the base to get my bearings; I walked by this one pier. At the very end of the pier was what looked like a VW Bug with a huge dent right down the middle from the front to the rear. The wheels were bent such that the top of each wheel leaned into the vehicle and the bottom pointing outward. As usual, there was another group of people in civilian clothes looking this vehicle over. I learned from sailors and later actually had a long talk with the skipper of the Submarine that hit this car. When an insurance claim was filed with the insurance company stating that one United States Submarine had hit this auto, it caused everyone in the auto insurance industry to want to see this accident evidence.

Months later, I learned who the skipper was as I had to work very closely with him on intelligence matters. During this period and in the privacy of his secure intelligence office, he told me what happened. The Thames River has a fairly strong current flowing out to sea. Diesel boats do not have very much power in navigating in tight quarters. Typically, when a Submarine is assigned a specific pier berth and unable to quickly move into the pier area out of the main river current, is advised to make any available pier. This means that the skipper's parking spot at the end of the intended landing-pier is no longer true. He is usually moored at a pier, which has another skipper's vehicle occupying the similar spot. Most skippers would move up river a little further than their assigned pier. Make the 90-degree turn as they drift down stream and give the boat a kick in the butt as they begin to line up with their pier. It takes at least one minute for the throttleman to throw all the huge levers into the proper position and apply the current to the electric motors.

Well, this one day Hank Morgan (the skipper) moved above the pier that was assigned to him. Once they made the 90-degree turn pointing towards the piers, instead of ringing up 2/3 or full, he rang up all ahead flank to ensure he would move quickly out of the main current of the river. Once he knew they would make it, rang up all back full; in other words, put the screws in reverse. The throttle man in his haste to respond conked out the diesels providing electrical power to the motors. It takes time to shift from diesel providing electrical power to drawing it from the boat's main batteries. In the meantime, the boat was still moving at a fast rate towards the end of the pier. Since the boat was a WW II Fleet boat with a long sweeping bow, as it hit the end of the pier, rode up onto the pier and on the top of the skipper's VW bug parked at the end of the pier.

Of course there was a court of inquiry into this accident and I have it from very reliable sources the following basic events took place in this hearing. The boat suffered about $300,000 damage to its bow and sonar equipment. They were going to charge the skipper with damage to government property under his responsibility. Hank Morgan happens to be one of J.P. Morgan's grandchildren and was in the navy for the love of it. It seems he became very upset with this group of senior officers and finally had them admit that this entire hearing was because of the cost that the navy will incur repairing the boat. Hank right then and there pulled out his personal checkbook, wrote a check for the full costs of repairing his boat, and presented it to the President of the Court. Then he asked, "Are there any other charges you would like to resolve?", requested permission to leave and walked out of the room. The entire Court sat there for a few minutes in silence before anyone finally recovered from the shock.

Once I was finally settled into Submarine school, I received word to report to the Deputy Commander Submarine Force Atlantic Intelligence officer. This is when I met Henry P. Morgan of the J.P. Morgan family. He had just assumed the duties in that capacity, and discovered that he held my NAVSECGRU Category- III clearance while I attended submarine school. He wanted to know all about the cryptology field and me. During the time I attended school, he would periodically have me report to his office at times just to tell sea stories. Other times we would discuss what equipment was being installed on boats heading north off the coast of Russia and the Arctic Circle.

Part of our screening process was a repeat for me in the pressure tank, the escape tank and a very detailed hearing test. This is when I learned I had a serious hearing problem. While I could detect slight frequency shifts, any frequencies above 4,000 cycles would drop off the end of the chart. They had me placed in a special sound room for a series of tests to ascertain if it was correctable or permanent. It was permanent and that one out of every four words, I would not recognize. This created a problem for Captain Beach and me, as the Skipper of the U.S.S. TRITON had to agree to a waiver before I could continue in the program. Fortunately, he agreed as I discovered later many crewmembers already had hearing problems because of the noise generated by diesel engines used to recharge the batteries.

The escape trainer was very unique. It was only a couple of years prior to my arrival that they used the Momsen Lung in the escape tank. In other words it was like a regular scuba rig allowing you to breathe while working your way to the surface. The current procedure now was called the Blow and Go method. What we would do is exit from the 18 foot level one time and then twice from the 50 foot level. Once everyone in our group had finished all three, they asked for volunteers to exit from the 114-foot level.

How it works is you inflate your life preserver and take a series of deep breaths and exhale as deeply as possible. Then you take a deep breath and exit through the opening and then blow all the air out and continue to try and blow as a couple of instructors with scuba gear watched you do this. Finally they would let you go floating to the surface. My second exit from the 50 feet level created a problem for me. I followed through on all the instructions and they release their hold on me and I started to float to the surface. Then they noticed I stopped trying to blow and quickly pulled me down and back into the 50-foot level airlock. I had to do some fast-talking to the instructors to let me complete that exit. I told them they were so good at telling us that I was just too relaxed and asked to finish the exit. The instructor in the airlock finally consented.

Once everyone was done, they asked for volunteers for the 114-foot ascent and I raised my hand along with about six or seven others. So we climbed down the stairs that spiraled down around the outside of the tall tank. We entered an air lock and they jacked the pressure up to equal that at the bottom of the tank. We entered into this area and in the middle was a round tube protruding down into the water. We were told one at a time to ventilate our lungs, take a final depth breath before going under the water, and up inside this tube. The wood handle was placed in our hands and we were signaled to blow out all our air and hold our face up looking to the top of the tank. When I did everything they instructed, I was released and I began actually shooting up and spiraling around this cable that this handle I held was traveling on. Before I knew it, I had shot almost completely out of the water, while I sprayed air and water all over from my mouth. In fact, this was the easiest one while the worse was the 18-foot level. I think it was because it took almost as much time at the 18 feet as it did at the 50 and the 114 was roughly equal to the 50 feet level in lapsed time.

Once we were finished and prepared to dry off and get dressed, the senior officer there asked which one of us was named HADLEY. I raised my hand and he remarked, so you are the

165

one. If we knew that on your 50' ascent you would have been disqualified so I asked why. It seems that during the initial period of the blow and go method, they used a 70 mm X-ray film as part of the physical examination before being subjected to the escape tank. This one sailor, also named Hadley, had a small spot on the film and they assumed it was dirt in the developer. This sailor also volunteered for the 114 level and was the last one to exit. Unbeknown to everyone it was not dirt on the film but an air pocket. Thus as he came up to the surface, this air pocket expanded and popped or pushed his lung completely out through his mouth and he died in a matter of seconds later. The results of this inquiry, all future X-rays would be full scale to ensure the detection of any problems in the lungs.

Once I started Sub School, a number of senior enlisted and officers would ask me why I was attending school since CT's were not part of the billet structure on submarines. When I told them I was reporting to the TRITON, that would satisfy their request. During the weekends, I would visit the local saloons in New London and Groton since there was little else in the form of entertainment available to sailors. I remember one time in this restaurant and sitting on one side of a horseshoe shaped bar. On the other side was a group of five or six young people drinking and voicing their opinions on foreigners in the country. It quickly became apparent to everyone else in the place that his or her families dated back to the Mayflower landing. Finally, I could not keep my big mouth shut. I remarked loudly enough to be heard across the bar that I agreed whole heartily with them on their idea of all these foreigners going back to their homeland. They immediately expressed great satisfaction with this remark. Then I asked them when would they pack up and go back to England. Their reply in shock was that their families trace back to the Mayflower. I acknowledged that fact to them but I also presented another question to them. Were there not some people already here at the time and who

showed you how to survive in this country?
They acknowledged that there were only the
local Indians. I then told them, they were
my ancestors and again I asked when you
are going to pack up and leave. Well, they
finished their drinks very quickly and left
the bar. The next thing I knew I had another
drink placed before me. I told the bartender
that I didn't order it. His reply, it is on the
house. In very quick order, it seemed that
just about everyone in the bar who heard this
diatribe by a bunch of smart-ass kids also
bought me a drink. It seems they enjoyed
the method of putting these bigots in their
place. When a number of them learned that
my grandmother was an Indian, they truly
understood why I had to put them in their
place.

During my tour of duty in the New
London area, I was routinely confronted
with this bigoted view by so many of the
New England citizenry whose families have
lived there for generations. Their
superiority at times was overpowering for
many naval personnel from other parts of
the country. Most of the property owners in
the New London area were ripping off the
sailors, charging ungodly rental fees for old
frame homes with no insulation. It was so
bad that many married sailors not drawing

sub pay kept their families either at their previous duty station area or hometown. It was more expensive to live there than in Washington DC.

The CPO club was another interesting place to visit. There were a number of women in their very late twenties to fifties who would come to the club every Friday and Saturday night. Many of these females were divorced or whatever, but always looking for an evening of free drinks and a potential night of sex. There were a number of these whom this lifestyle had, over time, a very adverse effect on their appearance. Usually, after a number of drinks and the soft lighting in the club, many took on the appearance of beauties. ["The Girls All Get Prettier At Closin' Time" – Mickey Gilley song] That is until you wake up and see them in the harsh cruel light of day. I remember this one Chief who was attending Nuclear Power school and having a hard time maintaining passing grades. He would visit the club every Friday night, get smashed, and eventually wake up the next morning with a strange woman in her bed. By Monday, he would swear that he would never do it again, until Friday came around. Finally, this one Friday he took home this one woman that most of the Chief's could not get drunk enough to consider her advances. That following Saturday morning, he came back to the barracks swearing, "That was it". He said that when he woke up and looked over to see who was in bed with him, he noticed she had no eyebrows; false teeth were out and looked like death warmed over. This scared the hell out of him and quietly got dressed and slipped out before she woke up. Like the drunk who finally reached the bottom, he claimed, " he had finally reached his bottom". Most of us assumed he would be back up at the CPO club that weekend, but he proved us wrong. He never went back, spent his time going to church on Sunday, and other activities strictly on the base for the next two months until he graduated. I even experienced a couple of these events as well, which pushed me into other more reasonable activities.

A number of the CPO's in the barracks attending Nuclear Power school were married without their family here. So they would start a number of pinochle games every Friday that would essentially last until Sunday; then they would go back to hitting the books.

During the Armed Forces weekend of 1959, a number of Army vehicles and a tank were put in place for display before visitors to the base during this weekend. A couple of sailors watching the army personnel setting up their displays asked don't they lock the tanks to keep anyone from driving them. They replied that it takes a week of training for anyone to learn how to start one, let alone drive a tank. That was the wrong response to a bunch of sailors.

That night at the CPO club, there was a social function that the Commanding Officer of the Base was attending. The CPO club was located near the top of a rock hill via a narrow winding road. The parking lot was packed to capacity. About the time the social function was ending and the CO was departing the club, there blocking the road was this Sherman tank. It seems there was not enough room for the tank to turn around and backing down the winding road was really not a viable option. Therefore, the crew of sailors quickly climbed out of the tank and ran like hell while the Commanding Officer stood there in total shock. About this time reports began to come in all over the base. It seems that every item of Army equipment had been removed from the display area and abandoned at a variety of locations. The Army Duck vehicle was found in Rock Lake at the very top of the rock hill that contained the CPO club.

The next day, the s*#t really hit the fan around the base and they called on ONI to investigate charges of sabotage to military equipment. Many of us in my class began to sweat and figured we were in deep trouble. One of the investigators called me into an office and began to ask me questions and I tried to evade giving answers. I did tell the investigator about the remarks by the army personnel implying that sailors were too stupid to operate such equipment without lots of training. I detected a hint of a smile on the investigator and after a few more minutes let me go and told me that he will be getting back with me. The rumor was that this implied challenge by Army personnel reached both the Admiral and Commanding Officer. After this interview, it became apparent to me that they began going through the motions of conducting a feeble investigation. By the time we graduated, no one was charged, no report issued and this incident simply died a death of omission. You see, we had one sailor in my class who had been in the National

Guard and was a tank driver, plus a couple of others besides me had experience in heavy equipment before coming to Sub school. We just could not pass up the challenge that the Army presented us.

The day I reported on board the U.S.S. TRITON SSRN-586, the boat was just barely livable for those not married and who had just moved their gear off a barge dedicated to the TRITON crew during the initial construction phase. Captain Beach and LCDR Adams, the Executive Officer, had a short private meeting with me and wanted to know how to address my being on board. It was common knowledge when CT's deployed on Submarines going to the Arctic Circle they had different rating badges on their uniforms. Therefore, they were surprised that I was there with my gold CTMC rating badge on my uniform. Therefore, I told them that I was to be assigned to the Operations Department and in charge of the one compartment called SUPRAD. I also stated that I was, with an understanding that I was to be fully involved in all crew activities, except whenever we went on special missions. Later I learned they had held quarters before I arrived to advise the crew they were not supposed to discuss my being on board. Therefore, I quietly made the rounds of the crew indicating that my role was to help work on improving overall submarine communications capability.

FROM: Stanley S. Earle, USS SEA DEVIL SSN-664 –

How To Simulate Submarine Life At Home.

This guide was designed for those who would like to, but haven't had the chance to enjoy an extended period of time at sea in the U.S. Navy. Happy Sailing!!!

When commencing this simulation, remember to lock all family and friends outside. Communicate only with letters that your neighbors will hold for three weeks before delivering, and will lose one out of every five of them.

Surround yourself with 120 people you don't like. Good choices for this include, but are not limited to: people who chain-smoke, snore like a Mack truck on an uphill grade, pass gas loudly and often (preferably with child-like giggles), and use four-letter expletives in speech the way kids use sugar on cold cereal.

Do not flush toilets for the first three days to simulate the smell of 70 persons using the same commode. After that, flush once daily.

Remove all plants, pictures and decorations. Paint all furnishings gray or white. Paint all rooms either gray or light blue.

Air condition the bedroom and bathroom to approximately freezing temperature. Heat all other rooms to approximately 100 degrees F.

To make sure you are living in a clean, happy environment, clean everything once a week from top to bottom. Work hard all day, even if it only takes three hours. Whenever possible, repeat your efforts. When complete, inspect your work, criticizing as much as possible. Never be satisfied with a good solid effort.

Since you'll never be able to go to sick call, unless summoned, stock-up on Band-Aids, aspirin, Robitussin, and Actifed. These have been proven as cures for every disease known to man.

Unplug all radios and televisions to cut yourself off completely from the outside world, but, have a neighbor bring you Time and Newsweek from last month and a Playboy with all the pictures cut out.

Listen to your favorite cassette six times a day for two months. Then, play music that causes acute nausea until you are glad to get back to your "favorite" cassette.

Once per day, plug in your TV to watch a movie that you walked-out on last year. Then watch an episode of "Thirty Something" that you didn't like the first two times you saw it.

Monitor all operating home appliances hourly, recording all parameters (plugged-in, light comes on when door is opened, temperature, etc.). If it is not in use, log as "secured".

Study the owner's manual for all appliances in the dwelling. At regular intervals, take each one apart and put it back together again. Then, test each at intervals. Take each one apart and put it back together again, once more. Then, test each one at the extreme limits of its tolerance. Expect breakage.

Work in 18-hour cycles, sleeping only four hours at a time to ensure your body doesn't know or care if it's daytime or night time.

Set your alarm clock to go off at the "Snooze" interval for the first hour of sleep to simulate the various alarms of watch standers and night crew going off at odd times. Place your bed on a rocking table to ensure that you are tossed from side to side for the remaining three hours. Alternately, use a custom-built clock that sounds like a fire alarm, police siren, and a rock band combined, so that you'll not become accustomed to ignoring your alarm.

Cut a single bed mattress in half, both lengthwise and widthwise, and put a firm board underneath it. Enclose three sides and add a roof that prevents you from sitting in any position (18 inches is a good height). Place a dead animal or two under the mattress to simulate the smell of your berthing mates and to add lumps.

Prepare all foods blindfolded. Use all the spices that you can grope for and add onions, hot peppers, or both, to everything. Cook all food until it is extremely rare, dried out, burnt, greasy, or burnt on outside and raw on inside (difficult, but possible). Cook nothing you like. Serve all food cold. To eat, remove blindfold and eat as fast as humanly possible.

Periodically shut off power at the main breaker and run around screaming "PROPULSION PLANT CASUALTY!" Do this until you sweat profusely or else lose your voice, then restore power.

Buy a gas-mask and scrub the face plate with steel-wool until you can't see out of it. Wear this for two hours every fifth day, even to the bathroom.

Prepare yourself for an emergency that will require you to evacuate the building, knowing that when you do, the biker gang you hired will simulate sharks and cut off your arm and legs. Study first-aid for sucking chest wounds, until you can quote the book verbatim.

Wear only approved coveralls or proper navy uniforms. Even though nobody cares, once a week wear a clean, pressed uniform for twenty minutes first thing in the morning, then, change back into coveralls.

Cut your hair weekly, making it shorter each time until you are bald or look like you tangled with a demented sheep-shearer.

Go outside once every month and go directly to the worst part of town. Wear your best clothes, so that you stick out like a sore thumb; then enter the raunchiest bar you can find. Ask the bartender for the most expensive imported beer he carries. Drink as many of these as you can in four hours, then hire a cab to take you home by the longest route he can find. Tip the cab driver, even after he doubled the fare because you were dressed funny.  Lock yourself in for another month.

This simulation must run a minimum of six (6) months to be effective.  The exact date of the end of the simulation will be changed no fewer than seven times without your knowledge.  This is done to keep you guessing as to when you can return to semi-normal life.  It is also done in hopes of screwing up any plans you have or would like to make.

We hope you have enjoyed this simulation as much as we have enjoyed the last six months.  Thank you.


Donated Sea stories.

I was a young and impressionable Ensign, one of the first class since WWII to be sent to Submarine School in 1960 to undergo the six-month initial training that preceded the rigorous one-year qualification requirements on board an operating submarine to be a Qualified Submariner.  On one of the underway 3-day training cruises, during which there were not enough bunks to accommodate the additional personnel, we would sometimes hang out somewhere on board and almost surely hear some sea stories about everything from recent x-rated liberty to incidents at sea.

On one occasion, someone noted that they had enjoyed the recent film, "Operation Petticoat" about the antics on board a pink submarine. The movie is actually a classic collection of embellished WWII incidents based upon fact; including the pink submarine, rescued nurses and the torpedoing of a bus.

A grizzled old Chief, who wore the Submarine Combat Pin from his WWII service, commented that he had been on one of the rescue missions, and that those nurses were not quite as attractive as in the movie, but looked more like "old shoe leather".

Then, when something in the conversation triggered another recollection, he recounted an experience when they had fired a torpedo and the poppet valve on the torpedo tube, which was designed to vent air into the submarine as water rushed into the tube to counter weight loss from the torpedo firing, failed to shut. Sea water quickly filled the torpedo tube and proceeded to surge through the valve and associated pipes into the bilges. When the Torpedoman tried to shut the back-up valve, he found it to be "frozen open"; they had been at sea for over 6-weeks and no one had checked the valve operational. By the time the valve was shut, they were waist-deep in water, and the sub had bounced into the bottom where they sat through a depth charge attack.

Some time later, after I had qualified in submarines on my first boat, USS BASHAW SS-241, I was assigned as Weapons Officer prior to an anticipated special "two-month", cold weather training exercise.

We had been working closely with the Sub Base Torpedo Shop as we were going to be carrying some of the latest torpedoes. One of the especially-trained torpedo experts working with us wanted to join us even though he was not a qualified submariner. I thought that he was an excellent submariner candidate and lobbied with our XO to get him assigned. As it turned out, we were very fortunate that the Navy chain of command approved the assignment.

We had been out at sea for about six weeks when one of the new torpedoes malfunctioned, resulting in some harrowing moments. When we were able to assess the damage to the torpedo, it was obviously beyond repair, and according to the printed doctrine, should be jettisoned to sea.

I noted to the Captain that I was concerned about leaving one of our newest torpedoes, however damaged, in relatively shallow waters where a fisherman might find it and provide valuable information to unfriendly people. I suggested that, because we had an expert on board, we could dismantle the torpedo, wrap the sensitive parts in plastic to return to base for analysis and clues as to the failure, and then jettison the non-classified parts.

The Captain was a "Navy Brat" graduate of the Naval Academy, and very "by the book", but he reluctantly saw the logic and agreed.

The torpedo was then disassembled and the non-classified parts put back into the torpedo tube. When the time came to jettison the junk to sea, as Weapons Officer, I was in the Forward Torpedo Room with the first class Torpedoman.

We had almost completed our check list when the Captain opened the watertight door and entered. I was surprised inasmuch as this was a special operation, all watertight doors were shut, and I expected the Captain to be in the Conn. He was obviously nervous, probably because of the nature of our training mission and this out-of-the-ordinary evolution.

We quickly finished the standard check-off, but remembering that sea story, I then told the Torpedoman to check the back-up valve. The Skipper was nervously in a hurry, and said, "Don't bother, go ahead and fire." Upon which I snapped to attention, saluted, and said, "I stand relieved, sir."

Of course, the Skipper realized that this was serious protocol, and I was turning over full responsibility for the order to him. He then said, "OK, check the back-up valve." Upon checking, it was frozen open and required a few minutes of banging on the valve-wheel to free it.

We then fired the tube, and, you guessed it, …the poppet valve failed to close. The deck plates were still open so the Torpedoman was able to quickly jump down and shut the valve as water was beginning to enter the bilge.

I retired as a Captain after another 20+ years in the Navy, and during that time I never discouraged the telling of sea stories, but rather suggested that one should listen for the elements that could serve as "lessons learned."

FROM: Tony Richardson Ufland –

"Wow – I am reading this and didn't realize the way I sleep and roll over are lingering habits from the boat!  LOL."

FROM:  Walt Barden –

<u>"Lass and the golden flapper"</u>

Hi Jim, You may have come across this before but I would submit the title of our boats "weekly patrol report" for a title of your book.  It was called "Deep Reading".  I am also a cancer  survivor and like you treat each day and new friends as a very special gifts.

I do have a sea story that you may have heard:

It involved a young lady who was the guest of one of our "more senior members" who was aboard late in the evening during crew turnover in Holy Loch.   She had no idea what the sign "Secured, blowing sanitary"   meant and proceeded to use a certain head located between the boss's room and his no. 2. That distinctive "whoosh" and a blood curdling scream alerted the below deck's watch that something was definitely amiss. Trust me when I tell you that neither her nor the CO's privy was a pretty sight. She may well have been the only lass to ever receive an actual "golden flapper award."

There was also the true story of a boomer CO who turned over the wrong boat to the relieving CO at our change of command ceremony. Will give you the details of that one if you wish. Smooth sailing shipmate and keep the faith.

Later:

Glad you liked the "Lass and the golden flapper" story. For the Co and the COC story you need to understand a little background. The boat undergoing the change of command was the USS FRANCIS SCOTT KEY SSBN 657. Our new skipper who had just finished his first patrol with us we nicknamed "Liquid Lou" and he did enjoy a good night ashore with his rag hats

To say that we "aided" him in return to the boat the night before change of command in Charleston would be a gross understatement. He was formerly the skipper of the USS TECUMSEH SSBN-628 before taking command of the KEY.

The following morning he was aided by the COB and a few trusted wardroom rats in getting himself up and ready for the big change of command ceremony. Blue Crew lined up on one side of the missile deck and Gold Crew and Skipper on the other. Naturally the Squadron Commander was present. The Gold Crew CO read his orders and turned to our Skipper. "Captain, we stand ready to relieve you." Lou looked at the Gold Crew CO and said, "This has indeed been one of the most successful and interesting patrols of the TECUMSEH and I do stand ready to be relieved." The skipper of the Gold crew reached out a hand to Lou and said "The KEY"

Lou looked him straight in the eye and replied "I gave you the @#&%ing keys yesterday, Captain."

With that the squadron CO remarked on how "stressful" the deterrent patrols could be and that the crews did need to "let off a little steam and relax when they got back in."

It may not have been word for word, but the story is true. Hope you like it and good luck on your book. Blessings, Walt Barden.


FROM: Glenn Gumpman –

I was trying to train this MM2(SS) nuke. For the first 3 or 4 weeks, his only reply to anything I said, whether it be a statement or a question was: "So!" I wasn't quite sure what to make of that…


## *A  SUBMARINE*

(A World War I poem found by a submariner in 1966 at the

Submarine Base, Groton, CT / Author unknown.)

Born in the shops of the devil,

Designed in the brain of a fiend;

Filled with acid and crude oil,

And christened "A Submarine."

The poets send their ditties,

Of Battleships spick and clean;

But never a word in their columns,

Do they mention a submarine?

I'll try and depict our story,

In a very laconic way;

Please have patience to listen,

Until I have finished my say.

We eat where'er we can find it,

And sleep hanging up on the hooks;

Conditions under which we're existing,

Are never published in books.

Life on these boats is obnoxious,

And that is using mild terms;

We are never bothered by sickness,

There isn't any room for germs.

We are never troubled with varmints,

There are things even a cockroach can't stand.

And any self-respecting rodent,

Quick as possible beats it for land.

And that little one dollar per dive,

We receive to submerge out of sight;

Is often earned more than double,

By charging batteries at night.

And that extra compensation,

We receive on boats like these;

We never really get it all,

It's spent on soap and dungarees.

Machinists get soaked in fuel oil,

Electricians in $H_2SO_4$;

Gunners Mates with 600W,

And torpedo slush galore.

When we come into the Navy Yard,

We are looked upon with disgrace;

And they make out some new regulations,

To fit our particular case.

Now all you Battleship sailors,

When you are feeling disgruntled and mean;

Just pack your bag and hammock

Be grateful you're not on a Submarine.

FROM: Bill Allen, ETC(SS), USS
FRANCIS SCOTT KEY SSBN-657; USS
HENRY CLAY SSBN-625 –

<u>I know what WWII feels like.</u>

I was on the USS FRANCIS SCOTT KEY,
SSBN-657. We were on patrol someplace in
the North Atlantic. Normally about once a
week on the same day at about the same
time, we would get a radio message in
telling us to Station Battle Stations Missile
for a Weapons System Readiness Test (a
WSRT-A drill). NOT ON THE REGULAR
DAY, NOT AT THE REGULAR TIME we
got a message in to station battle stations
missile. But before the message was
verified after its initial decoding, the
Executive Officer passed the word over the
IMC to "station battle stations missile for a
tactical launch". The alarm was sounded
and everyone reported to their assigned
stations…Mine was in Damage Control
Forward in the Mess Decks. It was dead
silent in the 425 foot submarine…You could
have heard a pin drop. No one said
anything. I know what I was thinking…My
wife wasn't alive anymore, my parents were
dead, the United States wasn't there
anymore…That would be the only reason

we were doing a "tactical" launch. About 5 minutes passed...again dead silence. A Fire Control Technician had to manually pressurize one of the missile tubes (the automatic function was broken) and in doing so over pressurized the missile tube and lifted one of the huge relief valves on the missile tube which sounded like the launch of a missile. Shortly after that, after the incoming message was properly decoded, the Executive Officer comes back up on the IMC to say "Now station battle stations missile for a WSRT". It was a drill!!!...you could sense that the entire boat sighed. Why the initial announcement wasn't corrected immediately, no one knew. The Commanding Officer wanted to see if we had the same problem the Air Force had. It seems the Air Force had intentionally done this and found that about 50% of their missile silos would not fire because both officers would not pull the trigger. The Captain wanted to know if we would have the same problem....NOPE! We were ready to kill millions of people!

## The Hazards of Topside Watch.

I was on the USS HENRY CLAY, SSBN-625. We were in the shipyard in mid-winter in Portsmouth, NH tied up to the pier and in the middle of a refueling overhaul. Because of the low temperatures and slippery decks we had two topside watches stationed. It was early morning when one of the topside watches heard a metallic clink and then a large splash. When he went to investigate he found that the other topside watch had fallen into the water. The kid was rescued and taken to the hospital to thaw out. The problem was that the top side watch who fell in didn't have his gun...IT HAD BEEN LOST OVERBOARD!! The Navy takes losing a weapon pretty seriously, so they sent divers down in water that was close to freezing. The divers did find the belt, the holster and the lanyard the gun was supposed to be attached to, but didn't find the gun. The kid that fell into the water was questioned and he said that when he fell into the water he had to discard all of that stuff to keep from drowning. End of story...Right? No...Not the end of the story. NOW>>>THE REST OF THE STORY as Paul Harvey used to say... About five years later, the Navy still hadn't forgotten about that lost gun. After a continuing 5-year investigation, they held a raid on the sailor's apartment in Charleston, SC, and guess what they found...The 45-cal pistol that been "lost" in the river in

Portsmouth. This was the kid's original story...It seems on the night of the incident in Portsmouth, NH, the kid was bored, took his 45 off of the lanyard and was spinning it like it was a six-shooter. It slipped off of his finger, hit the steel deck (that was the clink the other topside watch heard) and fell into the water. In a panic, the kid took off his belt, holster, gun and lanyard and threw them into the river and then jumped in himself in an attempt to cover up what he had just done. To his chagrin, the Navy found it was just a ploy to steal the WWI vintage .45.

The Senior Chief.

This one deals with a senior chief mechanic I was stationed with on the USS OMAHA SSN-692 when we were out of Pearl Harbor. We were in port and the senior chief and his wife were at home in bed sleeping one night. The senior chief had to go to the bathroom. When he got up he woke his wife up. She thought it was funny that he went down stairs to use that bathroom instead of the one off of their bedroom. So she was laying there listening for him when all of the sudden she heard a blood curdling scream coming from down stairs. She ran down the stairs, opened the bathroom door and turned on the light. Her husband, the senor chief was in the corner of the bathroom in a semi-fetal position pointing at the commode. His wife looked in the commode and then looked at him and said, "That's why the call them "cock" roaches."

I was on watch in Machinery Two Upper Level on the USS FRANCIS SCOTT KEY, SSBN-657, on patrol in the North Atlantic some place. Part of my watch station included the "tunnel" which is a shielded space over the reactor compartment. I had to go in there twice and hour to inspect and take log readings. So here I am, in the "tunnel" inspecting and taking readings when I notice a napkin with what looks like a turd lying on the tunnel deck. I go back and tell the Engine Room Supervisor about it and, and being fairly new on board, I asked him what to do about it. He said to just throw it in the sanitary and flush it. I did that. A few days later, I was approached by one of the officers who was conducting a pre-Captain's Mast investigation into this "turd" incident…It seems the Engineering Watch Supervisor that was on watch with me at the time I found the "turd" was also the Chief of the Boat and he had found out about this "turd" and didn't like some "coner" (someone who worked forward of Engineering) messing with his nucs so he initiated an investigation. The investigation eventually identified a Fire Control Technician who thought he would play a trick on the nucs so he got some dark- and light-colored caramel, made himself a "turd" and put it on the deck in the tunnel for me to find…He did a really good job too. The kid was taken to Captain's Mast where he just got his hand slapped with a warning to act more professional.

The "Family Gram".

When I was stationed in New London, Ct., I was sitting around the table one night talking with my best friend and his wife. The subject came around to Family Grams…Those 25-word maximum communication devices that the wives of boomer sailors were allowed to use to communicate with their at-sea husbands. I started talking about the habit my sub, the USS FRANCIS SCOTT KEY, SSBN-657, had of publishing some of the more interesting family grams they saw coming over the sked. The wives had just 17 words to say what they wanted to say to their husbands so some of the wives got quite inventive. I noted one particular fam-gram that I remembered. The wife wrote something to her husband to the effect that the meat was in the oven just waiting for him (the husband) to come home and eat some. Leo and I looked up and saw his wife turning a bright red and then she said "Does everyone in the fleet see these family grams?" Leo had to explain to her that all of the family grams go to all of the submarines and then each sub just picks out the ones that belong to them. I don't think she ever wrote another family gram.

[AUTHOR'S NOTE: I never received a Family Gram but I remember reading plenty of "Z-Grams".]

<u>Don't ever lose sight of your wife on a submarine.</u>

 When I was stationed in New London, a tour of an FBM was offered. My friend and I thought it would be a cool thing to do; show our wives what we worked on…He was on the USS GEORGE WASHINGTON SSBN-598, and I was on the USS FRANCIS

SCOTT KEY, SSBN-657.  Just getting
ready to take the girls down to the
submarine was challenging.  Leo and I
thought we were ready to go until the wives
came down from the upstairs bedroom.
Both girls were wearing dresses.  Both of us
immediately challenged the girls' fashion
choice for the tour.  We asked
them…."Okay, ladies, just how do you think
you are going to get aboard the submarine?
They thought for a minute and said "by
climbing down a ladder."  We said
"Exactly…And what are you
wearing?"…They both went back upstairs
and changed into slacks…And yes, there
was the diligent sailor standing at the bottom
of the ladder helping all of the ladies
down…And he was always more than
accommodating when they were wearing
dresses.  Now we have our wives on the
submarine…in the berthing area in Ops
lower level…showing them where we slept
while on the boat.  Leo and I got into a
conversation on something and then
suddenly realized that our wives were no
longer with us.  It didn't take us long to find
their giggling voices as they had climbed
into someone's rack just to see how it
felt…Luckily the sailor wasn't in the rack
too. Next we are up in the control room.
Our wives sat at the planes station.  They

played with the periscope. And again…being distracted again…our wives disappeared. With a little bit more panic and time we followed our wives' voices….They were in the Captain's stateroom shooting the s*#t with the boat's Commanding Officer. We apologized to the CO for our wives interrupting him and took our brazen wives home.

FROM: Charlie Backes, USS SAND LANCE SSN-660 –

<u>My Admiral Rickover encounter.</u>

The USS SAND LANCE had five reactor operators that qualified RO initially. As part of the initial engineering testing that goes with a new submarine, each shift had to have their qualified reactor operator and shift perform a fast-scram recovery. For you forward types, this involved an emergency shutdown of the nuclear reactor and a subsequent fast startup. For all submarines built during this timeframe, Admiral Rickover personally observed these fast-scram recoveries. This is about "my turn in the barrel", so to speak. Three of the RO's were selected to perform the fast-scram recovery while we were at sea. The admiral had come on board with all his accompanying fanfare and needs. A time was selected and the RO's taken to Machinery Room #2 to await their turn. I do not remember which position I was in, but I do know I was not the first. I am sure many of you remember how large Maneuvering was (or wasn't), especially the engineering types. When my turn came up they called me into the Maneuvering Room. Maneuvering normally held four watch standers: The Engineering Officer of the Watch, (EOOW), the reactor operator (RO), the electrical plant operator (EO) and the steam plant operator (Throttleman). When I got to maneuvering there must have been twelve people in the space normally used by four. I managed to squeeze in the room and relieved the watch. Admiral Rickover was in the chair normally used by the EOOW and the EOOW was standing. Also, this was not just the RO that was tested, but the whole shift; so all four watch stations were being relieved. When things settled down a little someone in Machinery #2 opened the scram-breaker for a partial-scram which allowed us to do a fast-scram recovery. When the reactor is shutdown one of the first things each watch station is required to do is to reduce electrical loads to minimum to keep the reactor as hot as possible. If the reactor gets below a certain point the RO is required to do a full-scram and we all are in deep doodoo. Part of this rig for reduced-electrical in the engine room is to shut off the vent fan supplying the Maneuvering Room with cool air. The temperature goes from 72 degrees to 98 degree in about five minutes.  Here we are with the reactor shutdown, the boat rigged for reduced-electrical, and a nervous reactor operator asking permission to restart the reactor. This permission is granted by the EOOW and a fast-scram recovery is started by <u>ME</u>. A normal reactor startup is not all that eventful; but with Admiral Rickover at my right elbow and not enough room to breathe, things got a little tense. My job was to withdraw the control rods in a manner that led to a controlled, critical reactor and to do a plant heat-up within limits. I was doing this when I started "bumping" rods out to control the conditions. Someone, namely Admiral Rickover, did not like the way I was bumping rods and he yelled "You're breaking the machine." I got control of myself and the plant and completed the startup back to initial condition with T-ave (read T-average) in the green band, the turbines on-line and making a 1/3 bell. At that point I was relieved, in more than one way, and got the hell out of Maneuvering. I think I have told that story about a hundred times over the years about how I got yelled at by Admiral Rickover.

A Sea Story.

The story goes that one submarine pulled up next to the pier and tied up. It was promptly met by a big black lady driving a pickup full of iced down beer which she started to sell to the crew. The Captain caught wind of this and called his crew back on board. He then proceeded to tell the lady to remove the truck from the pier because she was interfering with his crew. She drove the pickup to the end of the pier and walked back to where the submarine was tied up and told the Captain to remove his submarine from HER pier. It turns out she actually owned the pier. The Captain had to recall his crew and pull the sub back away from the pier while the mess was straightened out. He got the facts and was told to apologize to the lady, and to formally ask if he could tie up to her pier. She accepted his apology and granted permission to tie up again whereupon the submarine was again met by the pickup full of beer. I suppose the moral of the story is: you have to be careful who you try and boss around, they might be bigger than you think they are.

FROM: John Cunningham, QM3(SS), USS DIABLO SS-479 –

Seven missing days from my Navy career – or – why did I bother?

During the summer of 1949 I lost 7 days out of my career which are unaccounted for, and can never be retrieved. Indeed, a look at my service record shows none of the 7 days.

It all started in New London, CT. I had just been sent to New London for reassignment after riding my qualification boat the U.S.S. Ex U-2513 to Portsmouth, NH for decommissioning. As a point of reference, the entire crew of the U-Boat had been sent to New London. The trip to New London was quite a story, but perhaps that is for another paper one day.

In order to put my story in perspective just a little background is necessary. At the time of my sojourn I had been in the Navy about 14 months. I was a Seamen 1/C (SS). Oh, I know they had changed the rates and I was really a SN (SS), but I liked the thought then, and I still like the thought today of being a Seaman First Class. I had served on the U-Boat for approximately seven months, and had been qualified in submarines for about one month.

A review of my service record shows that on 8 Jul 1949 I was transferred from the USS Ex U-2513 to CO, Submarine Base, New London, CT. The record further shows that on 22 July 1949 I was issued orders to depart New London, and that I was to report to the USS DIABLO SS-479. Additionally the order indicated that I was granted 10 days leave and 2 days travel. Finally the record shows that my leave expired at 2400 4 August 1949 and that I returned to Naval Jurisdiction at 1800 4 August 1949. The latter date and time is important as will be shown below. It is interesting to note that there was no indication in the orders where the DIABLO was located. I guess someone must have told me that she was based in Norfolk, VA.

DAY 1

Now the water, so to speak, gets very dark and murky. I did indeed return to Naval Jurisdiction on 4 August 1949 at about 1800 hours. However, it was not to the DIABLO. In mid- afternoon of 4 August I went to the Submarine Base, Norfolk, VA. The DIABLO was nowhere to be found. I was informed that she was on duty at the Naval Academy, Annapolis, MD taking Midshipmen on training cruises.

What to do? My leave was about to expire. I had no choice but to report to the Naval Receiving Station at Norfolk. Despite my youth and lack of experience, I had been in the Navy long enough to know that I did not want any part of duty there. I knew that it could be weeks, or perhaps even months, before I was able to get on board the DIABLO. I sincerely believe that when I reported to the Personnel Office it was probably about 1700 hours, because almost all of the personnel had left for the day. There was a duty Yeoman there who took my orders. I believe he was a 1/C Yeoman. I asked him to cut me orders to report to the DIABLO in Annapolis. At first he balked. He informed me that all I had were travel orders, and there was no way he could authorize leave, or travel money, or whatever. I told him that I did not need any money (that was a stretch) or any leave. All

I needed was authorization for one day of travel to Annapolis. Finally, I convinced him and he cut the order. I feel certain he probably signed for some Duty Officer who was not to be found.

Thus began a saga, which if not recorded, will die with me, because there are absolutely no records. If a serious historian were to examine my service records he would find a couple of discrepancies, and perhaps chase down some of the saga, but full details would never see the light of day. The first such discrepancy can be found in my service record that shows that "I returned to Naval Jurisdiction at 1800 4 August 1949." A real sleuth would find that according to the DIABLO's ships log the DIABLO was not in Norfolk, VA on 4 August 1949. In fact, the best I can determine she left Norfolk on 2 August 1949.

Hence, the first question the history sleuth would ask would be: Where did I report, if I did not report to the DIABLO? One might find historical records in the Archives of the Navy Receiving Station, Norfolk, indicating that I reported there. However, as I related above in my encounter with the duty Yeoman, I rather doubt that any such record was kept.

Indeed if the sleuth were to examine all of my service records, he or she might conclude that I reported on board the DIABLO on 1 August 1949 (see below); however, then the sleuth would have to ask why I cut my leave short 4 days? And, he or she would have to deal with that record which shows that I returned to Naval Jurisdiction on 4 August 1949; thus the discrepancies.

Now, what really happened? I left Naval Receiving Station Norfolk late in the evening of 4 August. I hitch-hiked to Annapolis. Such was not an uncommon thing in those days. People were then very kind to service personnel in uniform, and with the help of several kind drivers, I was able to find my way to Annapolis, although it took all night. I had a somewhat serious experience with one driver in Washington, DC, but that too is another story for another time. Somewhere along the way I grabbed a bite to eat, and used most of the money I had.

## DAY 2

When I reached Annapolis it was just starting to dawn, and I knew I would be unable to report anywhere until at least 0700 or 0800 hours. I had exactly seven cents left in my pocket. I went into an all-night diner and purchased a cup of coffee. It was five cents. Yes that was the cost in 1949. I had two cents left, so I bought two one penny postcards. Yes they were only a penny then. I used one of the cards to write home. And now, oh how I wish that card had been saved by my parents.

I nursed that lone cup of coffee for as long as practical, picked up my sea bag (yes I had been lugging that keeper of all my earthly possessions with me everywhere I went), and headed for the Naval Academy. Naturally I found that sure enough the DIABLO was serving at the Academy, but she was out to sea. Eventually I wound up at what I believe was the USS REINA MERCEDES, a captured Spanish cruiser from the Spanish-American War that was rescued, refitted, and taken into U.S. Navy service. I believe in 1949 it was used to house enlisted personnel assigned to the academy. I marched up the gangplank saluted the flag and the deck watch and informed him I was reporting aboard.

Then the fun began. The deck watch was not at all amused, but he called the CPO, who was probably the equivalent of a duty officer. The chief was also not amused and asked to see my orders. I whipped them out and I am sure all old salts can imagine what happened next. The chief was quick to respond that my orders said I was to report to the USS DIABLO. However, by that time I was in no mood to stand on a simple set of flimsy orders.

I explained to the chief that I was tired and sleepy and hungry. I also explained to him that I was a Seaman in the U.S. Navy, I had no money, the DIABLO was not in port, and it was the Navy's responsibility to take care of me. I sat down on my sea bag, and prepared to at least make it a pillow. After considerable blustering, and after listening to my sad tale of woe, the chief disappeared. I suspect he went to contact someone of higher authority. In any event he soon returned, and proceeded to lecture me about the fact that they didn't have a billet for me, and hence no meal allotment. But out of the kindness of their heart they would give me breakfast, and then I had to be on my way.

At that point I could have cared less about where I would be on my way to. I was led to the chow hall and handed a tray. It was obvious that most of the men had already eaten, because there were only a few remaining in the chow hall. Despite my now sluggish senses, I was able to note that there was plenty of food remaining, which I am sure ended up in the garbage bin. Thus my so-called "freebie" breakfast did not cost the ship a thing.

Frankly, I cannot fully remember what happened over the next few hours. It must be remembered that I had been awake for at least 24 hours and most likely closer to 36 hours. I had lugged a sea bag all over the Norfolk Navy Base for a few hours, and then hitch-hiked to Annapolis. I don't know if the chief on REINA MERCEDES let me get a few hours of shut eye or not. But somehow before 1700 I ended up at the Naval Station, Annapolis, which was across the Severn River from the Naval Academy.

There was more "fun" to come. When I tried to report into the Personnel Office none of the Yeomen knew what to do. I guess eventually they got a Duty Officer to pick up the ball. At first he balked at allowing me to report for duty. But after I explained to him that I was a Seaman in the U.S. Navy, and I was there to await the return of my submarine, he relented and took my orders. But then he said that they had no place to house me, so he would just give me a liberty card and I could come back when the submarine returned. I explained that I was dead broke and his was a gracious offer, but the liberty card would do me no good.

Parenthetically, I would like to add here that had I wanted to do so I believe I could have taken that liberty card, walked off the base, and right out of the Navy. As will be recorded below the Navy had simply lost me. The DIABLO would have eventually started looking for me, but the only thing they would have found was that record which said I had returned to Naval Jurisdiction. They could not have charged me with desertion because the record said I was there. That is, that I was in the Navy somewhere.

Finally the officer said that he had a few bunks in one barracks and he would send me there. Wow! Was I in for a shock? I soon wished I had taken that liberty card and just disappeared. I found myself in a barracks which housed men awaiting other than honorable discharges. That is, undesirable, bad conduct, etc. I do not believe there was anyone there awaiting an honorable discharge; but quite frankly, I really did not try to find out. I felt I was in enough of a pickle.

After chow I took little time in getting a shower and getting into the sack. But my shuteye was sparse and much interrupted. What a place! To this day I do not know why my sea bag wasn't ransacked while I was in the shower. Maybe it was because the other residents wanted to wait and see what I was there for. Or maybe it was because they thought I might come out of the shower with a weapon. Whatever the reason the Lord spared me.

But oh what a night!? I was first awakened by guys running around all over the barracks and yelling and carrying on. Then, after catching a few more winks, I heard more sounds and I saw one guy brandishing a knife. Then I saw another guy trying to cut into someone's sea bag with a knife. I don't know why he didn't open it from the top. Maybe it was secured with a lock or something. But I certainly did not feel inclined to try and find out. Another night I thought I heard gun shots, but I never saw a gun. However, I quickly learned that it was better to try and stay out of harm's way and mind my own business. But I did take the precaution of lashing my sea bag to the head of my bunk.

## DAY 3

When day light came I was up and about and wandered off to the chow hall. As I recall I wandered around the base some (it was pretty small). And then I wandered over to the pier where I expected to catch the DIABLO. I think after lunch I tried to catch some more sack time, because most of the guys in the barracks were off on working parties or some other kind of duty. For the life of me I could never figure how the Navy ever got those guys to do anything. Because, after all, they were being kicked out of the Navy. In any event, after evening chow it was back in the sack, but only for fitful sleep, with one eye open, so to speak.

The next morning after chow it was over to the pier, and there she was. The DIABLO in all her glory. Finally I was to rejoin the Navy. But it was not to be. I went aboard and got no further than the deck watch. It went something like this: DW - "Who are you, and what do you want?" Me -"I have been assigned to this boat and I am reporting for duty." DW – "Where are your orders?" Me - "They are over at the Naval Station." DW - "You need orders." Me - "Would you please call the Duty Officer?" Reluctantly he did so. But the confrontation with the Duty Officer did not go well.

However, he was kind enough to go below and check for paperwork which would show that I was to report to the DIABLO. Would you believe it? No such paperwork existed. The DIABLO had no records showing that I was to report aboard. The reader should be reminded that I had left New London on 22 July with orders to report to the DIABLO. But here it was 7 August and the DIABLO had nothing to show that I was coming. Fantastic! But then as we often said: "There was a right way,

and a wrong way, and the Navy way." My
guess has always been that my paperwork
was residing somewhere on the sub tender,
and had arrived there after the DIABLO left
for Annapolis. Even that seemed like a long
time. 22 Jul to 2 Aug? But then maybe the
Navy was using pony express in those days.

The Duty Officer did allow me one
privilege. He allowed me to go below and
mingle with the crew and meet my new
shipmates. That led to a humorous incident
that was the killer. One of the guys, I believe
it was one of the men that I attended
submarine school with, but to this day I do
not remember who, came up to me. He
whipped out his wallet and handed me a 20
dollar bill, and said that was what he owed
me from a loan. Wow! Now I was in glory.

As a result I hastened from the boat and
dashed over to the Naval Station Personnel
Office. I asked the first Yeoman I could find
if he would call the Duty Officer. When he
presented himself I asked him if I could
have the liberty card I had been offered. No
dice. Sorry, but it was no longer available.
Why? According to him they had found
some duties for me to perform. Hence
another day shot, and another night of poor
sleep.

DAY 4

Up and about and off to the chow hall. But when I returned to the barracks I was confronted with yet another big surprise. A CPO came up to me and said he had some work for me to do. I have often wondered what would have happened if I had told the chief to stuff it, that I didn't belong to the base and he had no authority to give me work. The reader should remember, however, that I was a lonely and very frustrated SN, therefore anyone with a few stripes seemed like an authority figure. Anyway he took me into the head and handed me a bucket of suds and a brush. He told me that for the remainder of my time on base I was to scrub down the walls of the head. Whoopee! Something to do! Ha-ha.

Needless to say the rest of the day was spent either in the head or the chow hall. I would scrub maybe a four or five square foot area and then sit down and wait for it to dry. Sometimes it took a long, long time for that area to dry. Maybe even a couple of hours. But I always had my bucket and brush at the ready in case the chief should show up to examine my progress. The truth of the matter was I think I only saw the chief a couple of times after our first encounter. Hence, I soon figured out that it was just make-work, and the second and third days were spent just sitting or standing in the head and hoping that my delivery would come sooner rather than later.

## DAY 5

Another day at the office. Oops, the head. At least I got three long sabbaticals to the chow hall.

## DAY 6

Breakfast and then a break from head duty to go check for the DIABLO. And there she was! That time I was received in a much warmer way. To this day I do not know whether someone had checked with higher authority perhaps with a phone call, or calls, or if somehow they had received my paperwork. Or if possibly they believed my story and decided to accept me aboard. But I was informed that their temporary duty was over and they would be leaving the next morning for Norfolk. However, in order to take me aboard I had to have those travel orders I had been issued in Norfolk. Holy cow! Time was of the essence so off I went to the Receiving Station.

My saga was over, right? Not so fast! I was informed that they had to cut me new orders. My response was: "So cut them and I will be on my way." "Sorry sailor no can do." "Why not?" "Because there is no officer present to sign the orders." "You have got to be kidding, right?" "No!" "Well, when will the officer return?" "Tomorrow morning." "What time?" "0800." "Oh woe is me, because the DIABLO is leaving in the morning." "Sorry, good luck."

DAY 7

This HAD to be the day!? Up bright and early. Skipped chow and headed for the Personnel Office. Me – "Please cut my orders so I can catch my submarine." Yeoman – "There is no officer to sign the orders." Me – "I understand, but he will be here at 0800, would you please prepare the orders so he can sign them as soon as he gets here?" Yeoman – "Oh, OK." At about 0810 I had my orders and sea bag on my shoulders, and I was off to the DIABLO. Even today, I cannot remember if I ran or walked carrying that sea bag. But one thing I know for sure. The DIABLO was still at the pier and I was welcomed aboard.

As I recall they drew in the gangplank and threw off the lines even before I could get below. I have always wondered if they waited for me, because it was probably about 0900. But on the other hand, would they have waited for a lowly SN? I shall never know. Maybe the skipper didn't want to get an early start. Or maybe he had to wait for some other ships to clear the channel. Whatever! I was on board, and we were on our way to Norfolk.

Thus ended my sojourn. However, the story is not complete. As indicated above my service record has recorded that I returned to Naval Jurisdiction on 4 August 1949. Please see Figure 1 taken from my service record. So, when did I report on board the Diablo? I say the date was 10 August 1949. But, if you believe what is recorded in my service record it was 1 August 1949. How can that be? I was on leave in West Virginia on 1 August. Please note the reproduction of the "Enlisted Leave Record"(Figure 2) taken from my service record. As may be noted there are some incorrect notations. Or, more likely some outright falsifications.

The leave record must be examined in detail to prove the above. Therefore, what does the history sleuth do with the above information? There are no other records, which would show what happened between 4 August 1949 and 10 August 1949. I am the only person who knows what happened. Hence this saga has been put to paper, because the history sleuth could only determine that something was amiss. He could certainly not determine when I actually reported on board the DIABLO. He would be able to determine that I did not report on board on 1 August.

Presumably the history sleuth would make the following analysis: Based upon the information recorded in Figure 1, I left Submarine Base New London at 1000 22 July 1949 bound for the U.S.S. DIABLO SS-479. I had 10 days leave and 2 days travel time. Also as noted from Figure 1, I returned to Naval Jurisdiction at 1800 4 August 1949. But where did I report? A review of the DIABLO Ship's Log would show that on 4 August the DIABLO was enroute to, or in Annapolis. Hence, I certainly did not report aboard the DIABLO.

As detailed above, I actually reported to Naval Receiving Station, Norfolk, VA. There might be archival records which show that is where I reported. But as detailed above, based upon the unusual circumstances of my effectively extending my travel time to Annapolis, I would doubt that there is any such record. Unless the sleuth should examine historical records of Naval Receiving Station, Norfolk, and unless it is recorded, he would have no way of knowing that is where I reported.

The sleuth could determine that I reported to some Navy facility on 4 August 1949. He could determine that the DIABLO was in Annapolis on 4 August. He could determine that I did not report aboard on 1 August. The DIABLO left Annapolis on 10 August. However, he would be left with the question of when I reported on board the DIABLO.

A detailed analysis of my leave records gives the most complete description that something is amiss in my service records. The reader will note in Figure 2 (the first page of my annual leave records) that after Basic Training in Great Lakes, IL, I was granted 12 days of leave on 14 Sep 1948. The result was that I was negative 10 days of leave. On 12-20-48 I was granted 14 days of leave from S/M Base, New London, CT, prior to reporting on board U.S.S. Ex U-2513. Again the result was negative hence I was minus 24 days of leave. The reader will note that the record showed I reported on board the U-2513 on 1-4-49, but then the 4 was marked out and replaced with a 3. That is indeed the date I reported aboard the U-2513.

The record also shows that on 6-30-49 I had accrued 30 days leave and was then at plus 6 days. The reader will also note that originally the entry had been plus 5 ½, but was then changed to plus 6. Now it may be noted that the leave records are quite messy and difficult to decipher.

On line 6 there is a record, which one would assume was made at S/M Base, New London, CT, However, note that in the "From" column the date was entered as 7/22/49, which was the actual date I left New London (see Figure 1). But the 22 in the "From" column was changed from 22 to 23. That is the first obvious and deliberate false change of the record. Next, it may be noted that in the "To" column a date of 8/2/49 is entered partially on line five and partially on line six of the record. That is the second deliberate falsification of the record. Next the reader will note that on line 7 of the record there are multiple false recordings. In the "From" column a date of 7-24-49 is recorded. It may be noted that the 4 is a mark-over of another date which cannot be distinguished. Then there are two dates recorded in the "To" column of line 7. The first is 8-4-49, but the reader will note that date is scratched out and 8-1-49 is entered with some initials.

Now the next entry on line 7 is undoubtedly where the history sleuth would come unglued. The reader should note that in the "Annual" column a 10 is recorded. But it is marked out, initialed and replaced with a 6. It should also be noted that in the "Balance Available" leave column it appears that a 0 was entered, although there is some other entry underneath the 0, which is not legible. It should also be noted that line 7 was recorded on the U.S.S. DIABLO. The latter was obviously a deliberate falsification of the record, because the reader will note in Figure 1 that I was granted 10 days of leave – Not 6. And indeed, as will be noted later, had the records been correct I would have cheated the Navy out of four days of leave.

From the above analysis it should be apparent that my service record was deliberately falsified by an officer on board the DIABLO. One can only guess as to what transpired in the making of the records. As previously recorded the DIABLO most probably departed Norfolk Naval Base on 2 August 1949. The entries on line 6 of the leave record may have been changed to conform with someone's idea that I reported aboard the DIABLO on 2 August. The reader should note, however, that whoever the recorder was his math was not good. 7/23/49 to 8/2/49 constitutes 10 days, which would have been 8 days of leave and 2 days of travel, or 10 days of leave. Either way none of the record would fit with the numbers recorded in Figure 1.

Line 7 of the record is even more confusing. Again one can only guess as to what transpired. It can be assumed that one of the other officers, perhaps the exec, noted the previous entry and realized it was not correct. So, he entered the numbers 7-24-49 to 8-4-49 and the 10 days of leave. However, he must have realized that his math was off. 7-24 to 8-4 is only 11 days, hence not 10 days of leave, but only nine, if one subtracts the 2 days of travel. Also, whoever the officer was, he undoubtedly knew that I had reported on board in Annapolis. But he had only the orders from the Receiving Station at Annapolis, which did not jive with the orders from New London as shown in Figure 1.

Thus, whoever owned the initials "SY" compounded the felony by changing the 8-4-49 date to 8-1-49, and charging me with only 6 days of leave. Why 8-1-49? Again, one can only guess, but if the DIABLO left Norfolk on 8-2-1949 it may have been early in the morning. The record falsifier knew that I could not have reported aboard on 8-4, and certainly would not have made it on 8-2; hence 8-1 was a good number because that would have been the day before the DIABLO sailed. 7-24 to 8-1 is eight days so now at least the math was correct – six days of leave and two days of travel. Therefore the record keeper was happy. Theoretically I had gained four extra days of leave. And, of course, I was never to know the difference.

It would be natural for the history sleuth, if he had accomplished the analysis recorded above, to have asked the question, why go to so much trouble? Why not just record that I reported on board the DIABLO on 10 August 1949, which was the true date? Again one can only guess. Presumably the officers on the DIABLO did not, could not, or would not; believe my story of what happened between 4 August and 10 August. Whatever their thought process, the final records they recorded still did not, and do not, agree with the record that shows I returned to Naval Jurisdiction on 4 August 1949.

Parenthetically, some smart Yeoman somewhere realized the errors in the leave records. As noted on line 8 of Figure 2 on 12/17/49, I took 16 days leave which put me at negative 16. But then on 6-30-50 I had accrued 30 days so I was at plus 14. The second page on my leave records (not shown) shows a 20 day leave in 1951 putting me at negative six. But on 6-30-51 I had accrued 30 days which put me at plus 24. Then in late 1951 I took another 30 days leave which resulted in a negative six. I took another four days of leave in May 1952 leaving me at minus 10.

I was discharged on 6-11-1952 with 28 ½ days of accrued leave. Based on the above numbers that should have put me at plus 19. However I was only credited with plus 15 and that was what I was paid for. Hence a Yeoman at the Receiving Station in Charleston, SC noted the discrepancies in my leave records and charged me with the four days not recorded on the DIABLO. One can only wonder why said Yeoman didn't question the veracity of the records. But then he was probably only interested in the leave records, not the rest of my service record.

There, dear reader, you have it. Seven days missing from my Navy career, and no record to show it. Since I am the history sleuth, my recollection and a falsified service record, is all I have to prove my story. But so be it. If you have read it, at least it has been told.

FROM: Jerry Emerson, QMC(SS), USS JALLAO SS-368 –

Sometime in 1962, in the South Atlantic enroute to Bermuda, during a transit from NLON to conduct test and evaluation of equipment. We had our normal ship's complement with the addition of about 15 civilian contractors. JALLAO was on the surface at about 15 knots on a beautiful sunny day. I was QMOW in the Conning

Tower and we had two lookouts and the
OOD, up on the Bridge with the ship rigged
for dive. During the watch, civilian after
civilian came into the Conning Tower and
asked the OOD for permission to come to
the Bridge. As required, I maintained a
count of the number of personnel on the
Bridge. About the mid-watch, the CO came
up to the Conn and asked the QMOW,
"How many people are on the Bridge?", to
which I replied, "13, Sir." The CO reached
above the helmsman and rang the Diving
Alarm. What confusion and chaos that
started! The Radar Operator and I were
pushing civilians into the back of the
Conning Tower and almost throwing others
down the lower hatch and into the Control
Room. When the OOD got down and we
closed the upper hatch, we could hear and
see the ocean above lapping around the
hatch. The CO's comment was, "The
JALLAO is always ready to dive." I do not
know what he said to the OOD later. At the
time, this was NOT a very humorous event,
but when thinking about it later on, it was
hilarious.


FROM: John Ezell, USS FLASHER SSN-
613 –

SUBJECT.
Meals Underway:

Last breakfast before pulling in from
WestPac – fried chicken and apple pie
breakfast.  Better than "surf and turf", or
Thanksgiving dinner underway, because
after breakfast you knew you'd be home and
alongside the pier before dinner.

FROM:  Paul J. Greene,

From his book:
(p. 121)
            The next morning when we went to
sea, the captain told me to work with "Red"
in the navigation room.  Red told me that he
was the only on one board who knew how to
navigate and he had been there three years
and had not had leave. The Captain came
into the conning tower and told me that he
expected me to learn enough about
navigation in three weeks to let Red go on
vacation.  I had never even seen the ocean
before.  A book could be written about this
captain.  He was a mustang, someone who
has come up through the ranks to make

officer without having gone to officers' school.

The first morning out, when I was alone in the conning tower with Red on leave and the Captain on the Bridge, I never felt so stupid and scared in all my life. On most ships you will find at least 6 or more in the conning tower. The Captain called to me and said, "Are you ready to get underway Greene?" I said, "Yes Sir" and had no idea what he meant or what I was to do. I stood there with all those charts around me and all the queer looking navigational instruments and I knew I should be doing something, but for the life of me I couldn't figure out what. I thought this had to be a dream.

We had just gotten underway from the dock when the Captain bellowed down and said, "Greene, get on the signal light, the battleship USS MISSOURI BB-63 is challenging us." He said, "You do know how to use Morse Code on the light, don't you?" I told him, "Very little." He said, they want to know where we are going and what our orders are. (They were the senior ship in the harbor and it is their duty to keep a log of all harbor activities.)  He said, "You get on the light and start flashing 'a-s' over and over and I will give it 'all ahead full'". Just keep flashing until we are out of range. I found out later that "a-s" is a code that means to "stand by" or "wait".  That's how my first day at sea as navigator started; me signaling a "lie" to the Flagship with an Admiral on board.  I was on board about three months and really learned about navigation first hand.

My friend, Bill Yarbrough, was on a small ship which tied up at the same dock as my ship.  He also was learning navigation; therefore, whenever we would see one another at sea, we would practice signaling communications.  Bill was on a patrol craft or "PC";  I would signal, "PC I c u, u c me?"

(p. 123)

Our Captain on this little vessel was a character.  It seems like every day he would pull some stunt.  On one particular day we had the battleship in sight that we were to service when we spotted a giant shark at our fantail following us. The Captain got his M-1 rifle and went back on the fantail and tried to shoot it. He kept hollering for the helmsman to change course. After about thirty minutes the battleship called and asked us what was wrong and why we were late at being on station. A battleship usually carries an Admiral and thousands of men. There is no foolishness on this ship. Everything is done according to the books. It is regulation, regulation, regulation. My Captain said to radio them and tell them that we were having rudder problems, but it was nearly fixed and we would be on station shortly. Here I go again, telling a lie, and to an Admiral! If the truth was known about this, the Captain would have been wearing a white hat like the rest of us, and probably working in the Engine Room. Once he was sitting in the Captain's chair on the Bridge with his M-1 rifle, shooting at sea gulls and couldn't hit one so he just shot out the forward anchor light on the ship. He said, "By God, I'm going to hit something before we arrive on station." This ship was 100% like the TV series "McHale's Navy". We didn't even have a cook on board.

(p. 127)

When we finally got into Pearl Harbor, it was on a Saturday night. The next morning Busko, our Chief Cook wanted to go ashore because he had sent his wife and kid on over and he wanted to see them and spend the day. There was a young sailor on board who was "striking" for Cook, and Busko got everything ready for him and told him to serve the Sunday meal. The kid was apprehensive about this but very conscientious and he was willing to try. About noon, the officers and men who had duty and had their wives in Pearl were allowed to bring them on board for lunch. He was a little late getting everything set up, and just before announcing that lunch was ready, he got a grease fire started in the galley. He panicked! He quickly ran into the Control Room and got on the 1MC and yelled, "FIRE, FIRE, FIRE IN THE GALLEY! FIRE IN THE GALLEY!" He ran back towards the galley and quickly stopped and ran back to the 1MC and yelled, "listen men, this is no s*#t"!!

(p. 127)

I usually volunteered to take someone's place on the weekend so they could spend the weekend with their wife and kids. I had nowhere to go and nothing to do except sit in the Conning Tower all the time, correcting navigational charts. The very next weekend, on a Sunday, while all the men and their wives were seated at the table eating, the sailor with the Below Decks Watch, decided to blow sanitary tanks. I don't know why they call it sanitary; it is anything but sanitary. Let me briefly explain, all human waste is collected in the Sanitary Tank. When you use the bathroom, you must first turn off the sea valve, then open the inlet valve. When finished, you must close the inlet valve and open the outlet valve then bleed in air; then you reverse this operation. During each shift, the Below Decks Watch is to check the tank, and if it's full, it is to be blown. Now this is a real trick and a complicated maneuver. You blow the tank out to sea, but you must first be sure all the valves to all the inlets are closed because you have the dish water and everything else coming into the tank. Well, as you may already suspect, that's what happened. He failed to close the valve going to the kitchen sink, which is adjacent to the Mess Deck where everyone is eating. All at once everyone on the Mess Deck was suddenly inundated with crap from the tank. The food, the ladies' hair and dresses were stained with this disgusting stuff. Everyone had difficulty understanding how to operate all the valves in the head just to use the commode.

One of our crewmembers wrote a poem about this:

I've been aboard the BAYA, for nigh on to a week,

Sitting here with both legs crossed, unable to take a leak.


I'm afraid to ask instructions, too ashamed to ask the crew,

If I don't figure this thing out I don't know what I'll do.

Push this lever; turn that valve, which one
do I do first?

If I don't find the answer soon, by bladder's
gonna burst!


I sure don't want to flood the boat, I cannot
take a chance.

But if I don't do something, I'm gonna wet
my pants.


I fell asleep in Sub School when they gave
the demonstration.

I'm sitting now in misery from lack of
urination.


I've held it in for over a week, that's as long
as I can go.

Won't someone show me how it works, my
kidneys are about to blow.

There's no one I can turn to, the situation's
mighty bleak.

I'd give my reenlistment bonus for a chance
to take a leak.


The pain is quite unbearable, I'm about to
throw a fit,

Unable to pee was bad enough, but now I
have to s*#t!!!

(p. 128)

Next, we began to get cockroaches in the
Galley. The Captain heard about this and
ordered every compartment to hold Field
Day and clean everything. That means
polish all brass, etc. The Captain told Busko
he had better get rid of all the cockroaches
before inspection. Busko didn't do
anything. I told him he only had two more
days and he had better get busy. He said he
had everything under control. On the day of
the inspection, everyone who was not a
Department Head had to be on deck in dress
uniform for inspection by the Executive

Officer, and all others would stand by their department for the Captain's Inspection. When the Captain got to the Galley, Busko was standing at attention and the Captain said, "Busko, did you get rid of all the cockroaches?" Just at this time, Busko saw one crawling across the table, he quickly jerked his hat off and hit it, saying, "Yes, Sir; all but one and I got him now, Sir." Now, this is what Busko told me, but he is known for his exaggerations.

I think what got this cockroach thing going was our Chief Engineman, who was a tall, lanky sailor from Georgia. He was eating one day and when he got through he asked Busko if he had "any Rocky-Road gedunk with boot topping?" (This is translated as boat-talk for vanilla ice cream with nuts and chocolate syrup.) Busko told him to look and see. He got the ice cream and found a half gallon can of chocolate syrup. It was almost empty, but he poured what was left over his ice cream. This can had been open for some time with two big "church key" holes in the top. He was sitting across from me eating and there were

only three of us in the Mess Deck at the
time, when suddenly he jumped up and
hollered. Those long legs swung over me
and in two steps he was over at the sink
heaving. He later said he thought it was nuts
he was eating, but they didn't crunch just
right, so he sucked the chocolate off one and
took it in his long fingers to take a look, and
it was a cockroach looking back at him!!


(p. 129)

One day we were on the surface, and the
waves were really rough. The boat kept
rolling from port to starboard. During the
rough seas like that, we would often place
wet towels on the mess tables to keep the
dishes from sliding off. On this particular
day, Busko decided to make soup for us
because of the rough seas. He had a big
aluminum pot that held fifteen or twenty
gallons. He tied down each side of the pot
with a rope so it wouldn't slide off while the
ship was rolling so much. The Captain told
him to let him know when it was ready and
he would dive under the water where it

would be smooth enough to eat. Well, this all sounds great, but the problem was when we dived, the Diving Officer got too much down-angle on the boat, and the pot wasn't tied off to hold in that direction. Yes, all the soup that he had been working on all day, our dinner, was now a mess on the deck. This gave new meaning to the term "Mess Deck".

(p. 130)

Another time Dan was going ashore and I asked him would he just one time go ashore and come back under his own power and not be beat all to pieces? He assured me he would, and I actually believed him this time. It was four a.m. and I was on the Mess Deck drinking coffee and the deck hatch was opened. I saw a foot coming down the hatch ladder trying to find the next rung, then another foot laboring to get solidly on a rung. I saw how long the legs were, and I knew it was Dan, and he was drunk. When he finally got down and turned around, his face was bloody, his hat was gone and his kerchief was crooked, his cuffs unbuttoned and one sleeve was torn off. I said, "Dan, what in the world has happened to you?" His speech was slurred, but he said, "Paul, I remembered what you said and I did come back by myself. I did real good until I got right here near the Base and saw this drunk S.O.B. laying all coiled up on the ground. I just kind of nudged him with my foot and said, "Get up from there you drunk S.O.B., and you know what Paul? I thought he would never stop getting up."

FROM: Paul "Mad Dog" Hanes –

SUBJECT.

Meals Underway:

Scotch Woodcock (breakfast).

"Mystery Meat."

FROM: Gary Hogeland, USS BLACKFIN SS-322 –

Sometime during the spring or summer of 1961 I had the privilege of serving as a Sonarman on the on the USS BLACKFIN SS-322. We were engaged in local.ops off of Pearl . We fired an exercise MK 14 torpedo. I was on the sonar stack at the time and monitored the fish as it left the tube and reported to the conning tower a "hot-straight-and- normal" run. I proceeded to do a 360 degree sweep for any possible ships in the area.. As I was scanning along the port beam I heard the faint but very distinctive sound of high speed screws, aka torpedo. I reported a circular run to the conning tower and the captain, whose name I have forgotten, but I'm sure could be found in historical records, ordered an emergency surface. Before the ole BLACKFIN could surface the torpedo struck the sail on the port side but dislodged itself after impact. leaving a hole in the sail. They were the subject of a lot of finger pointing and chuckles as we pulled back into Pearl that day.


From: Lebonville, "Shorty" Renaud J.,

USS FINBACK SS-230 –
( he is going on 91 years old this year of
2014; he made four War Patrols, and was
aboard when FINBACK rescued then young
naval aviator George H.W. Bush, and has
memorabilia to prove it)

FINBACK's Captain was John Tyree.
Once Shorty was on the helm with a great
following sea. The mess cooks had finished
dumping the garbage and he was having a
hard time keeping the course. This sea was
easily moving the boat up to 20 degrees off
course. The Captain asked, "Who is on the
helm?", to which the answer was passed up,
"Lebonville." When Shorty got relieved and
went up to the Bridge, the Captain asked
him, "What course have you been steering?"
Shorty gave him the correct answer. The
Captain pointed out the garbage that had
been previously dumped and remarked to
Shorty, "We have passed that garbage twice
now." When Captain Tyree left the boat,
he became Assistant Presidential Aide to
Franklin Roosevelt.

FROM: Ross Knight , USS HALFBEAK
SS-352 –

I love the time I spent on the USS
HALFBEAK in Groton, Ct. We did JOOD
for Officer's Sub School. It was called
"bumper drills." Every Friday the junior
officers would back the old Halfbeak out
into the Thames River and bring her back in
to the pier; over and over again. The boat
was rammed into the pier so many times it
got to be called the "wrinklebeak." Then
after we secured we had a grand lunch and
early liberty (unless you had the duty!).
This was 1970.

FROM: Glen Myers –

SUBJECT.
Best nicknames on the boat:
        An XO we called Chewbaca; during
drills when he was heading to the casualties,
you could hear the Chewbaca "ARRRRR"
follow him to the scene.

FROM: Jeff Nieberding, ET1(SS), USS
THOMAS JEFFERSON SSBN-618 –

First patrol.

Early summer of '77 and I'm standing on
the dock waiting for the small boat to Ford
Island. There are several destroyers (coulda
been frigates for all I know) tied up nearby.
It's late on a Saturday and Pearl Harbor is
sleepy. I think to myself, was it like this 36
years ago before the Japanese descended
from the skies? The small boat arrives and
soon I can see the Arizona and the ever
present oil slick. We debark on Ford Island
and I am surrounded by history. After two
years in the Navy I have arrived at my first
real duty station.

I'd filled out my dream sheet at prototype
and requested a boomer out of Pearl.
Always heard that dream sheets where just
that, but I got what I asked for. I had been
assigned to the USS THOMAS
JEFFERSON SSBN-618 Blue crew reactor

controls (RC) division and they were due in
Pearl in a few days after completing a patrol.
As I was checking into the BEQ the Chief
on duty told me I had lucked out to pick up
the boat on an off crew.

Off crew progressed nicely as I got to know
my new shipmates and started picking up
the culture of being a bubblehead. These
guys are different I thought to myself, none
of them are quite right, even the officers are
off a little. The Captain would wear a T
Shirt that said F*&# Forty, guess he did not
like turning the big 40. Being only 20 at the
time it was an alien concept to me. Looking
back now I realize they were normal and it
was the rest of the world that was off a little
bit.

Too soon I found myself along with the rest
of the crew on a 7 hour MAC flight from
Hickam to Anderson AFB Guam. Landing
on Guam in itself was an adventure for me.
We kept dropping lower and lower and all I
could see out of the window was blue water,
"Where the hell is the runway?" was going
thru my mind but nobody else seemed
concerned so I suffered in silence. Gazing

out the window and still only seeing blue we abruptly touch down; come to find out that the end of the runway at Anderson is a cliff.

After gathering our seabags we were packed into a bus for the long drive to Polaris Point in Apra Harbor. We drove thru Agana and numerous other small villages along the way, gathering stares from the locals that did not always seem friendly. Since the Gold crew was still out on patrol and was not due in for a couple of days I figured they put us up in a comfy barracks until the boat arrived. Boy was I in for a shock. There was no barracks, there was this thing called "the Barge". My hat is off to you diesel boat boys because this barge was as close to being on a diesel boat as I would ever get. It was a dark, hot cramped, humid and smelly metal box tied up to the pier.

The next morning the COB took all of us new non quals on a bus trip around the island. I was surprised at the amount of WW II wreckage still on the island. The island itself was quite beautiful, even if it had some ugly scars of history on it. The COB relayed that the last Japanese defender had surrendered only a few years ago. We returned to Polaris Point in time to participate in the beer ball game and cookout, our last fling before the boat comes thru the breakwater into Apra Harbor.

With the arrival of the boat the next day the chaos of turnover began. My LPO had warned me to watch the Goldies closely because their only thought was getting out of Guam and back to Pearl for those 30 days R&R. A concept that I did not fully grasp as of yet. Soon the Goldies were gone and the boat was ours. I of course got a choice top bunk right outside of the head, not that I got to spend much time in it.

Refit is just a clever way to spell work, 12 hour days were the norm and 16+ not uncommon. In addition, being a non qual I was putting time in on ships and engineering quals. On the plus side my shipmates were so concerned about my well being they made sure that I qualified shutdown electrical operator so I could stand the 0000 – 0400 watches. The long days soon delved into a blur of work and an occasional foray to Andy's Hut By The Sea to consume mass quantities of beer. It is truly amazing how much a bubblehead can drink and still get the work done.

Another unsung joy of refit that I discovered was stores load. Being in Engineering Dept. and thus the largest department on board we got to be topside to handle stores. Good, I thought, we get to be in the sunshine. For some reason I had forgotten that we were in Guam and that if the temperature dropped into the high 80s people were looking for a coat. Not to mention the rain squalls that you can see coming but you cannot escape. It was also during this time that I discovered that a #10 can can be lethal in slippery hands, especially if you are at the bottom of the torpedo room ladder handing off the can you had just received. And what are all these round weights we are loading for?

Soon enough we were underway for a couple days of sea trials after refit. Going out to make sure everything works and look for leaks I was told. Leaks I asked. Yeah, we go out and dive to test depth to look for leaks, came the reply. Holy s@#*, there has got to be a better way I thought. But noooo,

508

that's what we did. I remember being in the machinery two upper level when the klaxon announced that we were going to dive. I guess I was expecting some kind of spiritual event or a revelation when we slipped beneath the waves. Nope, just a slight down angle and if you listened real close (I was) you hear a gentle swish as the ocean swallowed us. After some angles and dangles we proceeded to test depth in steps followed by announcements on the 1MC for all compartment to look for leaks at each step.

The boat returned to Apra Harbor after a couple of days to tie up loose ends and make the final preparations for getting under way on patrol. This also provided the last chance to consume beer for the next 75 days and send that last letter home. Most of us did just that.

There was no fanfare as we got underway for patrol. Just a fact of the cold war that most of what we did was unnoticed, did not seem odd to me, that was just the way it was. On the second day at sea MMCM (SS) Mowery told me (I was just a piss ant 3rd

class) to clean the after escape trunk.
Having learned early on not to mess with
Master Chiefs (unlike Ensigns which were
fair game) we proceeded to open the lower
hatch so I could access the escape trunk. On
my way up into the trunk the Master Chief
told not to dog down on the upper hatch as
we would never be able to open it upon
return to port. Wonderful I thought, I was
already nervous enough being in the trunk
with the sea just inches from my head.
Trying not to think about it I busied myself
in that time honored Navy tradition of
cleaning that which did not need it. After
several minutes I heard an extremely loud
noise in the trunk which I was sure was the
sea coming to visit me. I launched myself
out of the trunk into engine room upper level
in a desperate attempt to escape death. As I
rolled to a stop I was greeted by hysterical
laughter. The engine room upper level
watch, and I am sure the Master Chief did
nothing to dissuade him, had cracked open
the 700 psi bleed air in the trunk right next
to my ear. I looked around and noted that
there was quite an audience, including the
EOOW enjoying the festivities at the

expense of the non qual. I am sure that brown stain remained on the deck until the boat was scrapped.

The patrol soon settled into the familiar routine of a 1/3 bell at 130 ft with occasional trips to periscope depth. I quickly qualified throttleman and began working on quals in earnest. To add to the fun this was an ORSE patrol so there were plenty of drills to participate in. Getting familygrams and reading news that the radiomen had made up to monkey with somebody. But I made progress and by the end of the patrol I was a "half-qual".

Hump night arrived along with the Hump night poker games and skits. I let MMC (SS) Louthain talk me into doing a take off on Carnac which Johnny Carson had made famous. We had a blast and the crew loved it. I had laughed until I could laugh no more. So I did Carnac on every patrol after that.

The maneuvering watch was set and we were entering Apra Harbor to end a successful patrol. Soon the mountains of porno would appear on the decks in berthing as we cleaned up and got ready to give the boat back to the Goldies. On the 7 hour flight back to Pearl I pondered what had happened and marveled at the fact that it seemed like we had just emerged from a time machine while the rest of world had moved on. Nobody really knew what we did nor did some care I suspected. What mattered was that I needed to do to get ready to do it again. I had Dolphins to earn.

FROM: Steve Oliver –

SUBJECT.

Favorite Songs:

We had a record player on board and the only album was "Pure Prairie League".

[The author would name the most popular song on this album, but he does not want to be blamed for installing that incessant tune in your head for the rest of the day. Go look up the song and do it to yourself.]

FROM: Bernie O'Neill, IC3(SS), USS SAND LANCE SSN-660 –

I want to share what I consider the best part of my life, so far, and thereby enlighten others who may be considering a similar path in military life. In addition, since I so thoroughly enjoyed this adventure, perhaps some readers may find these items interesting or simply entertaining; in any case, I would have achieved my purpose in compiling this information. No matter what your personal reason is for looking over these few pages, I sincerely hope you take away with you the same sense of pride and dignity that has implanted itself in my heart and soul. It is my wish that I can effectively express my total respect, deep appreciation and gratitude to the U.S. Naval Submarine School instructors of New London, Connecticut; my fellow crew members of the USS SAND LANCE SSN-660, and the women and men of the Portsmouth Naval Shipyard, in whose hands we placed our very lives. Thanks to each and every one of these individuals, we all made it safely home to our families and friends.

The time frame was the later part of the 1960's and early 1970's. The Vietnam War was a major part of the daily news, and the military draft lottery was displayed on television as if it were some game show from time to time. I had recently graduated from Milford Mill High School near Randallstown, MD.

I was fully aware of the brutality of the war, and knew at some point that I would soon be faced with the decision – do I volunteer, or do I wait on the draft? After High School I began my formal work career as a Telephone Central Office Installer Technician for the Western Electric Company, located in Cockeysville, MD, a subsidiary of American Telephone and

Telegraph (AT&T). In 1968 as a single and
eligible male draft candidate, I gave much
consideration to my military options, so I
began investigating different military
services and alternatives, none, by the way,
was to flee to Canada as some less than
honorable citizens did.


The Sales Pitch.

One summer afternoon I somehow found my
way down to the U.S. Naval Reserve
Training Center, located at the historic "Fort
McHenry", home of the "Star Spangled
Banner" located on Fort Avenue in
Baltimore City, MD. I was approached by
one of the recruiting officers and provided a
memorable tour of the Training Center. To
the rear of the building there was an aging
World War II diesel-powered submarine
christened the USS REDFIN SS-272, and
no, it is not the same boat tied up to the pier
in the Baltimore Inner Harbor today. I was
invited aboard and there mingled with some
very good-natured and cordial individuals
who were charged with keeping the inner

mechanical equipment fully functional on this vessel; who, by the way, were very successful at their assigned task. I then continued my tour with the recruiting officer and moved on to see a Navy Reserve Construction "Sea Bee" Battalion drill area, then another area designated as "The Naval Communications Technical Squadron 5-1" which had numerous meritorious service awards to the U.S. Naval Active Fleet posted on their drill hall area bulletin board. (This Security Group would later be part of my Naval duty tour.)

We soon got down to business and after I had filled out a plethora of paperwork, I was asked, "Well, have you given any thought as to which unit you may be interested in joining here at the Reserve Center?" I clearly remember being impressed with several of the proactive drill units and their missions and promptly said, "No, not as of yet!" The next response from the recruiter was, "Well, how about the Submarine Service?" My answer was, "Well, I thought that was a dying branch of the service in a post World War II era." He laughed and said, "No, I think that you'll make an excellent submariner and you'll find it very challenging and technically educational. So, with such glowing comments and encouragement, I said, "OK, Submarines it is!"

I was soon placed on a waiting list for "Active Duty for Training" at the noted U.S. Naval Submarine Training Base in New London, CT. It seemed like forever waiting for orders to Submarine School, so in my own enthusiastic way I went and requested early assignment to report for training. I arrived in New London by train after departing from the Pennsylvania Railroad Station in Baltimore, I was sent off by my fiancée and her parents. Upon arriving at the Submarine Base Information Office, I was greeted by the Officer of the Day (OD), and one of the First Class Petty Officers assigned to shore duty in personnel administration. I was then given the grand tour of the Naval Enlisted Submarine School facilities. I was promptly shown where I was to "bunk". The place looked like a long building with hundreds of bunk beds lined up side by side on both sides of the building and down what appeared to be an endless hallway as far as one could see. The quarters were painted a bright blue with individual lockers of a dark "pea green" and crowded sleeping accommodations that were "poor" at best, folded mattress about three inches thick, however, I was here to be trained, and that was where my focus would remain at this time. Reporting for duty over the weekend had its advantages. I was able to take a quick look around the Sub Base and local town before beginning training bright and early Monday morning.

Monday morning I found myself in class with a group of about 35 feisty but determined enlisted sailors. The Instructor entered our classroom and immediately took control. After a brief introduction of who everyone was, and where they were from, the Instructor asked a final question, "Has everyone heard of the Navy Great Lakes Basic Enlisted Training Facilities?" He then proceeded to make the point that that particular facility was not a place where anyone of us would ever want to be. He made the following motivational statement, "Anyone who successfully completes this Submarine Training would not have to report to "Basic Training at the Great Lakes Facility". Enough said, it worked for me and I immediately was convinced and made up my mind that if this place was not all that great, then the "Great Lakes" had to be much worse, so it was my intention to succeed right here and now.

On Tuesday we all had to go through physicals and psychological evaluations. I made it through the medical physical and the psychological training including the hyperbaric chamber training where four of the ten of us who had been squeezed into the chamber (which was constructed for four or five people) had their ear drums burst and several began bleeding, but in spite of all this, I was determined to move on, so I did, right to the eye examination and an immediate release; the problem – eyesight measured 20/40 vision without correctable lenses.

I was promptly advised to pack-up and go back to my reserve unit in Baltimore and await further instructions. Upon arriving home I went directly to the reserve center and inquired what I had to do to obtain permission to complete my submarine training. "Well", the Officer of the Day said, "you need a 'Waiver for Glasses' and that requires the signature of the Commanding Officer of the Reserve Facility. Hearing this I made sure to get my waiver, and the rest is history. I promptly returned to New London to complete my submarine training. Upon my return, it was pointed out to me that the newly-forming class got a break from nature – lightning had struck the 100 foot tall submarine rescue escape training water tower on the base and placed it out of commission for an extended period of time, long enough for me to get through Sub School and not have to worry about the challenging "blow and go" exercise which was a mandatory part of Submarine Training and another filtering point for the faint of heart. Quite frankly I have never missed not having to go through that ordeal, however, I bet I would have entered that tower and completed that task in record time (smile).

## First Duty Assignment – Nuclear Submarine Precommissoning Crew.

Time flew and Submarine School was down-right challenging – having to learn all about hydraulics, pneumatics, electro-mechanical and electronic life support systems and ship maneuvering and control systems along with onboard communications, diving controls and their importance to my survival and the overall survival of the crew. Classes were finally over and I had obtained a 4.0 rating on a 4.0 scale for my personal student rating. It was now time for all of us to obtain our orders and be notified of where and which submarine we were going to be assigned. Several of my classmates were sent to boats actively serving in the Viet Nam arena, others were sent to Ballistic Missile Boats, often called "Boomers" and still others Nuclear Fast Attack boats and some even went to Diesel boats. Me, well, I waited and waited and waited, finally one day after about 3 weeks, I went to the base Personnel Office and asked if anyone could find out

what was the status of my orders. The reply
came one day later when I was informed that
somehow I was assigned to a Nuclear
Submarine billet and nobody had completed
a security clearance background check on
me. So a little while later the Security
clearance was completed and I was ordered
to a pre-commissioning unit located in the
Portsmouth Naval Ship Yard
in Portsmouth, New Hampshire. Upon
obtaining my orders I was asked by the
Officer of the Day: "Hey Sailor, how did
you rate such choice duty?" My response
was simply a big smile and I replied "I have
friends in "High Places". I then promptly
went packing to Portsmouth, New
Hampshire, without a clue about how
fortunate I was to have this type of duty
assignment right out of submarine school
training.

I again traveled by train to my destination.
Upon arriving in Portsmouth I was soon to
find out that the Naval Base while officially
in Portsmouth, New Hampshire but was
actually right next to Kittery, Maine and in
walking distance to Pease Air Force Base, It

was at Pease my wife and I would entertain ourselves at the air base movie theatre. I entered the Ship Yard through Kittery, Maine carrying my duffle bag over my shoulder and was greeted by a U.S. Marine Guard. I displayed my orders and was told someone would be over to show me to my quarters in a few minutes. Sure enough I was escorted to a Navy Barge, "Well here you are pal," my escort said – "Welcome Aboard!" Within a few minutes I was given my quarters – a third rack high bunk bed on a shipyard-floating barge. Again I thought this is to be temporary and I can live with that. As soon as I unpacked I inquired where the "Sand Lance" was located. I was again escorted to the dry dock area where all at once I saw the entire boat elevated out of the water. It was astonishing to me to see such a sight. I then moved to the boarding area and was showed the entire boat inside and out. The inside at that time was nothing but cables and piping as it was still entirely under construction.

So, I asked how long until we are ready for sea? The escort smiled and said: "well we have had to nearly rebuild this entire boat ever since the "Thresher" was lost, you see we learned a great deal from that tragedy and we are putting backup systems onto the backup systems to increase the safety factor, it's going be awhile."

The USS SAND LANCE (SSN 660) was going to be the first 637 Class Submarine to go to sea from Portsmouth Naval Ship Yard since the loss of the USS THRESHER (SSN 593) during her sea trials after her 1963 modification. It was also during 1968 the USS SCORPION (SSN 589) was lost at sea.

<u>In Memory of those on "Eternal Patrol"</u>

The Loss of the USS THRESHER and USS SCORPION

On the morning of 10 April 1963, the Thresher proceeded to conduct sea trials about 200 miles off the coast of Cape Cod. At 09:13 hours, the USS SKYLARK ASR-20 received a signal indicating that the submarine was experiencing "minor difficulties." Shortly afterward, the Skylark received a series of garbled, undecipherable message fragments from the Thresher. At 0918 hours, the Skylark's sonar picked up the sounds of the submarine breaking apart. All hands were lost -- 129 lives.

Well time moved on ever so slowly so it seemed. I personally became home sick and had accumulated earned leave time that I promptly used to return home and see my family. Prior to joining the Navy, I had discussed getting married to my then girlfriend and on my way off the boat to go home Senior Chief Sonar Operator Gerry Pollard, Chief of the Boat remarked to me "O'Neill, I don't want to see you go home and get married young man, you get back here safely and single you hear me?" "OK, Chief I replied, I'll see you when I get back." Well making a long story short – about a week later I telegraphed the boat and requested extended leave since I had done just eloped and married my high school sweetheart.

I still have a copy of that Western Union telegram to this day. "Married on May 09, 1970, requesting extended leave." Needless to say, it was granted and I had a little explaining to do upon my return for what the Chief of the Boat (COB) had said. However it all worked out in more ways than one. My wife and I have a wonderful family and raised 5 beautiful and loving children. It was not without pain as we lost our oldest child Colleen Lorraine, to meningitis and two other premature male children at 6 months of development during pregnancy. We named the first Brian Scott and the second Brendan William. All three are at rest together in St. Joseph's Cemetery in Hanover, Pennsylvania.

Away For Helmsman/Planesman Training.

While the SAND LANCE continued to be constructed many of the crew had individual training assignments to attend to, one such requirement was to have qualified back-up Helmsman and Planesmen. These two functions are responsible for the literal steering, diving and navigational control of the submarine. My training for this crew role was conducted onboard the USS GATO (SSN 615).

Chief Of Naval Operations,1971.

It was during this time in U.S. Navy history when a new style Chief of Naval Operations took Command of the Naval Fleet. His Name was Admiral Elmo Zumwalt Jr. His personal philosophy was to openly communicate with every member of the "New Navy". So when I completed standing watch and assisting with the check off and acceptance of the many newly installed shipboard systems, I found time to write Admiral Zumwalt. His reply is contained herein. I was an enlisted sailor who had made a case for more coordinated family leave time and starting what some would call today a "Mentoring Program" whereby new enlisted personnel who expressed a desire to make the Navy a Career would basically be taken under the guidance of a "Naval Officer Mentor". It would be the Officer Mentors role to coach, and provide a path of advancement for Enlisted Sailors up through the ranks and eventually lead to a Commissioned Officer role in the U.S. Navy.

In addition to personal communications to individual Naval Personnel, The Admiral was noted for Fleet wide communications called: "Z-Grams." This was his way of showing his open style of communications and quickly attempting to alter the internal Naval Culture to a new more personal and caring military life where "everyone" was appreciated and respected. It was, in my humble opinion a battle that he would ultimately lose, for better or worse.

Elmo Russell Zumwalt, Jr., was born in San Francisco, CA on 29 November 1920. Graduating from the U.S. Naval Academy in June 1942, with the accelerated Class of '43, he served mainly in destroyers during World War II and continued in surface ship assignments after the war. In 1950, Lieutenant Commander Zumwalt received his first command, USS TILLS (DE-748). Subsequent commands included USS ARNOLD J. ISABELL (DD-869), in 1955-1957, and USS DEWEY (DLG-14), in

1959-1961. Promoted to the rank of Captain in July 1961, Zumwalt attended the National War College and held responsible headquarters' positions in Washington, D.C., until receiving a further promotion in July 1965. Rear Admiral Zumwalt then commanded Cruiser-Destroyer Flotilla Seven and served in the Office of the Chief of Naval Operations. He became Commander Naval Forces, Vietnam in September 1968 and was promoted to the rank of Vice Admiral shortly thereafter. On 1 July 1970, Admiral Zumwalt received his fourth star and assumed the post of Chief of Naval Operations, the youngest officer to ever hold that position. During the next four years, he guided the Navy through a period of difficult personnel, fiscal, technological, and operational challenges. Admiral Zumwalt retired from active duty in July 1974. He was thereafter active in political, policy, and business pursuits until his death on 2 January 2000.

Getting Down To The Business At Hand.

The day finally arrived and we took the
SAND LANCE out for Sea Trials along
with many shipyard contract technicians and
Hyman Rickover - Admiral, USN. "The
Father of the Nuclear Sub." I was very
honored to be aboard this submarine during
sea trials with this individual. The man
expected the highest level of personal
performance and he obtained it from this
submarine crew. The Crew and SAND
LANCE completed all tests with excellent
results. The hardest part of our preparations
was making sure the submarine met a list of
some thirty-five personal requirements
which were received in hand-written form
prior to the Admiral's arrival, enough said,
the Crew Members know what that entailed
and we were ready!

Congratulations were due to the Entire Crew
of the Sand Lance as we completed our sea
trials with notable success. Now it was back
to the shipyard and make ready for
redeployment to our first assigned homeport
that was to be Charleston Naval Base, SC.
Our in-transit time took about two weeks as
we operated off the east coast for a short

while. The Sand Lance was an impressive vessel the Officers and Enlisted Crew gave her a hard workout on the way down from Portsmouth, NH to the Charleston Naval Base she performed well and we were all proud of her.

Charleston became my port of departure from active naval service, as luck would have it, my tour of duty was about to expire - release from active date (RAD) and the next deployment of the SAND LANCE would take six months and that would place me beyond my enlistment contract. So it was with mixed emotions I prepared for departure. To John McGuire, IC3/SS my shipmate and fellow IC Technician, I say to this day I felt poorly about having to be the one between the two of us who was to go ashore rather than remaining with the Sand Lance during the upcoming southern deployment.

First Unqualified Enlisted Crew Member "Submarine Qualified" Aboard the USS SAND LANCE (SSN 660)

During my tenure aboard the SAND

LANCE I consistently worked at obtaining my "Qualified In Submarines" status. It was an even greater honor to become the first enlisted sailor to receive my coveted "Silver Dolphins" as a Plank Owner of the Commissioning Crew, an accomplishment that would be again recognized by the Decommissioning Crew some 20 years later at the SAND LANCE inactivation ceremony, which I attended along with Captain William A. Kennington, USN the first Commanding Officer of the SAND LANCE and a few other members of the commissioning crew Harvey Cybul, The Navigation Officer, Michael Hess, Engineering Training Officer, Nathan "Ike": Isenhour IC1/SS my senior enlisted supervisor and former Lt. Michael Hewitt, SAND LANCE Engineering Officer, Mike was the guest speaker for the inactivation ceremony in New London, CT. and a he made a great delivery of the speech.

IC Electrician – Responsible for:

All Shipboard Interior Communications, Dial-X Telephone System, Intercommunications Systems, Air Quality

Control, Steering and Diving Electro-mechanical Servers and Systems Controls, Electrical Power Distribution, Combat Information Center Power Controllers, Sound Powered Communications System.

Contributing More In Different Ways.

I returned to the Naval Reserve Center at Fort McHenry, Maryland and finished my tour of duty with the U.S. Naval Security Group Division 5-1 Communications Technicians, where I received the "Sailor of the Quarter Award" after my active duty for training in the summer of 1973, I constructed the first active naval communications monitoring station at Fort McHenry. This Naval Reserve Communication Technician (CT) Unit subsequently received numerous awards and commendations for their contributions to protecting radio communications security from serious breaches by Active Duty Naval Vessels.

Ironies of Life.

To say that I enjoyed my Navy tour is an

understatement, I have always had a great respect for the military service and I would suggest all young Americans spend at least two years in service to our great country in one of our time honored armed services. It would be some twenty years after my tour of duty in the Navy that I would find out that at the same time I was stationed at Portsmouth Naval Shipyard, there was another SSN Submarine christened the USS JACK (SSN 605) in the shipyard at the same time as the USS SAND LANCE which had one of my second cousin's on board Michael G. O'Neill and neither one of us knew the other existed at that time. Michael's Father is Captain Martin George O'Neill, USN Retired Commander of two US Aircraft Carriers, the USS FRANKLIN D. ROOSEVELT (CV 42) and the USS TICONDEROGA (CVA/CVS 14) he (Martin) was honored with numerous Naval heroic service medals, more than one dozen.

FROM: John Pankratz, USS BASHAW SS-241 –

SEA STORIES.

"Sea Stories," sailor's recounts of incidents, usually embellished and often with expletives, are a famous, if not infamous, part of the navy.

I was a young, impressionable ensign, one of the first class since WWII, to be sent to submarine school in 1960 to undergo the 6 month initial training that preceded the rigorous one year qualification requirements on board an operating submarine to be a submariner. On one of the underway 3-day training cruises during which there were not enough bunks to accommodate the additional personnel, we would sometimes hang out somewhere on board and almost surely hear some sea stories about everything from recent x-rated liberty to incidents at sea.

On one occasion, someone noted that they had enjoyed the recent film, "Operation Petticoat" about the antics on board a pink submarine. The movie is actually a classic collection of embellished WWII incidents based on facts, including the pink submarine, rescued nurses and the torpedoing of a bus.

A grizzled old chief, who wore the submarine combat pin from his WWII service, commented that he had been on one of the rescue missions, and that those nurses were not quite as attractive as in the movie but looked more like "old shoe leather."

Then, when something in the conversation triggered another recollection, he recounted an experience when they had fired a torpedo and the poppet valve on the torpedo tube, which was designed to vent air into the submarine as water rushed into the tube to counter weight loss from the torpedo firing, failed to shut. Sea water quickly filled the torpedo tube and proceeded to surge through the valve and associated pipes into the bilges. When the torpedoman tried to shut the back-up valve, he found it to be "frozen open"; they had been a sea for over 6 weeks and no one had checked the valve to be operational. By the time the valve was shut, they were "waist deep in water" and the sub had bounced into the bottom where they sat through a depth charge attack.

Sometime later, after I had qualified in submarines on my first boat, USS BASHAW SS-241, I was assigned as weapons officer prior to an anticipated special "two-month, cold weather training exercise."

We had been working closely with the sub base torpedo shop as we were going to be carrying some of the latest torpedoes. One of the especially-trained torpedo experts, working with us wanted to join us even though he was not a qualified submariner. I thought that he was an excellent submariner candidate and lobbied with our executive officer to get him assigned. As it turned out, we were very fortunate that the navy chain of command approved the assignment.

FROM: Ted Curtin, USS ATULE SS-403 –

We were headed southwest somewhere off
Newfoundland, homeward bound after a
cold-war adventure off the Faeroes, where
we had patrolled submerged for about six
weeks, listening for the passage of Russian
subs possibly bent on mischief in the open
Atlantic. It was the time of the Suez Crisis,
and we had been part of the execution of a
long-standing operation order that flung a
cordon of submarines and patrol planes
across the "Gap", the various straits that
separate Greenland, Iceland and the United
Kingdom. We had been called from our
homes under secret orders, our plans for
scheduled deployment to the Mediterranean
cancelled in the furor over the Egyptian
takeover of the Suez Canal and the ensuing
fighting. Our task had been to lie still
beneath the surface, listening for the sounds
of submarine engines and calling in the
planes to locate, identify and track the
intruder. Now we had been relieved by
another sub, and were on the surface,
speeding our way back home to New
London.

Our boat was the ATULE, a World War II
Fleet submarine converted to what we called
a "GUPPY", streamlined and with better
batteries and equipment. I was the new
Chief Engineer, recently reported aboard
from the older GROUPER, on which I had
qualified in submarines. Our skipper was
Willy Knull, a mild-mannered, soft-spoken
man of considerable experience, and the
crew, officers and men alike, were a good
and generally well-seasoned lot. Our recent
patrol had served to bind us into a smoothly-
working team.

I had just been called for the "night watch",
eight to midnight. It was winter, and as the
cliché goes, "a dark and stormy night"; so,
as I was assembling a nearly-dry set of foul-
weather gear, I was happy to get word that
the Captain had decided to submerge for the
rest of the night, because of poor visibility
and the rough ride we were getting. We
were near the regular shipping routes, and
submarines are hard to see, even in good
weather, so he felt we had rather be both
safe and comfortable, even if it delayed our
return home.

So, there I was, leaning against the plotting
table in the Control Room, braced against
the constant violent rolling and pitching, the
boat shuddering every so often as a
particularly big or erratic wave slammed
into our low-lying superstructure. I felt even
more grateful not to have to suit up and
climb into that dark maelstrom. We
reported up to the Captain in the Conning
Tower that the on-coming watch was
assembled and ready, and we heard him
shout up to the bridge, "Take her down!"
The diving alarm blasted its familiar
"Oooga-oooga", the 1MC carried the OOD's
shouted "Dive-Dive!", with a background
noise of shrieking wind, and the watch on
deck came tumbling down the ladders into
the Control Room, streaming water from the
foul-weather gear that encased them all but
their eyes. Then the bottom of our world
fell out!

Normally, when a submarine dives, at least
the diesel-powered fleet boats, the sound of
the diving alarm is followed by a well-
ordered, coordinated sequence of events.
The engines are shut-down and propulsion is

shifted to the electric motors and battery at full speed. All the outside openings are shut, while the vents are opened, allowing the huge ballast tanks to flood and give the boat negative buoyancy. Large steel hydraulic planes extend from the boat's sides, one pair forward and one aft, like stubby airplane wings, to control the angle of the boat as she goes up or down underwater. As she submerges, usually at a down-angle of 5-degrees, the Officer of the Deck becomes the Diving Officer, and he and his crew make adjustments to drive the boat down to the ordered depth and level her off on an even keel.

That is what is supposed to happen, normally. As I stood there waiting for the wet crew to complete their dive, things suddenly went awry. Just as the Chief Petty Officer of the Watch (COW) scanned the "Christmas Tree", a lighted board that showed whether hull-openings were open or shut, and reported, "Green Board, pressure in the boat", signifying that all was well and safe for diving. The boat lurched into an alarming down-angle, throwing us all off balance. She seemed to be heading for the bottom, pointing her bow more than 45 degrees down, and things began to fall out of their stowage spaces with a tumult of thumps and bangs, accompanied by a shower of dust and debris long hidden in out of the way places, while we all hung on and wedged ourselves in place as best we could. As Engineering Officer, I was the ship's senior diving officer, so I got right behind the Diving Officer, to give what assistance I could, as he urged his planes-men to get the angle off and pull her up.

The Skipper took over from the Conning Tower, as submarine doctrine provides, and took the classic action called for, Stop-Back-and-Blow. He ordered, "All Stop, All Back Full; Blow all Main Ballast." On a dive, the stern planes situated right behind the propellers, have the greatest effect on the angle of the boat; and ours weren't having any effect in leveling us. The Captain's orders stopped the full speed force of water over those planes, began to pull the boat backward (toward the surface) and immediately began to lighten the boat by

blowing the water out of the recently
flooded ballast tanks, making the boat
buoyant again.

Soon we were wallowing on the surface,
breathing out various sighs of relief while
we tried to figure out what had happened. I
recalculated the figures in the diving book, a
log of the distribution of all the liquid
weight in various tanks, which affects the
trim, or angle of the boat when submerged.
We checked out all our control mechanisms,
and all seemed normal. So, we tried it
again.

And the same thing happened! Again we
plunged rock-like toward the bottom, which
was a couple of miles down. Again we
stopped, backed and blew, and once more
we reached the surface where we rolled
about much like a log in the surf while we
double-checked all of our equipment,
procedures and calculations. Nothing
seemed to indicate an answer, until finally,
one of the young lookouts who was on the
dive as stern planes-man, said, "Mr. Curtin,
these planes aren't working right. See, I can
spin the wheel in manual with one finger,

and it should take my might!" Back I went
to the After Torpedo Room, where the stern
planes had a pointer attached directly to the
control-arm, and it was moving properly.
Yet, something was radically wrong when
no resistance could be felt in moving the
planes by hand. All our heads were now
together, yet all that collected experience
found no explanation, and we decided we
had no choice but to go home all the way on
the surface.

I climbed into damp, salt-encrusted foul
weather gear and took my watch on the
bridge an hour or so late, immediately cold
and wet, but still alive.

Though quite drained by the harrowing
experience, my mind was still pondering the
whys and wherefores of the event, since it
was my bailiwick as Engineer. Through it
all there had been no panic, not even among
the newer unqualified hands, and I don't
recall being afraid though we had been in
great danger. My reaction had been one of
anger and frustration on the malfunction; but
the more I reflected on it the greater was my
gratitude and pride in the behavior of the

crew, who worked calmly together, a smoothly operating team of professionals, secure in their knowledge of what they and their boat could do together.

All our thought on the problem was to no avail as we pounded our way slowly down past Nova Scotia, through snow and ice that coated our superstructure, and more storms that battered holes in the aluminum plating of our "sail", the streamlined structure around the bridge, was not until we were alongside the floating dry-dock in New London that the answer came. A diver came to inspect the stern planes, and as was their method, jumped off the deck to land on the planes themselves, only he kept on going. There were no planes there at all! Somehow, sometime during that first storm, the planes had taken such a blow from the sea that the shaft had broken in two, and the planes had fallen right off! At last we knew just how precarious our position had been. And now we had our own "sea story" to match countless others we'd heard, most of which began with the words made famous by the wartime novel "Shore Leave" – "and there I was…"

FROM: Pat Taylor, USS ATULE SS-403 –

…taking water over the bridge on USS ATULE in 15-18 foot seas. The two 18 year old lookouts. Went on for two full days and nights while we were en route to Argentina. All our boats, 5 from Key West and 5 from New London, were heading to report on the Russian sub that had left our area passing over into USS GRENADIER SS-525's patrol zone, and then got surfaced when she ran [illegible] can flat trying to get away when she counter- detected the 525 boat. "Big Secret". We were all told by the Admiral up in Argentina where the spooks debriefed us, and showed the pictures that our "playmates", the P2 a/c got of the Soviet when we called the plane in to vector on the surfaced sub. They were draping canvas all over the sail area, and as the pictures show, it proved that the Russians had converted some of their boats to carry two ballistic missiles in their enlarged sail. Of course, when we got back to KWEST 12 days later, there on the pier, along with all the wives/sweethearts, was Admiral Jerauld Wright, CINCLANTFLT, with a big band and a case of Jack Daniels whiskey for the GRENADIER, who got the credit for the first forced-surfacing of a Russian sub. It seems that the picture had been labeled "SECRET" in Argentina, but now had been on the cover of "Life" magazine a week before our arrival home.

## The exercise shot that almost got the boat into trouble.

I have the MK 14 gyro on my desk as a keepsake. It had been part of an expendable exercise fish we fired. For all I know, maybe one that was readied over in the Med. We had been given this one fish to "play with" and got in a little trouble over it. We opposed a sortie coming out of Naples, a carrier task group with a screen of destroyers, a fleet oiler/AO, and a fleet Ammo ship/AE. We were the two "orange" subs and were tasked with penetrating the

screen and giving the DD's some ASW
exercise. We got in under the tin cans, and
came up about 2,000 yards off the bow of
the Ammo Ship. The Captain (Don
Kirkpatrick) had said we were going to use
the expendable if we had the chance, so it
had been made ready and the tube loaded. I
was the TDC operator at Battle Stations, and
we had a beautiful firing solution set-up at
1,600 yards range with a 75-80 degree angle
on the bow. As I recall the weapon was set
to run at about 25 feet, or maybe a little
more, and it went out "straight and normal."
We all got to watch the wake as it ran down
the [illegible] "target". The troops on the
Ammo ship saw it too, for we could see
sailors on the port rail pointing to the wake
headed for them. Well, as it turned out, the
fish did not run and sink; it blew it's head
like a regular exercise unit, and we saw it
pop to the surface after our target went by.
The Captain ordered a quick surface, and
called for the search light to the bridge as
soon as we got up. He had the
Quartermaster send a flashing light message
to the AE, saying, "Bang, bang – You're
Dead!" After a moment's pause the AE sent

back from her bridge, "You would be too!"
It was a message that we did not understand
the meaning of. We rigged for recovery and
brought the unit back aboard, and before the
[illegible] was up, the CO of the AE, a four-
striper Aviator, sent an official message to
the ATULE asking that our CO pay a call
on him when the two of us were slated to
enter Palma in the Majorca Islands in
another eight days. The Captain thought it
to be a nice social call and remarked, "I
wouldn't be surprised if the old man invites
me to have a sip from his private sea stash!"
Well, he was surprised alright. Our Skipper
came back to the boat with his tail between
his legs like a whipped pup, and related to us
that we better start reading the Sixth Fleet
Regs, because there was a chapter in there
that said under no circumstances were any
exercise weapons, torpedoes especially, ever
to be fired at the Sixth Fleet Ammunition
Ship for it carried the entire arsenal of
aircraft-launched atomic weapons in reserve,
and there were to be no "sympathetic
detonations" triggered by fleet exercises!
That was a good time to be the Engineer and
not the Weapons Officer. It was Weps'

chapter and verse that he was responsible for knowing once we entered the Mediterranean. The Captain took all the blame in front of the 4-striper who grudgingly allowed that he was not going to report the incident to COMSIXTHFLT. You can believe we all opened the new fleet regs and studied them for any more "no-no's" during that deployment! The Skipper of that Ammo ship explained his response, "You would be too!", by pointing out that any submarine that might have been sailing within 10 miles of his ship blowing up with all the Fleet ammo on it would have gone down as quickly as he would have. Anyhow, I got the gyro out of that weapon. We never fired it again and took it back to the BUSHNELL at the end of our trip, and except for a little WD-40 spray on it every 5-10 years, it doesn't seem to need any tender care and still spins fine.

Reminds me of a short story I passed to Roy Purtell/SEA OWL this morning, in response to one of our Engineman's swipes at submarine junior officers allowing that they best just "stay out of the way." It recalled an ATULE event as follows:

Enjoyed reading EN Hemmings' rag about our old diesels having served with them all. There are a few among us that would trade a Fairbanks-Morse for an oily Jimmy, though I am sure those snipes stood proud keeping those GM engines running.

While I can accept junior officers "getting in the way" of leading torpedomen, snipes, or even the leading commissaryman. I think most of them learned the hard way about when to let the Chiefs and First Class PO's do their thing. There were times too, when coming home with smoke pouring from all four exhaust holes, where we had a part and a place in the scheme of things.

As Engineer on USS ATULE SS-403, coming back from a Med patrol in the late 50's, I was confronted with telling the skipper we would most likely have to change our Movement Report such that we would not be able to arrive in CONUS on our scheduled ETA, for number three Main Engine was down cold with a gross leak in the exhaust manifold. A 12-knot SOA just wouldn't get us there on time! Then I remembered having learned of a "new glue" not yet in the Supply System. The Engineer of the boat we relieved inbound in Rota passed on to me a couple of boxes of something called DEVCON, a new two-part steel epoxy mix with a rating to withstand up to 1,000 degrees F. He said he hadn't the opportunity to use it and had purchased it "open-purchase" before they left the States, and "did I want it, just in case?". As the Captain stewed over the prospect of a late arrival home, I remembered these two boxes of "stuff" under my bunk n the three-man stateroom. I lugged this magic mix back to the engine room, sat down with the First Class and we poured through the instruction sheets. Before the Captain had the out-going message to the Squadron put together, I raced forward to ask him to give us 12, maybe 18 hours to get No. 3 back on line, and he did. We [illegible] worked with two EN's around the clock making "putty" to fill a 2-inch hole and crack in the liner and held heat lamps to the curing mix, and we got the

engine pouring smoke in 10 hours, on-line
and doing 80-90 in twelve hours.

While I never took the course at Annapolis
that Hemming seems to think [illegible]
exist ( we learned boilers, super-heated
steam and down-comers in my day). We did
learn to think "outside the box." By the
same token, 12 years later, as skipper of
GRAMPUS on one of those 5-month
UNITAS deployments around the tip of
South America. I learned from the CO that
made the trip the year before, that navigation
was "lousy" way down south of Chile, due
to the always present overcast in the
Humbolt Current. No stars, no sun for
sometimes days on end. The charts we had
ordered for that deployment (the subs are
almost running solo on that annual ASW
cruise), did show a lot of small radio
direction finding stations along the west
coast of South America, even out on the
Galapagos. This time I took the initiative to
"open purchase" from Radio Shack, no less,
a $380 RDF receiver that we could plug into
the Conn, take to the Bridge, and get cross-
bearings from the beach at any time of the

day or night. It got to the point where we were sending the position of the [illegible] force to the Admiral at 12-noon and midnight, a position that the flagship couldn't fix for themselves. So, once in a while a JO learns from his mistakes, and sometimes learns from his new leading division petty officers; and sometimes after 15 years of smelling diesel with his shipmates, he gets to pay his way on his own two feet!

POEM – Contributed by John Rupertus, FTG2(SS), USS CHOPPER SS-342 and USS ATULE SS-403 –

### ***This Old Navy Just Ain't What It Used To Be.***

From Puget Sound Naval Shipyard

Navy Day – 27 October, 1940:

The old salt spat at a passing rat

And borrowed a match from me;

Then scratched the match where his pants
were patched,

And spoke most fervently.


I'll swear, by gum; it strikes me dumb

About this new Navee.

Without a sail, nor even a brail

And the dog-watches drinking tea.


"T'was some years back, that I took a crack

At serving Uncle Sam,

And 'taint the same, except maybe the
name,

As 'twer in those days, by damn!"

We went aloft, if the old man coughed,

Or if it began to blow;

And we got a root from a gov'ment boot

If we's a-went up too slow.


A trick at the wheel, an arm o'steel

From lots of plain beef, y'see.

We got our rum and a slap o'slum

Almost every day.


And we had to risk it, with moldy biskits

If stores was runnin' low.

Today I seed how these youngsters feed

The mess that they get each day.

And strike me pink, if I don't think,

That I'd went in a swell café.

It's kinda strange, this terrible change,

What's come to an honest trade.

They print the log, an' instead of grog,

Drink sody and lemonade.


An' tellin' me true, like I'm tellin' you

They clean up most every day.

Which only shows, how a sailor can go

Mad for a little pay.


It used to be, that a man at sea

Was a sailor, it makes me boil.

To see the way they cruise today,

With radiums, gas and oil.

And not content to remain where meant,

On top – where a ship shoulders sail.

They go and man, a sheet-iron can,

And dive like a blasted whale!


They think they are smart, but frazzle my
heart

And shiver me timbers too.

If under the seas's any place to be

For a self-respected crew.


The old salt spat; then donned his hat

Gave a hitch to those pants of his.

He'd said his say, so he creaked away,

All itches and rheumatiz.

For a sailor man, since the flood began

And Noah put to sea.

He raised this 'plaint, "Aye, the Navy ain't

What the Navy used to be.!!

FROM: Gene Rutter, USS ENTEMEDOR
SS-340 –

The "Noodle Patrol"

My boat, USS ENTEMEDOR (SS340) had
pulled into Copenhagen in the mid fifties.
Usually stores replenishment is one of the
first things done. However, in this
case.....the following day, muster was held
and we were deployed on an immediate
basis. We left Copenhagen without
replenishing the groceries (Stores). So.....for
the next seemingly endless number of days,
we ate NOODLES. Had never realized the
different ways they could be done, much to

the credit of the cooks. As a result I lost about 25 pounds, and would not eat noodles for the next 30 to 35 years. When we got back to New London, there were two large 100 pound crates, filled with lobster. Our crew gorged itself. Did not know until years later that the cooks, who would get the stores were told not to bring anything back unless they had some very specific items, which were due on the day we left Copenhagen.

Birth of our first Child

We were deployed during the birth of our first child, a girl, in August 1958.

One of the officers on the Entemedor (SS340) prepared a kind of joke. He had a bulletin typed, showing items such as Top Secret, Classified, and also that I had taken "Action" nine months prior to the birth, had the Captain sign the bulletin and passed among the crew. Must admit it was appreciated and provided some laughs for the crew.

FROM: Richard Schrum,

USS POLLACK SSN-603 –

While I was the supply officer on USS POLLACK SSN-603 I was assigned to supervise the after capstan when coming into port. When coming into the pier at St Thomas I stepped backwards and fell into the line locker. I quickly jumped out of the line locker but the bridge phone taker announced to everyone on the sound powered phones that Lt Schrum had fallen into the line locker. For the next 3 months my new nick name from the crew was "line locker"

When coming into New London, CT in a dense fog the USS POLLACK SSN-603 was on the surface going very slowly and ringing the fog bells, etc. A cabin cruiser came out of the fog to our starboard side and with a bullhorn the lady asked if we were a lighthouse? CDR Scott Chester the CO on the bridge said in a loud voice (no bull horn) no we are a US Navy submarine.

Finally, as supply officer I purchased a stainless steel Stanley thermos bottle for the crew to use to send coffee to the officer of the deck when he was on the Bridge while on the surface. One OOD left the thermos on the bridge and we submerged and spent the next 30 days underwater. When we surfaced the next OOD found the thermos to be in great shape and we continued to use it.

FROM: Seen on facebook:

635(G) early 80s had Kevin Cat Fish Lee and his pal "I'll save ya" Joe Boyer. Cat Fish returning from liberty in Scotland fell off the brow to the tender and Joe not knowing how to swim a stroke jumped in to save him. Now that's a shipmate.

We had a young A-Ganger come down to AMR one morning proud to show off his new tattoo. He pulled up his shirt and said "I'm f****n Psycho"! Too bad that the tattoo across his chest was spelled

"PHYSCO". Needless to say his nickname was Physco for the remainder of his tour.

We had a CTM rider that everyone called "Scruffy." They didn't have much broken stuff to work on, so he helped the cooks out quite a bit instead. Either the CO or XO went to recognize him for his efforts and realized they didn't know his real name either, so "Petty Officer Scruffy" was thanked for his extraordinary efforts in the galley.

On TULLIBEE, there was a yard period when some of us weren't getting amorous partners on the beach as often as we'd prefer. The T2 "Fransciscan Monastery" was led by MM1(SS) Bob "Bingo" Bode, aka "The Monsignor." One morning after not making it back to the barracks, my absence was noted and I was demoted to "Junior Candle Trimmer."

On the JACK, one of the SK's came to me and another person for a final run-through on Sonar before going to our Chief for his Sonar qual-sig. We spent a good ½ hour convincing him that the towed array was actually a "toad array," because it was shaped like a frog! It took a LOT of convincing on our part, but he finally believed us. We waited until he was almost out of the mess deck heading for Sonar before we told him the truth (only to keep the Chief from ripping our heads off).

Someone stole the XO's stateroom door, on the VON STEUBEN. When zone bones failed to turn up the door, which was hidden in M1LL overhead, he decides to get back at the crew. He hangs a CPO spread in his doorway and stations a 24-hour E-5, and above, Stateroom Security Watch, complete with watch cap, guard belt and flashlight. One division decided to ramp up the shenanigans when they bound and gagged the watch-stander, who was apparently snickering the whole time, and stole the CPO spread.


Sonar stuffed a bunch of pubes in an EAB before fire drills and gave it to the nub when the drill started.


A young SN on a Sub Tender spent over an hour going from one end of the ship to the other and back, and from lower decks to higher decks, looking for the fallopian tube calibrator, before a Chief took pity on her because she was pregnant and sent her up to Medical to have things explained to her.


On Olympia, the COW, an SK1, asked the nub standing lee helm where the EM log was. Nub had no idea, so the COW sent him back to the engine room to get it so the OOD could review it. After being given the runaround in the ER, the nub came back to Control without it. The COW suggested he try the XO's stateroom; perhaps it was on his desk, "but don't wake him." This was the XO who hung a "Danger – Sleeping Dragon" sign on his door when he hit the rack. Nub came back to Control a minute later, "He says he doesn't have it." COW, DOW, and OOD were still processing this remark with somewhat horrified looks on their faces when the XO walked into Control. His only comment was, "Guys, I know what you're trying to do – next time do it while I'm awake."

When pulling into port as a TM we had to shoot water slugs for timing purposes for the shipyard. Well, after shooting numerous water slugs going through the channel in King's Bay, GA., the muzzle doors shut on a rather large fish. Me, being the type of person I am as a TM2, I take the cut-off portion of the fish and put him into a zip-lock baggie. I shove him into the ventilation ducting that runs into the Torpedo Room and out the watertight door into middle level passageway, which includes the officers' staterooms and CPO Quarters. A few weeks later while I am in off-crew and the other crew is on the boat, I get a very heated phone call on how I am A-such-and-such, and it took the TM's two weeks to figure out where the rotten fish smell was coming from.

Taped a couple of fresh eggs in the overhead above the CO's stateroom. Took a long time to start stinking, but when they did….

Marbles placed in the overhead above the CO/XO's staterooms were fun, and they didn't make noise until the boat left port.

Prussian blue on the X-60J earpiece. Wait for the roving watch to be near the phone, then growl it.

Fixed the XO's OBA on John Adams, by tightening all the straps on one side so he'd have to turn his head to the side to see.

Best dit-dot bomb ever: We had a WEPS that was a complete booger-eater. We plugged in an EAB, removed the facepiece from the hose, and filled the hose with dit-dots. We removed the cover from the diaphragm and put a bent paperclip on it to use as a pressure plate, the routed the hose into the corner of the WEPS rack. The pressure plate went under his pillow. When he laid down in his rack, his head pushed the pillow down onto the diaphragm, lighting off the EAB air, blowing dit-dots all over his rack. Not only did the bomb work, but he got a huge goose-egg on his forehead from trying to rapidly sit up in his rack.

A TM doing my torpedo room walk-through damn near got me on a gag about MK 48 torpedoes having external combustion engines; where the pressure of sea water provided compression for the piston. I got my revenge – he sat on my Qual Board, and asked, "What can you tell us about MK 48 torpedoes?"

"Well, they're external combus..."

"XO, wait, what? Who signed your card? Uh, let's see, non-qual. Sir, I think this non-qual will be happy to provide some personal training, isn't that right, non-qual?"

CO on 704 hated the NAV; made him track a B1RD contact. Took him an hour before the NAV figured out he was tracking a seagull.

On the 683, we had the PM for the signal ejectors. The Chief in the Engine Room had a non-qual looking for a water slug. Could not find one so he had to make out a chit for one. Went to Supply, he sent him to the Torpedo Room to see if they had a spare. They said no, he needed his for PM going into port. So he went back to Supply, then he was sent to the Captain to have him sign the requisition. The Captain looked at it for a minute and said, "These slugs are getting expensive." He went back to Supply with the signed chit and they told the non-qual how he had been had. Had him going for about 45 minutes.

Pringles can filled with dit-dots. EAB hose EB-Greened to the bottom of the can and the manifold valve shut. Can and hose stuffed into the overhead as best as could be. MC-Roving Watch comes along checking the valves....POOF.

On the boats, I had stayed away from jokes on others, until the CO asked me if I could

leave a message on the Tektronix
replacement computer called an HP-9020,

(One in Control and one in Sonar) for the
other crew. I said, "Sure." And we picked a
particular date for no rhyme nor reason. He
kept on saying he wanted more than a
simple, "Hi? Gold Crew, ....Blue Crew." I
had actually written a front end menu for
both computers that had two submarines
facing each other similar to dolphins, kind
of. The one in Control was realistic and the
one in Sonar was cartoon-like. I had created
blue submarines for the Blue Crew and gold
submarines for the Gold Crew in the menu.
Now, to tell what happened: On the pre-
scheduled day, the first time they used the
menu and checked to see if it was on or after
the day that was planned. If it was it
rewrote the menu system and removed the
program I was using to check the date. First
a blue submarine came up and next to it a
gold submarine and a torpedo was shot from
the blue to the gold all the while it played,
"Pop Goes The Weasel," and on the Pop, the
gold submarine had a large red ball cover it.
From then on, the menu for the other crew
had upside down submarines. They could

still use the menu for our crew and it was right-side-up. And they could have someone witness the original torpedo shoot since it was on the menu.

Rest of the story:

On that day the other crew had a really big inspection that had not been scheduled, so the CO and I were unaware. Planning this gag out took well over 2 weeks work in my spare time and involved others on the ship. There was the cartoonist who drew the artwork, and a musician who came up with the music for "Pop Goes The Weasel." While funny, I am sure the other crew was not quite as appreciative. Best gotcha, and only one I did. And best of all there was NO trace <u>until today</u>.

We were under the ice and I had a non-qual deck himself out in a survival suit, KPOC and boat hook, then go up to Control and say, "Officer of the Deck – ready to take on mail."

Some guys came up with a "Hurt Feelings
Report" and made an actual form for it. Had
blocks like "Name of real man that hurt
you" and such-like…very amusing, and
added a little salt to the open gashes.

While I was the SRW, I used to soak
chemwipes in waste oil, and stick them in
the temporary ventilation routed to
maneuvering. Hearing them bitch at each
other about crop dusting was hilarious,
nobody had any idea what I had done…
ENG and EDO included…hilarious.

Used to tape the key down on the phones in
the ER and set them next to radiacs or
pumps all throughout the ER. EOOW had
almost every one isolated when I heard
"ELT 2JV!"

On 704 there was an escape hatch from
radio directly down into the galley above the
diswashing sink. We would open it and mess
with the nubs on crank duty. They would
look everywhere but straight up. We got
one guy convinced he was hearing voices
and was really getting freaked out. We did
have to let him off the hook before he got
himself Disqualified.

Was at the "smoke pit" after watch and a
nub asked me to sign his qual sheet. As a
joke I offered to sign his sheet if he took a
drag off his smoke through his nostril.
Before I could finish yelling, "What the hell
is wrong with you?!" he had taken the drag
and was coughing so hard his eyes were
bloodshot.

On 605, sending nubs back to ERLL to ask
MM2(SS) for a "Red Tag Special." M-Div.
grease locker nearby. Trying to remember
Mom's childhood advice of, "If they didn't

like you, they wouldn't mess with you," trying to get all the G.P. grease out of your crack.

Non-Quals coming aft for a can of "striped paint" were fun! They'd get taped up and hung upside-down from the overhead while we gave them "checkout" on the ship's gravity system.

Midshipmen were always fun. We actually caught one trying to enter the RC while underway because he couldn't figure out how to go forward. New ensigns were entertaining also because we Nukes got them first! Always had fun doing exactly what they told us to do. Scrammed the plant twice!

The CAMP Watch told an SKSA, that "MHC stood for "Mayonnaise, Horseradish, and Catsup," and was designed to send condiments for hot dogs back to the Nukes in the Feed Bay. I had to keep walking away to avoid LMAO.

Had a fellow RM on 694 that used to set up chad-bombs in snuff/dip cans. He'd load a Skoal or Copenhagen can with chad and then rig up a paper clip and rubber band inside. When some nub asked him for a dip they would get a ton of chad sprayed on them.

Speaking of Midshipmen, reminds me of the time we were on a Middie Op, had this big, tough Navy linebacker on board for his 2 weeks of heroism. He overheard a conversation in the Crew's Mess about "making a hot fudge sundae" out of a non-qual. There was a can of cherries, a can of whipped cream, some heated fudge sauce, and some ice cream with a scoop. The only thing lacking was a non-qual to put it on.

So, Mr. Midshipman Joe Palooka says, and I quote, "There aren't enough of you guys to do that to me." Let us draw the kindly curtain of time across this scene, except to note that the Captain came through to investigate the screams, filled his coffee cup, shook his head and muttered, "Middies," as he headed up to Control.

One of my favorites was to staple the arms and legs of guys' poopie suits shut just before a drill set. Then stand at the end of berthing and watch the hilarity begin at the first drill.

One MM1 Nuke used to draw a red line across nubs' necks while they were sleeping with a felt tip pen. He would usually follow up the next day with the comment to the nub about how he "could have killed them while they were sleeping." The poor guys usually wouldn't sleep for a week.

At quarters in AMR1, on 616(G), we all used to stand with our hands on the overhead pipes. We decided it looked like we were riding on a bus. When our MMCS would come in we'd let him talk for five minutes before informing him we couldn't hear him because he wasn't on the bus.

Had an MM1 who used to relieve me late for AMR1 watch. He slept right outside in the missile compartment, so I started using the Freon frisker with the tip removed to wake him. Gives you a pretty nice shock. After two or three times I never got relieved late again.

One midshipman complained to the skipper about his "greasing." The Captain then said, "At least you won't get hemorrhoids."

When I became COB as a very junior E7, I had no idea how much Toilet Paper to order, so I went to the boat alongside and talked to the Salty old Seadog COB there, and he told me, "two rolls per man per week." I went back to my boat and filled out my 1250, had second thoughts and ordered 1,000 extra rolls. Surely did not want to run out on my first patrol as COB. Towards the end of the patrol, I realized I had way too much TP, so I went into the Crew's Mess at lunchtime and announced, "This is RUMOR only, we are running out of TP." Within an hour all excess TP was gone.

We did an E.B. Green mummy-job to a yardbird on the lower level table, completely mummifying him and then left him for his mates to find.

FROM: Mike Hanlon, USS Finback in 1984
—

Again we were doing what we did best punching holes in the ocean and it was a quiet op; no big things pending, no ORSE, TRE, or any major exam, just protecting the nation. I went to take a shower and was pretending to be an ST and enjoyed nice long shower. But something was amiss....the shower drain was plugged and before long I noticed my feet were covered and I had to interrupt this wonderful escape to clean the dreaded shower drain! Oh God, was that disgusting as I dug out all the hair, soap scum and other foreign matter, then I thought to myself, I hope the guy before me hadn't put anything nasty in the drain trap on this casual outing. I finished cleaning the drain, jumped back into the shower, I was glad that the drain was clear and functioning properly. After finishing the shower I got all duded up, clean skivvies, clean socks, clean poopie suit, I looked like a rock star. The mess deck was full of something so I headed aft to shoot the breeze with one of my favorite shipmates. We always had a good time telling sea stories and just yukking it up. Another shipmate, the LELT, came aft and we had a real live shoot the s*#t session in the aft port corner of M2UL. We were all telling different lies and sea stories and people noticed how nice I smelled and looked and commented on it. I then had to tell the story of the dreaded shower drain and what I had just encountered. Now Pat was very straight laced and John and I could be pretty crude. John and I were aghast to hear this disgusting prattle because we couldn't imagine a subsailor clogging up the shower like that. Pat thought we were the crudest people on the planet so to prove our point, we started a survey of everyone that walked past us and as someone would pass, we would ask them, "hey when was the last time you used the shower on the boat?" We got numerous responses, ranging from one week ago, ten days ago, a month ago but my favorite response was from Mike, an electrician and he said....WHAT TIME IS IT??? It was a hilarious time on the boat, but Pat still thought everyone was kidding, which made us laugh even harder....Now you know the rest of the story. We were easily entertained.

FROM:  Dave Shepardson, USS JACK
SSN-605 –

<u>SUBJECT.</u>

Funniest Exchanges:

Shortly after I reported to the USS JACK
SSN-605, with the old AN/BQS-13, we
were doing some war-games and were
supposed to go active and the Sonar
Supervisor told the active operator to train
the system to 180 degrees relative, and do a
full power ping.  Over the 27MC came:
"Sonar/Conn…What was that?"
"Conn/Sonar, we just unleashed the acoustic
hounds of hell!"  "Sonar/Conn, Aye."

From:  An interview with Norman Fearing
Skiles, WWII Submariner –

We visited at the kitchen table and reviewed his memorabilia, including his scrap book.

He made Chief and was saved in 1953 and is a good Christian man active in his church.

He joined the Navy, for a six year hitch, to see the world with his buddy in September of 1941 at 18 years of age.

While at Sub School his first dive was aboard the O-9 boat, and it leaked profusely.

Sailed under Captain Sam Dealey aboard HARDER SS-257, and was out of Pearl Harbor for the 1st three war patrols, then moved to Perth, and left the boat with ten others that had made the first five war patrols with him just before she was sunk on her sixth.

HARDER had the HOR engines which broke down a lot, but they were able to move the boat at 23 knots, a full 3 knots faster than the other boats running the other engines.

On the 5$^{th}$ patrol the last DD (Destroyer) was shot at in very close quarters while submerged or at PD, but Dealey missed. A scout plane sent the enemy Destroyer over to the boat. The Japanese fleet was moving out of port when they picked the DD off. HARDER barely had time to prep the tubes for the shot. They were primarily there to count the number of ships the Japanese Navy was moving out of port. The DD ran above them while at 80' and dropped depth charges which really rocked them. He is unsure how the boat survived that pattern as the DD was right above them.

Another time on HARDER, they located a DD on sonar, and sent two fish his way but missed. Dealey made a high-speed dive while silent running and lost control of the boat. She went down to 700' or 800' and came back up to 250', and survived the depth charges that were dropped. They ended up sinking the DD which was also carrying 80 Jap survivors from a DD that they had sunk the day before.

He was on USS SARDA SS-488, with Chester Nimitz, Jr as CO, and William

Anderson (future CO of USS NAUTILUS SSN-571) as XO.

He was one time a Sonar Instructor at Sub School, NLON, because Radiomen at that time were the sonar operators. He left New London for USS SEA CAT SS-399 or the USS SEA POACHER SS-406, and was then transferred to USS CUBERA SS-347.

Says Nimitz was on USS HADDO SS-255 in a wolf-pack with USS HARDER SS-257 and HAKE SS-256 who were members of SubRon12.

A professor at one of the Australian universities wrote a book on HADDO referencing her being a destroyer killer.

He has a scrapbook with WWII pictures, some of which are at the Royal Hawaiian Hotel at Pearl Harbor, HI. Some of his pictures were confiscated by the censors at the time, and promised to be returned to him after the war, which did not happen.

At one time was on the relief crew aboard USS GRIFFIN AS-13.

He was on patrol once, and topside at night for one-hour shifts, when the CO allowed the Radiomen to come up for fresh air once in a while as the after-lookout. He was looking out astern at the phosphorescent wake and the bright moonlight for any aircraft that were forcing them to dive during the daytime hours. He was looking around through the binoculars when a QM3, who was on his first boat, accidently, hit the diving alarm. The COW automatically opened the vents and he moved fast to get below being covered from the spray coming out of the vents. The QM3 was thence nicknamed "Crash Dive."

Picked up USS HARDER after Radioman School in the Panama Canal as she was transiting to the Pacific and Pearl Harbor.

Favorite Sea Stories as seen on facebook –

Telephone Dillema.

While in Norway, on the last day before we got back underway, I went out to the bar with two other guys, one a dude from California, and the other an Indian straight off of the reservation. We're at the bar for a while, and they get into a contest, (I was the non-drinking peer-leader). The Indian orders two "Prairie Fires", (that's a shot of Tequila with a finger of Tabasco Sauce). So after a few of these, we all decided it's time to go. The Indian made his way to the boat solo, but my California friend and I go over the square to some pay phones outside a quickie mart. I'm struggling to follow the instructions on the back of my phone card, and my friend is sitting on the bench near the quickie mart door. After several failed attempts to call home, my friend gets impatient and demands that I give him the phone. He starts punching numbers, seemingly at random. Sometimes he's even looking at the phone when he hits the numbers. I swear I saw him palm the whole number pad one time. Anyway, after a bit, he hands me the phone and says he needed to sit down on the bench. As I watch him barely able to make it to the bench, I hear the phone begin to ring. It actually got through! I don't know how the phone company does it, but apparently phone cards only work when you're three sheets to the wind!

A Midshipmen Cruise.

On a midshipmen cruise the midshipmen took over our qualified lounge and refused to let us in so we tagged out the power to the lounge so they would leave and actually do the mock qual sheet we made for them... The Engineer Officer was the OOD that night and being a non-academy boy he gladly signed off on the tag out.

Same midshipmen cruise: Those guys wouldn't get up for Field Day; they said they didn't have to; so we broke 2 boxes full of chem- lights in a bucket made it glow. A couple donned chicken suits and grabbed a broke radiac meter. Then stuck the COB's mega phone through the curtains and announced... "slow reactor coolant leak"; then threw the glowing water on the deck of their rack space then sent the guys in wearing EAB's and the radiation meter screaming and yelling. The shocked and panicked look on their faces when they came running out in their boxer shorts was priceless!

EB Green.

Quietly EB-greening someone in their rack just before the battle stations drill or before field day; or placing the high-tensile tape on the outside of their curtain and watching them try and get out.

Rack Weighting.

Another good one was putting TDU weights underneath the mattress on somebody's bunk and waiting to see how long it took for them to notice the increased weight whenever they lifted up their mattress.

Submarine Dictionary, nuclear version.

Tweener- Not a nuke, technically not a Coner... Missile Techs.

Port and Starboard Duty- Identical to Vulcan Death Watches.

S.W.I.M.S.- (Acronym to remember the required actions for responding to a radioactive spill):

Stop, Walk away, Ignore the problem, Make up a story and Stick to it.

Incident Report- What any nuke gets published when he violates reactor safety protocols

Fact-Finding Mission- See also Witch Hunt. Directly precedes an incident report.

Green Screen of Death - What you get for standing watch in sonar staring at that monitor screen in a dark room and listening to the ocean. AKA 6 hours of extra sleep.

Red Screen of Death - Trying to stay awake at periscope depth at night watching those little f'ing red lights go back and forth and getting smacked in the back of the head by the Diving Officer for broaching the boat.

FROM:  Corry Clinton, USS RHODE ISLAND SSBN-740(G) –

A simple and effective prank is to daily cut off just a little bit of somebody's belt. They won't notice, but they'll soon be obsessed with getting fat. Over a long patrol, it really adds up. It's subtle, so I don't know how well it'd work in a book. And as a disclaimer, that was a friend's trick, not mine. As the COMMO I devoted myself to spreading rumors, which was often satisfying in and of itself!

FROM:  Dan Craw, ETC(SS),        USS TANG SS-563
USS GATO SSN-615
USS PHILADELPHIA SSN-690
USS BREMERTON SSN-698
USS AUGUSTA SSN-710 –
Heavy.

When I was on the USS GATO SSN-615,
out of New London we end up with a young
Sonarman with the nickname of Heavy.

We were operating off of NY/NJ in the
Narrow Bay Op Areas with a couple of other
boats, all taking turns tracking and shooting
weapons at each other. The time was Oct
1973. We had just finished shooting a
weapon and went up for our com period.
One of the messages was for all boats to
return to New London, load out and with-in
a day head for the Med as Israel was just
attached and it looked like the Russians
were going to step in.

We all raced in and tied up at State Pier, two
alongside the Tender and three alongside the
pier. We were alongside the pier and loaded
food, while the other two boats loaded war
shot weapons. Then we did a dance in the
middle of the river and went alongside the
tender and loaded weapons and the other
two boats loaded food. Then the next day we
all made a high speed run across to the Med.

So what does this have to do with a Heavy?
We were short a Sonarman and got one from
Squadron, just out of school, that was
waiting for his boat to come back from a
northern run. He showed up just as we sat

the Maneuvering Watch so they had him put his sea bag in the crews mess and sent him topside to help on the #3 mooring line. He was standing around up there watching all the line handlers throwing and retrieving their heavies. Finally he picked one up and was looking at it when someone asked him if he knew what it was; his answer led us to believe that he had invented the heavy. So one of the guys told him, you are so good at it, shows us. So this kid takes his heavy, separates the coil into two sections, one in each hand, raises both arms and swings them in different directions and let go with both hands and throws the heavy into the water. By the time someone stopped him he had thrown five heavies into the water. So it was easy picking a nickname for him. I think that other than the YN and Heavy, I was the only other person on the boat to know his name.

Heavy was put on Mess Cooking duty just after we got to sea and the very next morning was washing up getting ready for breakfast with the leading cook in the crews head when he turned, looked at Andy, the leading cook, and asked: "So how do we get our mail at sea".

The Mail Buoy.

When Andy heard the question, it was like a
light turning on above his head. All Andy
said at the time was, we could retrieve it off
of the Mail Buoy. The two of them finished
washing up and went in, prepared Breakfast
for the on/off going watches and cleaned up
after all had eaten. At that point Andy sent
someone for a complete set of rain gear, life
vest, heavy and a boat and grappling hooks.
He them gave them to Heavy and told him
to put on rain gear and life vest and to keep
the rest of the gear with him at all times until
we came across the "Mail Buoy". Andy also
told Heavy that the newest guy on the boat
was also ways given the honor of being the
"Mail Buoy Retriever". Andy told Heavy to
sit in the back of Crews Mess and wait for
the word from Control that they had located
the Buoy and at that time to proceed to
Control.

Heavy did as he was told, sit and wait, wait
and sit. All this time the crew was going
about a normal day a sea while transiting
across the Atlantic. Most would stop, take
one look at Heave sitting there, dress in the
rain gear and life vest, with the Heavy, boat
and grappling hooks, let a little laugh out,
shake their head and walk off. Others would
ask him what he was doing and Heavy
would answer: "I'm the Mail Buoy

Retriever". At that point they would laugh a little and walk off.

Heavy sat there until it was time for Lunch, served and cleaned up lunch and then resumed his "Mail Buoy Retriever" duties until dinner. At that point Andy told Heavy that they were not able to locate the "Mail Buoy", but someone would let him know if and when they did.

Heavy gave Andy all the gear and equipment back, served dinner and when to his rack. Just before the evening movie a messenger walked into the crews mess and told Andy that the Captain wanted to see him "NOW" in his stateroom. The crews mess broke out in screams, Andy broke out in a sweat. Andy waked in to the CO Stateroom and was told to close the door; Andy wanted to die. Our Captain, D. G. Harsheid, looked at Andy and said, "I understand that you had Heavy dress and waiting on a 'Mail Buoy Watch' all day". Andy took a deep breath and said, "Yes Sir". The CO then looks at Andy and asks, "Do you think you could get him to do it again"? *At which point Andy about piss in his pants* and with a big smile answered "YES SIR". The CO told Andy to have Heavy serve Breakfast and them wait and when the he was ready he would send a messenger down and tell Andy to get Heavy read.

The next morning, after breakfast the CO calls away the Fire Control Tracking Party and sends the Messenger of the Watch down to have Andy get Heavy ready and send him up to Control. A few minutes later in walks Heavy loaded down with more lines and equipment then he could hold. The Tracking Party was busy tracking the "Mail Buoy" under the supervision of the XO, Sonar was calling in bearing to it, the O.D. was preparing the boat to go to PD; for a new guy this must have looked like a major undertaking. At some point in time the XO walks up to Heavy, who was standing next to me and the Plotter, looks a Heavy and told him, if he dropped the mail bag back into the water, then that would be the end of his liberty in the Med. Heavy looked a little scared at that point.

For what must have seemed like hours to Heavy, but was only about 20 minutes or so while we prepared to go to PD, Sonar was tracking the Buoy. Then the Sonar Supervisor calls in and told the CO, "Con Sonar, we have been locked on the wrong Buoy. Instead of tracking the "Male Buoy" we had been tracking the "Female Buoy".

Sonar corrected itself and that we are now on the correct Buoy." Harsheid replied, "Very Well". The place broke out in loud laughter. I thought we were going to have to pick someone up off of the deck.

Finally the CO gave the word to proceed to PD and up we went. Heavy was standing their looking at me with excitement in his eyes and said, "Oh boy, I'm going to get the Mail". When we reached PD the CO called out a few bearing to the "Mail Buoy" and then told all in the Control Room that he was going to make a 1MC announcement. At that point he tells the rest of the crew what had been going on, that this was a good learning experience, something that goes on, on all the boats, that Heavy was a good sport about it as had the crew and he thanked all for that. It was about this time that Heavy figured out what was going on and joined in with the laughter that was going on. The CO then secured the Tracking Party and Heavy, turned the Conn over to the O.D. and life on the boat went on.

FROM:        Michael Atwell –

Acronyms.

PAPERCLIP – People Against People Ever Reenlisting; Civilian Life is Preferred.

BOHICA – Bend Over, Here It Comes Again.

FROM: David Bridges –

SNOB – Shortest Nuke On Board.

FROM: Daniel Brown –

Disgusting Memory.

Plastic COW or fake COW – The UHT (Ultra High Temp) treated milk that replaced the fresh kind when supplies ran out, usually after a week or two underway!

FROM: Quinton Dively –

## Junior Officers.

I thought it was pretty good before Blue Nose when the A-gangers stole the CO's stateroom door and hid it in the Torpedo Room. About an hour later the general alarm went off to "MAN BATTLE STATIONS". The CO took it in good stride but told the crew over the 1MC that whoever found the door would be greatly rewarded. Well needless to say they never found it.........and they tore my room apart. Then when the CO noticed that the JO's were laughing their ass's off....he thought they had something to do with it.......so he gave a direct order to the A-gangers to remove all of the JO stateroom doors, mattress's, pillows, & sh*#ter door and stack them in the CO's passage way and made the JO's stand watch (log book, kevlar vest & helmet, watch belt, and walkie-talkie) in the passageway after they got off watch. It was awesome. I know someone out there took pics of the ordeal. Needless to say that the JO's were not to happy with the enlisted.

FROM: Josh Hoops –

<u>Prank.</u>

The craziest prank I ever saw was when one
of my ELT's dressed up in Anti C's on the
midwatch, came up to control while I was
standing OOD, carrying a primary sample
bottle (with a loose cap), tripping and
spilling it all over the dive, helm and
planes... I noticed immediately that the
bottle said FTO all over it, but, the dive
(who just happened to be the COB... yes, I
said the COB) was not as observant... He
freaked out, got on the 1MC, and announced
"Spill in Control!". Needless to say, I (as
the CRA) was having to explain to the CO
why my ELT thought it was a good idea to
conduct spill training on the midwatch... in
control.

FROM: Steve Ishay –

ACRONYMS:

LIFER – Lazy Ignorant Fool Expecting Retirement.

Definitions:

Grotopotomus (Grotopoto-for short) – Female species in/near Groton, CT.

Bremelo – West Coast version of the Grotopoto found in/near Bremerton and Silverdale, WA.

FROM: Jason Lane –

CPO Door.

We took the CPO bunk door and hid it in the freezer while the MS's did inventory. They didn't get it back for over a week.

FROM: Matthew Larkin –

Revenge.

While I was cranking I had been having a prank war with an MM2 on our boat for several underways. I don't remember what all led up to it, but I woke up one morning with my toenails painted green. I swore my revenge. I made up a bunch of the large sheet pans full of green jello. I swapped out his mattress for the jello, and made his rack back up, sheets and all. Unfortunately, I got the wrong rack.

FROM: Jim Manning, USS FLASHER SSN-613 –

Loudmouth NQP Mitigation.

We had a Seaman Apprentice, short s**t, non-qual puke, loud mouth check aboard the USS FLASHER, claiming this was his boat. Yea that's what we said!
That day and probably averaging 3-4 times a

week he was wrapped head to toe in EB green tape and placed in various parts of the boat (the best place was shaft alley bilge).


FROM:  John Martinez –

Terms that I can remember and their definitions:

NUB - non-useful body; non-watch standing MO FO; without Dolphins

NUKE- most smartest people on any submarine

CONER - forward-riding personnel designated to protect the reactor and the precious engine room at all times; oxygen consumers

SONAR TECH - person designated to change out that roll of toilet paper over the multi-million dollar tracking system; person who cannot go through an entire watch without getting relieved to take a shower

ORSE - some kind of inspection designed to keep an entire crew of people up for 36 hours while NUKEs take pop quizzes on 16-

factor power formulas and walk around in daisy-chained houka-masks pretending to put out 'Back Draft' type fires and sleep on the floor in 1-hour shots.

MONKEY BUTT - condition in which continued wiping only results in the 'Red Ass.' Can only be alleviated by warm, soapy shower

SHAFT ALLEY - aptly named, area from which entire crew is screwed

MIDSHIPMEN OPS - morale-building underways designed to keep crews away from their children during the summer. I mean, why would I want to see my kids when they're home every day...

RICKOVER - mean, god-like figure known for teaching the Air Force how to spend wisely by building an entire building with a reactor from $600 hammers and $1000 toilet seats

GRADE 'D' but EDIBLE - type of meat served on submarines (seriously, that's what the damn package said.) no matter how long you cook it, will always remain gray in color

JASPER - peanut butter higher in quality

than JIF

MEGGER - party favor used to put your friends in a jovial mood. most effective when applied to exposed steel toe on a chukka boot

DECK DIV PETTY OFFICER - "smart" coner in charge of leading 'baby' coners in using paint-by-number method of painting submarine; 1 = BLACK

SNORKEL JUICE - extremely rare designer cologne. smell can only be removed by other toxic waste

NON-SKID - top-rated Navy-issued facial skin defoliator; also useful in keeping your drunk-ass butt from just slipping past the drunken lines

GMT - general misuse of time; usually during your 'on-coming' time; relative of FIELD DAY

BEQ - Nuclear version of "The Skulls." ; cannot go into it any further, I would have to 'kill you' if I told you anymore

FROM: Jeff Miller –

SKIP (Submarine Knowledge Impaired Person) -- Politically correct version of NUB.

FROM: Patrick Muldoon –

FOLO - First On Last Off = Any Nuke.

<u>Submariners.</u>

It is amazing the sarcastic and funny crap that a bunch of over-intelligent misfits, like us submariners, can come up with while spending long hours on watch punching holes through the water. I've never laughed as hard as I did after watch on our Med cruise sitting on the Crews Mess. We had some guys that should've become pro comedians.

FROM: Robert Smith –

FLOB NQP - Free Loading Oxygen Breathing Non Qualified Puke.

Boat Nicknames:

L.U.R.F. = (for the Engineer) Little Ugly Red-headed F@#%.

On 706 = Goomba and Spike

For two brothers on 727 = 1-ton and ½ ton.

A cook "Butch", nobody could remember his name, hence: Petty Officer Butch.

An IC'man 3rd named "Chuckie" who resembled the Chuckie Doll from the scary movie.

An STSC named "Flash" who only had one speed.

An A-Ganger named "Spooge".

"Spit Chunk" for a guy that sneezed his teeth to the deep six.

"Poopie" who blew sanitaries on himself while sitting down.

"Dome" = bald on top.

"Monk" = bald on top in the back only.

"Hungry" for a large and heavy eating TM. Stay out of his way in the chow line.

Y.A.F.I. = You're A Freakin' Idiot.

"Hatchplug" for a fat boy aboard.

"Wedge" – the 2$^{nd}$ simplest tool.

"Garsky and Hatch" – while Starsky and Hutch was on TV.

"Snaggle Puss" – for a TM that was beard-growing challenged.

For three Poles' names ending in SKI – Big Ski, Little Ski, and Middle Ski.

Radioman Chief named "Suitcase."

Sonarman named "Odd Body."

TM named "Hog Body."

A COB named "Buckets."

A cook named "Bubbles" found in head sick and blowing bubbles in the toilet.

B.I.F.F. = Big Ugly Fat F#$%.

"Wing Nut" = a guy with large ears.

"PooPoo" = MM-Nuke victim of sharting accident while on watch.

"Telegraph" = had two permanent oblong bald spots each side of head, ie: half-a-head.

"P.U.M.A." = Possibly the Ugliest Man Alive.

On 698(G) STS2 "Scumbag" and a career deck-ape "YOB" = BOY spelled in reverse.

For the COB on 704 = "Clueless Overweight Bastard."

"P9" for a nuke on 615-his name began with P and had 9 unpronounceables following.

ST on 620 named "J.A.F.O." = Just Another F@#%ed-up Observer.

"Poof" = Nuke Electrician.

"Biggie" for Bigelow.

A JO as "Dr. D." for looking like Doctor Demento.

"Beaner" for STS2 for looking Mexican.

"Boozer" a real last name, no attempt at re-naming.

"Uncle Pervie" for MMC who looked the part.

"WANG" for EMC resembling Emperor Wang from Flesh Gordon.

Aboard L.Y. Spear, "Cleo" a Lithographer with artistic ability like Leonardo DaVinci.

L.U.R.F.F. = Little Ugly Round Fat Fellow.

"Winnie" = short for real name Winthrop, former LELT.  Now goes by Win.

"SPRADOGG."  No explanation offered.

"Tommy Toolbox" EN1 on Gudgeon.

"Flapper" an A-Ganger, for 'sanitary incident' reason.

"Pizza Pie" for TM2 on Shark for occasionally making mid-rats Pizzas.

"Dirt" for a guy that was shower challenged.

"Bunsen" and "Honeydew" for a COB from LaFayette and Alabama resembling Muppet.

Yelling "Doc" brought both the HM and the Doctor on Boomers.

"Chewie" for resembling Chewbacca from Star Wars, and he resented the name.

"Nazi Dick" an XO who looked like an SS Officer.

On 619(B) – "Horsemeat," "Mule Dick," and "Godfather."

On 728 – "Colonel."

For 2 MT's reported aboard simultaneous names ended ING = "Ing-1" and "Ing-2."

"Fatty McWaste-a-rack" for an undieting Nuke.

"Tank" Nuke on 664 whose actual name was Tahnk.

"Skeletor" for XO on Maryland for being so gaunt.

"T. Spoon" for actual name of Tom Spoon for his whole life; also tattooed as such.

"Tattoo" for 5'2" height-challenged shipmate.

"Night Stick" for a scary MT.

"San-2" for a guy that did not take showers, even after field day bilge diving.

"Butter Bean" for resembling the wrestler in shape.

"Schmoo" for a Weapons Officer.

"Lurch" for a Nuke on 723 that stood well over 6', resembled the Adam's Family butler.

"Big Dan the Augment Man," XO aboard 615 on an '84 Med Run.

"Strawberry" – did not divulge the reason.

"Hurricane" - For a cook on 694, because of after-meal galley condition.

Three on 615-Allan, Allen and Alan; "Big Al," "Little Al", and "Captain" cuz he wuz.

"Notso" for a guy named Sharpe.

"Gibbles and Titts" for 2 nubs named Gibson and Tittle.

"Trixie" for a MT nub whose name was unpronounceable.

"Ranger Richter" for Richter of Whale.

"FERD" for Fernandez aboard 634.

"Skimmer" for a nub during the 'Great Dolphin Giveaway.'

"Diggler" he had to support himself or be on the ball valve.

"Catfish" because he looked like one.

"Kitty" because he smelled like sour milk.

"Darkness" no explanation needed.

"Fluffy" don't know how, but it stuck.

"Stevie-6" was born with six fingers.

"Spaceshot."

"Paper."

"Crappio" for real name Carpio.

"Big Dumb" for a stupid A-Ganger, also referred to as "Dumb," for short even by wives.

"Charley _____ [fill in the last name] for several junior men on 664, but not real name.

On Oly – "Jabba the Hutt," (EM), "Herbie Hosenose," (ST), "Gumby," (STCS), "Tyrone," (IC), "Spike," (ICC), "Lee-Hyphen," (ST), "Ginsu," (Nav.), "Brown-Eye," (Nuke), "Reactor Phil," (Nuke MM), "Gonzo," (IC).

"Turkey Lurkey."

"Turd."

"Drobot."

"Super Chunk."

"The Conductor."

"Princess Sassy Pants."

"Rack Kitten."

"Gay J."

"Schlong."

"B-10."

"Schnarf."

"Waffle."

"The Murms."

"Izzy."

"Gremlin."

"Mattress Back.
"Cheeto."

"Bean Dip."

"Cornholio."

"Yardog."

"Doughboy."

"Mickey," looked like Mickey Mouse on 664.

"Stain" – no nickname required.

"Buggles."

"Billydont."

"Wedge" because this nub got stuck in the outboard.

"Rat."

"Toad."

"Twiggy."

"Fast Eddy" QM on 664.

"Cool Breeze."

"Dancing Bear."

"Snake" a certain XO always said "Trust in me," from the movie Jungle Book .

"Skuz."

"Pillow Ass."

"Chunky."

"Lightning," a slow-moving boy from the deep South.

"Bullet."

"Conky."

"Tweedle Dee," from a certain wardroom.

"Tweedle Dum," from same wardroom.

"Dweeb."

"Frankenstien," for resemblance reasons.

"The Buzzard," for the same reasons.

"Weird Dave."

"Cock-La-Tue."

"Goobs."

"Bulky-Knit."

"Sugar-Bear."

"Dendo."

"Possum."

"Sparrow."

"The Brute."

"Hog-Head."

"Mumma," for a Nuke MM – short for Mummy.

"B.D.B.'s" = Brain Dead Boys, stood ERLL in rotation.

"Token."

"Lunchbox."

"Sharkbait."

"Grokno."

"Bulbous."

"Stem."

"Shorty Gordy."

"Wabob."

"House Mouse," for being the smallest man in the Division.

"Bubba," for an A-Ganger aboard Jack.

"Droopy," for resembling Droopy the 1960's cartoon dog.

"Willllburrr," for Weps on Jack, parody of Mr. Ed the 1960's TV show.

"Nnnervy," for RMC who got shocked a lot and shook like a Mexican jumping bean.

"Vegetable," for another A-Ganger.

"Balou," for resembling the bear in Jungle Book.

On Andrew Jackson, three brothers, "K-1," "K-2," and "K-3."

Twins aboard Cheyenne put in same duty section so swap-duty was preempted.

"Hee-Haw," for a dirt hillbilly striker on 625.

"Buffalo Head," for an Okie from Tulsa with a big noggin and bright red hair.

"D-squared, B-squared," for Deaf, Dumb, Blind and Bald.

"Samich," on 720 for last name of Reuben.

"Fuzzy."

"Mad Dog," named by TMC after biting the XO on the leg during field day, by mistake.

"Terminator."

"Iron Mike."

"X-Ray."

"Bad Dog."

"Baho Bulgebelly,"  his truck held just enough booze for 2 weeks.

"Hitch."

A QM named WilHELM.

A HM named HERTling.

"Scrotum", but the CO did not approve; altered to "Scroat."

"Big Daddy Rick," with the silent P.

"Mumbles," "Goober," "Wacko."

"Wrong Way _____," 635(G) for Dave the QM.

"Swimmer," for 664 Nuke MM who liked to jump in when drunk.

"Stark Naked," ENG caught him showering ERLL watch conden. purfier while H2O-rats.

"Smiff," for FT Smith on 664.

"Spot."

"Country."

"Hebe."

"Stretch."

"Eddie Two Star."

"Mikey the Hit Man."

"Shorty."

"Tiny," for a big MM on 664.

"Stormin' Norman."

"Butterball."

"Stump."

"Sully."

"GD-it."

"Flounder," on 605 resembled same in Animal House movie.

"Ballsio," Nuke MM.

"Flipper," real last name Dolphin on Gato.

"Gunny Wingnut," bull nuke who liked exercising drills with perpendicular ears.

"Three-Bladed Wingnut," Nuke MMC on Olympia for stand-out ears and long thin nose.

"Booger," cause he was hand-picked to be Asst. Nav. by CO.

"Moose," a Nuke MM.

"Flex," ESMer who liked to work out a lot.

"Rum Cake,"

"Johnny Gerbil Ass."

"Bed Wetter," for a new kid on board named Ledbetter.

"Splash," for an ELT on Parche.

"Cheese," an A-Ganger.

"Boney," for last name Bonebrake.

"Physco," with Physco tattooed on his chest (Psycho) misspelled by tattooer.

"Scruffy," for a CTM rider.

"Soupy."

"Rico Suave," on the 720.

"Bingo," on Tullibee.

"Squealy."

"Rerun."

"Little Kid."

"Seaman Shoeleather," after his Captain's Mast.

"Warhead."

"Rabbit."

"Lube Oil."

"Mr. Clean."

"Whip."

"G.I. Joe."

"Peaches."

"Pappy."

"Air Bank."

"Patches," for a guy with bald spots all over his head.

"Mush Mouth."

"Andy," real name Anderson.

"H-12," for a Germanic name beginning with H followed by 11 letters, on Aspro.

"Jake."

"Vanlooneybin."

"Tigger."

"Ox."

"Bull."

"Hambone."

# *GLOSSARY.*

**Ships Mentioned** (in order of appearance):

USS FLORIDA SSBN-728

USS CARBONERO SS-337

USS TANG SS-563

USS BARON VON STEUBEN SSBN-632

USS STONEWALL JACKSON SSBN-734

USS WILLIAM H. BATES SSBN-680

USS TUSCALOOSA CA-37

USS CHICAGO SSN-721

USS KAMEHAMEHA SSBN-642

USS NAUTILUS SSN-571

USS BECUNA SS-319

USS THRESHER SSN-593

USS PIPER SS-409

USS SUNBIRD ASR-15

USS SEAWOLF SSN-575

USS SEA ROBIN SS-407

USS GRAYBACK LPSS-574

USS GEORGE C. MARSHALL SSBN-654

USS TECUMSEH SSBN-628

USS CUTLASS SS-478

USS CARP SS-338

USS STURGEON SSN-637

USS TULLIBEE SSN-597

USS TINOSA SSN-606

USS HADDOCK SSN-621

USS SEA DEVIL SSN-664

USS TIGRONE AGSS-419

USS COBBLER SS-344

USS BAYA SS-318

USS HENRY CLAY SSBN-625

USS GUDGEON SS-567

USS POMFRET SS-391

USS GEORGE BANCROFT SSBN-643

USS TRITON SSN-586

USS SENNET SS-408

USS AMBERJACK SS-219

USS RAY SSN-653

USS SPERRY AS-12

USS CAIMAN SS-323

USS SEA OWL SS-405

USS CONSTITUTION "Old Ironsides"

USS INDIANAPOLIS SSN-697

USS GURNARD SS-254

USS ARGONAUT SS-475

USS ARCHERFISH SS-311

USS BALAO SS-285

USS CASIMIR PULASKI SSBN-633

USS JOHN HANCOCK DD-981

USS CAVALLA SS-244

USS THEODORE ROOSEVELT SSBN-600

USS SEAWOLF SSN-575

USS BASHAW SS-241

USS FRANCIS SCOTT KEY SSBN-657

USS TECUMSEH SSN-628

USS HENRY CLAY SSBN-625

USS OMAHA SSN-692

USS GEORGE WASHINGTON SSBN-598

USS SAND LANCE SSN-660

USS DIABLO SS-479

USS REINA MERCEDES IX-25

USS JALLO SS-368

USS FLASHER SSN-613

USS MISSOURI BB-63

USS BLACKFIN SS-322

USS FINBACK SS-230

USS HALFBEAK SS-352

USS THOMAS JEFFERSON SSBN-618

USS REDFIN SS-272

USS SCORPION SSN-589

USS SKYLARK ASR-20

USS GATO SSN-615

USS TILLS DE-748

USS ARNOLD J. ISABELL DD-869

USS DEWEY DLG-14

USS JACK SSN-605

USS FRANKLIN D. ROOSEVELT CV-42

USS TICONDEROGA CVA/CVS-14

USS CHOPPER SS-342

USS ATULE SS-403

USS GRENADIER SS-525

USS ENTEMEDOR SS-340

USS POLLACK SSN-603

USS SARDA SS-488

USS SEA CAT SS-399

USS SEA POACHER SS-406

USS CUBERA SS-347

USS HADDO SS-255

USS HARDER SS-257

USS HAKE SS-256

USS GRIFFIN AS-13

USS RHODE ISLAND SSBN-740

USS PHILADELPHIA SSN-690

USS BREMERTON SSN-698

USS AUGUSTA SSN-710

USS FLASHER SSN-613

USS  GROUPER AGSS-214

USS CARBONERO SS-337

USS OHIO SSBN-726

**12 K**

Referring to the 12,000 gallon per day still which converts sea water into fresh water by electrolysis.

**1250**

A requisition form for drawing from the supply system.

**9901**

The numerical designator of a Nuclear Power School graduate.

**"A" School**

Generally the first of a series of specialized training facilities for a particular rating.

**After Battery**

Crew's berthing spaces aft of the Crew's Mess on a diesel boat.

**After Engine Room**

Engine Room No. Two  aft of ER1 on a diesel boat.

## After Room

The After Torpedo Room aft of the Maneuvering Room on a dieselboat.

## Auxiliaryman

The Machinist's Mates in A-Gang that are in charge of most mechanical equipment in the Non-Engineering spaces.

## Baby Nukes

In process of matriculating Nuclear Power School.

## Bathythermograph

A recording device used to measure the temperature of the water immediately around the boat.

## Berthing

Designated sleeping areas containing bunks and lockers.

## Billet

The placement of a sailor into a crewmember slot.

## Binnacle List

A list of sick and off-duty personnel deemed so by the medical  staff, and reported to the XO.

## Bluejacket

Term for the enlisted sailor, who is issued his blue jacket in bootcamp.

## Blue Nose

The term for a sailor who has passed above the Artic Circle line of demarcation at approximately 65 degrees north latitude.

## Blue Shirts

Enlisted men below the grade of Chief Petty Officer.

## Bollard

A large line fastening pier mount used to tie up boats.  The shape of it was something like the old kids' punch dummies that you could not knock down.

**Boon-Dockers**

The high-cut black leather work boot issued in Boot Camp.

**Bow Compartment**

Forwardmost compartment housing the Crew's and Chief's berthing spaces and the emergency diesel is in the lower level forward on a 637-Class nuclear submarine.

**Breaker**

A resettable electrical circuit interrupter.

**"The Briny"**

The ocean; the salty sea.

**Brow**

The ramp allowing access to topside from the pier, or from another boat or ship.

**Brow Banner**

The banner that faced toward the head of the pier so people could see the name of the boat, it's hull number and ship's crest. It had grommets in its perimeter and was laced onto the brow railing with light-gauge white line, or probably in "today's Navy", Zip-ties.

## Buoyancy

That property of physical science that allows an object to float, hover, or sink.

## Camel

A small work-float used to chip paint, or paint the ship at the waterline.

## Caution Tag

A yellow tag, one level below a Red Tag.

## Cavitate

The name for the tiny bubbles that form on a fast-rotating propeller moving through the water, that creates noise in the water that an enemy can detect with their passive Sonar, when the bubbles begin to pop.

## Chain of Command

The proper order of rank from the Captain on down.

## Chit

A form to ask permission for something from the Chain of Command.

## CHOP

Pet name for the Supply Officer.

## "Chopper"

Pet military word for helicopter.

## Chronometer

Ship's clocks that have to be wound daily with a key by the Quartermaster of the Watch.

## Collision Alarm

A "siren signal" heard over all the 1MC loudspeakers.

## Come-a-long

A mechanical-advantage racheted cable winching device for taking up slack or extreme pulling ability.

## Control Room

The center of ship's maneuvering, steering and weapons tracking systems, below the Conning Tower on a dieselboat and below the Bridge Access Trunk and the forwardmost Operations Level compartment on a nuke 637-Class fast attack boat. The Lower Level houses the Pump Room.

## Critique

A post-drill evaluation of the mistakes and areas to be bettered in the crew's performance.

## D.B. Cooper

The guy in the 1960's that extorted a lot of money in a suitcase from the airlines, then flew away on a one of their jets and parachuted out with the money over the northwest territories and neither the money nor he was ever heard from again.

## Damage Control Trainer

A school especially for the member of the boat's Damage Control Team on the Groton Connecticut Sub Base where damage control procedures are practiced such as fire, flooding, toxic spills, etc.  These are in New London and San Diego.

## Danger Tag

A red tag about 3"x6" that is placed on equipment to indicate authorized non-use of the equipment for safety purposes.

## Depth Charge

A large canister about the size of a 55 gallon drum full of explosive, set to explode at various depths in order to kill a submarine.

## Diver's Tag

A "Danger" red tag to preempt causing trouble for divers in the water outside the hull.

**Diving Alarm**

A "klaxon horn" heard over all the 1MC loudspeakers.

**Drill**

Repeated casualty simulation to hone a crew to perfection through practice (aboard Submarines the surface navy qualifying statement "this is a drill" is <u>never</u> used; we treat every drill as the "real thing".)

**ECM**

Electronic Counter-Measures Room, the first room going forward from the starboard side of Frame #65 off of the Upper Level Operations passageway on a 637-Class where Electronic Intelligence is broken down identifying all incoming electromagnetic signals and emitters.

**ELT Room** (Nucleonics Lab)

The third room going forward from the port side of Frame #65 on a 637-Class where the Radiation Monitoring Equipment and testing is performed, and chemicals are stored.  Also where the dark-room is for developing film.

## Engine Room Compartment

Aft of the Reactor Compartment both upper level and lower level has assorted machinery for ship's services and propulsion systems on a nuclear submarine.

## Escape Trunk

A double-watertight door sealed access point, able to be pressurized for egress from the boat, one forward and one aft, for shallow-water escape from a sunken submarine.

## Fathometer

A recording device used to measure the depth of the water below the boat's keel.

## Field Day

When the entire crew "turns-to" and cleans up the ship.

**Fire Control**

The system occupying the starboard side of the Control Room on a 637-Class for targeting and firing weapons.

**Fireman's Suit**

Flame-retardant suits for fire-fighters on the Damage Control Team.

**Forward Battery**

The Officers' Berthing and Yoeman Shack aft of the Forward Room on a dieselboat

**Forward Engine Room**

Engine Room No. 1 aft of the After Battery on a diesel boat.

**Forward Room**

The Forward Torpedo Room; most forward room on a diesel boat.

**Foul Weather Gear**

Rain coat, winter coat, boots, etc. used as protection against the "foul" weather.

## Gedunk

Goodies, ie: chips, candy, icecream.

## General Alarm

A "bell-ringing" heard over all the 1MC loudspeakers; used to call the crew to "Battle Stations".

## GERTRUDE

The underwater sound-generating system for, local only, ship-to-ship communications.

## "Glow Boat"

What the Diesel Boat Sailors call the Nuclear Submarines.

## Go Critical

Start the reactor.

## Goat Locker

A pet name for the Chiefs' Quarters.

**Half-Way Night**

At or near the half-way point in a patrol, the crew entertain one another with fun antics, which may include sing-a-longs, skits, etc.

**Head**

Bathroom containing commodes and sinks.

**Helo**

Short for Helicopter.

**Hogan's Alley**

Port side alcove with a limited number of bunks in the After Battery on a diesel boat. Also the location of the Medical Locker.

**Inclinometer**

A curved device operating on the same principle as the bubble in a carpenter's level, that is calibrated to show the up or down angle of the boat, relative to level, which the stern-planesman controls. A second inclinometer shows the list on the ship athwartships.

**Jury-Rigged**

Put together in an unconventional manner, and sometimes comically, ie: Rube Goldberg.

**LP Blower**

The Low Pressure blower that sends low pressure air to some ship's service air lines and is connected to the ballast tanks for the finishing rate of a blow to empty the ballast tanks close to, or on, the surface.

**Liquidometer**

Gauge composed of a siphon for emitting a sample liquid stored in a reservoir or tank and a liquid level sensor for monitoring the level of the sample.

**M-Divver**

Someone in M-Division.

**Maneuvering**

The propulsion-control area of the power plant that turns the shaft operated by the Controllerman aft of ER2 on a diesel boat. Aft of the Engine Room.

**Maneuvering Room Compartment**

Where the Reactor Operator and Engineering section watch man the controls to propel the boat on a nuclear submarine.

**Mess Cook**

A helper to the Ship's Cook (Commissaryman).

**Mess Decks**

The Crew's Mess and Galley area where the enlisted Crew and Chiefs eat.

**Middie**

A short and pet name for Midshipman from the U.S. Naval Academy at Annapolis, Maryland.

**"Mustang"**

An officer who has come up through the ranks from enlisted status.

**NSN**

Navy Supply Number.

**Nav ET**

Electronics Technician/Navigation in charge of the SINS.

**Negative Tank**

A centrally-located ballast tank that the flooding of which would cause the boat to sink as is necessary for an "Emergency Dive", working in an opposite manner to the Safety Tank.

**Neutral Buoyancy**

That state where the ship is in hover, neither sinking nor rising.  Pumping tanks to sea will make the boat lighter and she will rise, and vice versa.

**"O-in-C"**

Officer in Charge.

**Old Salt**

> Any experienced long-time sea-going sailor.

**Operations Compartment**

> Aft of the Bow Compartment – In the Lower Level the Torpedo Room and Auxiliary Machinery Room, and in the Middle Level, the Crew's Mess, Officers' Staterooms, Wardroom, Head, Showers, Storekeepers Shack, Copier Room, Fan Room, and in the Upper Level ECM, Nucleonics Lab Room, Radio Room, Sonar Room, XO and CO Staterooms that share a Head and the Control Room on a 637-Class nuclear submarine.

**PANOPO**

> The 116 men of USS NAUTILUS SSN-571 were to first to "pierce" the North Pole under the Arctic Ice Cap and thus became a unique breed of Blue Nose, which anagram meant: "Pacific to Atlantic via North Pole".

**Parker Check Valve**

A uni-directional valve for the flow control of fluids or gasses.

**Pit Log**

Short for Pitometer Log. Extending below the keel of the boat, as well as on skimmers, a device used to measure the boat's speed relative to the water.

**"Ping-Jockeys"**

Pet word for Sonarmen (sometimes referred to as Sonar Girls).

**Piping Tab**

The definitive book showing all components of all systems aboard, classified TOP SECRET.

**PM cards**    Planned Maintenance cards with procedures to conduct equipment preventative maintenance.

**Polynya**

A "soft spot" in the Arctic ice cap, where there are partially melted pools of slush which are much easier to surface through.

**Port and Starboard**

Six hour watch time-segments followed by six hour rest time-segments.

**Pri-1**

Priority One, or quickly needed.

**Pump Room**

See Control Room.

**psi**

Pounds per square inch of pressure. The

pressure upon the boat's hull increases at a rate

of 44 psi per every 100 feet of depth.

**QMOW**

Quartermaster of the Watch.

**Quals**

The process of learning ship's systems and being "signed off" on line items of a Qualification Card that will eventually lead to Submarine Qualification and earning the coveted Dolphins.

**Quay**

Another word for pier or wharf.

**Radiation Area Sign**

A Magenta on Yellow sign with the familiar radioactivity trefoil icon.

**Radio Room**

Third room going forward on a 637-Class from Frame #65, off of the Upper Lever Operations passageway where the Radiomen stand watches utilizing the advanced communications and teletype equipment.

**Rag Hats**

Referring to enlisted men below the rate of Chief Petty Officer; those who wore the "Dixie-Cup" white hats.

**Reactor Compartment**

Aft of the Operations Compartment beginning at Frame #65 on a 637-Class is the forward bulkhead of this compartment and the Tunnel (above the reactor) leads the Engine Room on a nuclear submarine.

**Recirc**

Short for "Recirculate".

**Safety Tank**

On Nautilus and previous boats, a centrally-located ballast tank that was kept full so that pumping out the water to sea would make the boat lighter creating a positive buoyancy, enabling it to rise.

**Safety Track or Safety Rail**

The continuous safety rail flush with the topside deck and accessible near each hull-penetrating hatch to hook into with the "Life Belt" harness sailors wear in order to be safe from being swept or falling overboard while on deck.

**Sail**

Conning Tower or dorsal fin of a submarine.

**Screw**

Sometimes referring to the main propulsion shaft propeller.

**Shark Watch**

A rifle-armed crewman stationed during Swim Call to ward off sharks while men are in the water and usually stationed atop the sail.

**Shellback**

The term for a sailor who has passed the Equator line of demarcation at zero degrees latitude. Until earning that coveted name, you are referred to as a pollywog.

**Shoal**

A build-up of ocean bottom where grounding of the ship may occur.

**Sig**

Short for "signature" which are required on Qual Cards, Chits and Requisitions to indicate proper authorization.

## Silent Running

At sea, where non-essential equipment that can generate sound into the water, is turned off in order to not betray own ship's position.

## SINS

Ship's Inertial Navigation System located in the after port corner of the Control Room on a 637-Class where satellite cuts are downloaded to the mainframe computer that contain the required information  for locating the latitude and longitudinal coordinates of the boat on the surface of the ocean.

## Skimmer

Any sailor that is in the Surface Navy.

## Sonar Shack

Where all of the controls for active and passive sonar are located and where the Sonarmen stand their watch.

## Sound Isolation

Noise-making or vibrating equipment that is mounted on shock-absorbing mountings.

## Sound Trials

Operations at sea designed to calibrate own ship or other ship equipment, ie: Sonar and sound isolation.

## "SpringboardEx"

Any exercise in the warm Caribbean Sea waters.

## Squid

See  SKIMMER.

## Stateroom

A bunk room with or without its own head found in "Officer Country".

## Sub School

The school where about 20 out of 100 of the volunteers that try to be submariners learn or get transferred away from the program while learning all there is to know without actually being a crew member aboard a boat. The author did not attend Sub School, he earned his Dolphins the "hard way", and that aboard the oldest WWII submarine in the fleet.

**Submarine Escape Trainer**

A one hundred foot tower full of water used to train prospective submariners to "blow-and-go" simulating escaping from a sunken submarine. There was one in Groton and one in Pearl Harbor.

**Swim Call**

When the Captain authorized the crew to come topside and enjoy an oceanic swim.

**Swipes**

What the ELT uses to collect swipe-samples.

**T-Hull**

Referring to a Trident submarine.

**Target**

Any potential real or practice surface craft, submarine, aircraft, or land area.

**Techs**

Technical personnel in charge of sophisticated equipment.

**Throttleman**

Steam Plant Operator; he answers propulsion bells ordered from the Conning Officer via the Ship's Annunciator which is hand-operated by the Helmsman when given the order to alter ship's speed through the water.

**Trim**

The levelness of the boat forward and aft, adjusted by pumping water between variable ballast tanks.

**"The Tunnel"**

The passageway between water-tight doors on a 637-Class that allows access through the top of the "shielded" Reactor Compartment between the Operations Compartment and the Engineering Spaces.

## Upward-pinging sonar

An active sonar that had its pinger targeted on the ice ahead and above the boat to determine ice pack thickness for arctic underwater navigation and surfacing potential.

## Voice Tube

Where communications could be had between parties in a noisy space usually from upper to lower level of a compartment.

## Watch

The four, or six, hour time segments when crewmen are on station to perform their assigned duties, after which they are off-watch.

00-04   Midnight to 4 a.m.

04-08   4 a.m. to 8 a.m.

| | |
|---|---|
| 08-12 | 8 a.m. to noon |
| 12-16 | noon to 4 p.m. |
| 16-20 | 4 p.m. to 8 p.m. |
| 20-24 | 8 p.m. to midnight |

**Water Slug**

Practice firing of a torpedo tube without a weapon discharging to sea.

**"Z-Grams"**

When the Chief of Naval Operations, Adm. Elmo Zumwalt wanted to communicate his message to every sailor in the fleet from his office, he would issue his famous "Z-Grams".

# *ANAGRAMS.*

**1MC**          The main ship's communications system broadcasted from one of three locations: the Control Room, Conning Tower, or Bridge, and which is heard in all compartments.

| | |
|---|---|
| **7MC** | Ship's two-way voice communications circuit between the Bridge, Conning Tower, Control Room, Forward Torpedo Room, After Torpedo Room and the Maneuvering Room. |
| **21MC** | The Captain's Command announcing system. |
| **27MC** | Sonar and Radar Control circuit. |
| **AB** | After Battery. |
| **AC** | Alternating Current or Air Conditioning. |
| **AE** | Assistant Engineering Officer. |
| **AEF/MT** | Advanced Electronics Field/ Missile Technician. |
| **AMR2** | Auxiliary Machinery Room Two. |
| **CDO** | Command Duty Officer. |

**CIC**          Command Information Center.

**CO**          Captain of the boat
(affectionately referred to as "The Skipper".

**COB**          Chief of the Boat (most senior
          Chief aboard, directly
          responsible to the Executive
          Officer).

**COMM**          Communications Division (also
short for Communications Officer or COMMO).

**CONN**          Conning Officer (at sea, the
officer in charge of the depth and ship
maneuvering).

**CORPSMAN**          The enlisted medical personnel
aboard the boat, usually a PO1 or above.

**COW**          Chief of the Watch (at sea,
usually manning the Ballast Control Panel).

**DASO**          Demonstration And Shakedown
          Operation.

**DBF**          An old dieselboat sailor
anagram meaning, "Diesel Boats Forever".

**DC**          Damage Control or Direct
Current.

**DIV COM**     Division Commander.

**DCA**     Damage Control Assistant.

**EAB**     Emergency Apparatus for Breathing.  Connects to EAB headers via hose throughout the boat to prevent toxin inhalation.  The submariner has to know where all of the connections are for damage control procedures.

**EDIV**     Engineering Division (Engineering Officer commonly referred to as ENG).

**EDMC**     Engineering Department Master Chief Petty Officer  ("Bull Nuke" aboard boats).

**EHF**     Extra High Frequency.

**ELT**     The specially trained top of his class at prototype school who is concerned with radiological and chemical issues aboard the nuclear boats, they also read dosimeters which record how much radiation each individual receives over a period of time while aboard a vessel with a nuclear reactor.

**ENG** Short pet name for the Engineering Officer.

**EO** Electrical Plant Officer.

**EOOW** Engineering Officer of the Watch.

**ERF** Engine Room Forward.

**ERLL** Engine Room Lower Level.

**ESM** Electronic Surveillance Measures.

**FBM** Fleet Ballistic Missile submarine.

**FSN** Federal Stock Number.

**HF** High Frequency.

**HP** High Pressure.

**JA** Sound powered telephone circuit that a headset and microphone plugs into at all battle control stations.

**JO**          Junior Officer.

**JOOD**      Junior Officer of the Deck (at sea, in training).

**LF**          Low Frequency.

**LP**          Low Pressure.

**LPO**       Leading Petty Officer.

**MC**         Missile Compartment.

**MCUL**     Missile Compartment Upper Level.

**MDIV**     Machinery Division (A-Gang).

**MJ**         Sound powered telephone circuit.

**NAV**       Navigation Division (also short for Navigation Officer).

**NAVSECGRU**  Naval Security Group.

**NQP**       Non-Qualified Personnel.

**NUB**       Nickname for an NQP from which they all answer. Originally from the concentrated use of a #2 lead pencil, working it down to a nub.

**NUKE**   Nuclear Power Trained Personnel .

**OD**   Officer of the Day (in port, senior officer aboard with the duty section).

**OOD**   Officer of the Deck (at sea, senior officer of the watch section).

**OPS**   Operations Division (also short for Operations Officer).

**ORSE**   Operational Reactor Safeguard Examination – when a U.S.N. Inspection Team comes to the boat, and you had better pass.

**PDC**   Practice Depth Charge.

**POD**   Plan of the Day, published daily by the Executive Officer showing the times of planned evolutions to be conducted throughout the day until the next POD.

**POM**   Pre-Overseas Movement.

**POOD**       Petty Officer of the Deck or Topside Watch.

**PTG LO SUMP**   Port Turbine Generator Sump.

**RO**       Reactor Operator, usually an ET.

**SCRAM**       Reactor shut-down.

**SHF**       Super High Frequency.

**SOAP**       Ship's Overhaul Assistance Program.

**SPM**       Secondary Propulsion Motor (?) for close-in to the pier boat maneuvering .

**SSO**       Site Security Officer.

**TDU**       Trash Disposal Unit.

**TP**       Toilet Paper.

**TRE**       Tactical Readiness Examination.

**UHF**       Ultra High Frequency.

**UI**       Under Instruction.

**ULF**       Ultra Low Frequency.

**VHF**       Very High Frequency.

**WEPS** Weapons Division (also short for Weapons Officer); sometimes called the Gun Boss or Gunnery Officer.

**WESTPAC** Western Pacific Theater of Operations.

**WSRT** Weapons System Readiness Test.

**XJA** Telephone system used for general ship's service communications.

**XO** Executive Officer (second in command to the Captain).

# *Paygrades:*

### Enlisted:

**E-1** SR Seaman Recruit (paygrade while in bootcamp)

**E-2** SA Seaman Apprentice (paygrade after graduation from bootcamp)

**E-3** SN Seaman First Class

| **E-4** | PO3 | Petty Officer Third Class |
|---------|-----|---------------------------|

| **E-5** Class | PO2 | Petty Officer Second |
|---------------|-----|----------------------|

| **E-6** | PO1 | Petty Officer First Class |
|---------|-----|---------------------------|

| **E-7** | CPO | Chief Petty Officer |
|---------|-----|---------------------|

| **E-8** Officer | SCPO | Senior Chief Petty |
|-----------------|------|--------------------|

| **E-9** Officer | MCPO | Master Chief Petty |
|-----------------|------|--------------------|

### Warrant Officer:

| **W-1** longer in use) | WO1 | Warrant Officer 1 (no |
|------------------------|-----|-----------------------|

| **W-2** | CWO2 | Chief Warrant Officer 2 |
|---------|------|-------------------------|

| **W-3** | CWO3 | Chief Warrant Officer 3 |
|---------|------|-------------------------|

| **W-4** | CWO4 | Chief Warrant Officer 4 |
|---------|------|-------------------------|

| **W-5** | CWO5 | Chief Warrant Officer 5 |
|---------|------|-------------------------|

### Commissoned Officer:

**O-1**  ENS  Ensign (affectionately called a "butter bar" because of the single gold bar)

**O-2**  LTJG  Lieutenant (Junior Grade)

**O-3**  LT  Lieutenant

**O-4**  LCDR  Lieutenant Commander

**O-5**  CDR  Commander

**O-6**  CAPT  Captain

**O-7**  RDML  Rear Admiral (lower half; formerly Commodore)

**O-8**  RADM  Rear Admiral (upper half; formerly Rear Admiral)

**O-9**  VADM  Vice Admiral

**O-10**  ADM  Admiral

**O-11**  FADM  Fleet Admiral (reserved for wartime)

## _Enlisted Rates and Ratings:_

**(SS)** Qualified in submarines and allowed to wear the Dolphins (silver for enlisted and gold for officers)

**CS** Commissaryman (Ship's Cook)

**EMC** Electrician's Mate Chief Petty Officer

**EN1** Engineman First Class

**ET2** Electronics Technician Second Class

**ETN** Electronics Technician (Navigation – SINS)

**FT** Fire Controllerman

**GM** Gunner's Mate

**HM** Hospital Corpsman or Hospitalman

**ICC** Internal Communications Chief Petty Officer

**MM** Machinist's Mate

**MMFN(SU)** Machinist's Mate Fireman (Submarine Unqualified)

**MS** Management Specialist

**QM** Quartermaster

| RD3 | Radarman Third Class |
|-----|---------------------|
| RM1 | Radioman First Class |
| **SK** | Storekeeper |
| **StM** | Steward's Mate |
| **TM3** | Torpedoman's Mate Third Class |
| **YN2** | Yeoman Second Class |

## *FROM:  The Author:*

I began this project in 2009 and have been working on it (on-again/off-again) since then.  I have concurrently been re-writing a book of the War Between The States genre which tells the tale of my Great-great-grandfather's participation through his daily entries in the diaries he carried, both before and throughout the war, 1860-1865.  This submarine sea stories book is to help defray the costs of having two cancers, and maybe to get a dependable automobile, and buy something nice for all of my grandchildren before my time is up.  A portion of any profits from this project will be donated to

USSVI as promised when I began this job. I was aboard three boats during my six year hitch in the Navy. I was ordered, TAD to Nuclear Power School, to my qual-boat, USS GROUPER AGSS-214 after ET'B' School in Great Lakes, IL. After qualifying, I got married and then moved with my new bride to Groton, CT and checked aboard USS TRITON SSN-586. While there I envisioned what, as an ET, I would be doing as an RO, which I rejected while wanting to continue my electronics repair education in circuitry repair and Radar, IFF, WLR-6, Sonar watch-stander, SINS watch-stander, ECM watch-stander and also be a well and cross-trained forward puke, while remaining on the fast-disappearing diesel boats before they were all gone. At that point I would reconsider NucPwrSchool. The TRITON's Executive Officer said that I would not be able to rescind my orders to NucPwrSchool, and so I requested a Captain's Mast as my only option. The Captain read my orders to the XO and said, "XO, it says right here, 'Commanding Officer insures proper motivation prior to class commencement date', and the XO had to allow me my desire. He was a Nuke and hated me for my decision. I was sent to USS SEA DEVIL SSN-664, which I met in Ft. Lauderdale, FL while she was on her way back to SubRonSix in Norfolk, VA from Rosie Roads and weapons-loading. SEA DEVIL was my home from March 1969-December 1972, at which time I separated from the Navy on a threat from my x-wife where she said, "make up your mind; either the Navy or me!" Well, I had wanted to make the Navy a career, but that changed. I got out and tried to attend USF in Tampa, FL, but the GI-Bill money did not come in time for me to replace all of the money I had laid out for tuition, books, clothing, etc., and I was forced to quit school and go back to work. I have had such varied jobs as in sales, a cowboy ramrod on a beef-cattle ranch, restaurateur, office manager, carpenter, mason, woodshop inventor, AutoCad Certified draughtsman, construction project engineer, Conservation Technician at Soil and Water Conservation District, sign painter, logo designer, musician and song writer, poet, author, artist, association secretary, Chaplain and performed several ministries in my local Church. It has been interesting. I became 66 years old this week and if the Lord takes me now, I am ready to go to a much better place than here that is waiting for me to spend life eternally with Jesus.

For anyone who wants me to do another Submarine Sea Stories book, I encourage you to contact me at

xboatsailor@yahoo.com

with your story containing SUBMARINE BOOK in the Subject Line. If enough interest is generated, I will put together a Volume Two. Pass the word to your submarine cohorts that I am willing to accept this challenge again for all of the boatsailors out there, Vets and Active Duty. God bless you all....... Jim.

Made in the USA
Charleston, SC
20 October 2015